T0284824

A REALLY STRANGE AND WONDERFUL TIME

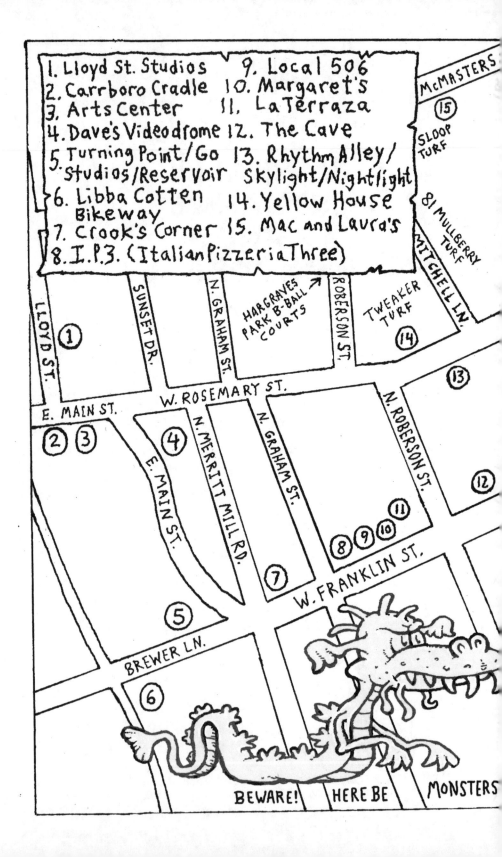

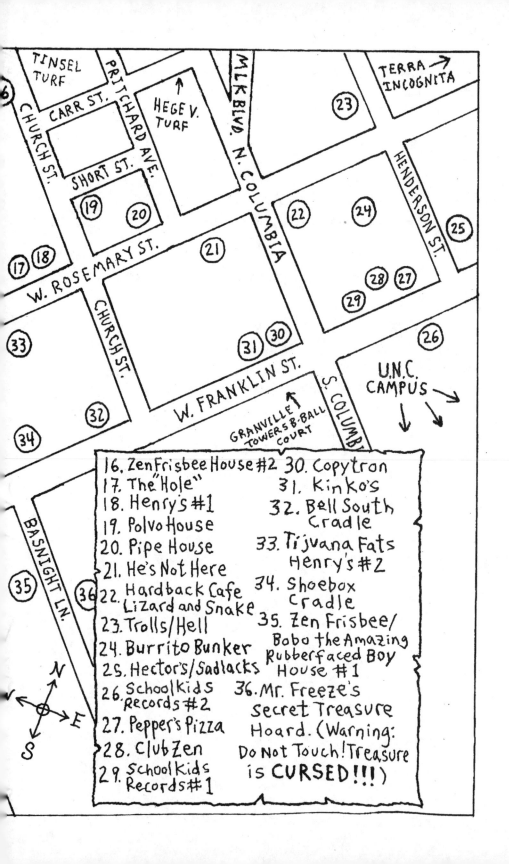

TINSEL TURF

CARR ST.

PRITCHARD AVE.

HEGE V. TURF

MLK BLVD. N. COLUMBIA

TERRA INCOGNITA →

㉓

CHURCH ST.

SHORT ST.

⑲ ⑳

HENDERSON ST.

㉕

⑰ ⑱

W. ROSEMARY ST.

㉑

CHURCH ST.

㉒ ㉔

㉘ ㉗

㉙

㉜

㉚ ㉚

㉛ ㉚

S. COLUMBIA

㉖

㉝

㉞

U.N.C. CAMPUS →

W. FRANKLIN ST.

GRANVILLE TOWERS B-BALL COURT

BASNIGHT LN.

㉟

㊱

N / W / E / S (compass)

16. Zen Frisbee House #2
17. The "Hole"
18. Henry's #1
19. Polvo House
20. Pipe House
21. He's Not Here
22. Hardback Cafe / Lizard and Snake
23. Trolls/Hell
24. Burrito Bunker
25. Hector's/Sadlacks
26. Schoolkids Records #2
27. Pepper's Pizza
28. Club Zen
29. Schoolkids Records #1

30. Copytron
31. Kinko's
32. Bell South Cradle
33. Tijuana Fats / Henry's #2
34. Shoebox Cradle
35. Zen Frisbee/ Bobo the Amazing Rubberfaced Boy House #1
36. Mr. Freeze's Secret Treasure Hoard. (Warning: Do Not Touch! Treasure is CURSED!!!)

Also by Tom Maxwell

Hell: My Life in the Squirrel Nut Zippers

A REALLY STRANGE AND WONDERFUL TIME

The Chapel Hill Music Scene:

1989–1999

TOM MAXWELL

hachette
BOOKS

New York

Hachette Books
Hachette Book Group
1290 Avenue of the Americas
New York, NY 10104
HachetteBooks.com
Twitter.com/HachetteBooks
Instagram.com/HachetteBooks

First Edition: April 2024

Published by Hachette Books, an imprint of Hachette Book Group, Inc. The Hachette Books name and logo are trademarks of the Hachette Book Group.

The Hachette Speakers Bureau provides a wide range of authors for speaking events. To find out more, go to hachettespeakersbureau.com or email HachetteSpeakers@hbgusa.com.

Books by Hachette Books may be purchased in bulk for business, educational, or promotional use. For information, please contact your local bookseller or email the Hachette Book Group Special Markets Department at Special.Markets@hbgusa.com.

The publisher is not responsible for websites (or their content) that are not owned by the publisher.

Print book interior design by Amy Quinn

Library of Congress Cataloging-in-Publication Data

Name: Maxwell, Tom (Musician), author.
Title: A really strange and wonderful time: the Chapel Hill music scene: 1989–1999 / Tom Maxwell.
Description: New York: Hachette Books, 2024. | Includes index.
Identifiers: LCCN 2023025994 | ISBN 9780306830587 (hardcover) | ISBN 9780306830594 (trade paperback) | ISBN 9780306830600 (ebook)
Subjects: LCSH: Alternative rock music—North Carolina—Chapel Hill—History and criticism. | Rock music—North Carolina—Chapel Hill—1991–2000—History and criticism.
Classification: LCC ML3534.3 .M395 2024 | DDC 782.4216609756/5609049—dc23/eng/20230622
LC record available at https://lccn.loc.gov/2023025994

ISBNs: 9780306830587 (hardcover); 9780306830600 (ebook)

Printed in the United States of America

LSC-C

Printing 1, 2024

To Emrys, my love of lifetimes

His disciples said to him, "When will the kingdom come?"

[Jesus said,] "It will not come by waiting for it. It will not be a matter of saying, 'Here it is' or 'There it is.' Rather, the kingdom of the father is spread out upon the earth, and men do not see it."

—Gospel of Thomas 113, translated
by Thomas O. Lambdin

Contents

The Infinite Past

IT ALL STARTED WITH THE CAT'S CRADLE. BY 1989, THE LIVE MUSIC venue had been open in various Chapel Hill locations for twenty years. It began life in 1969 as a tiny basement club that couldn't hold more than thirty people. Bill Smith Jr. showed up two years later. He came to the University of North Carolina at Chapel Hill from the venerable coastal town of New Bern but wasn't cut out for sitting still as a student. "Coming from eastern North Carolina, I'd had to behave for eighteen years," Bill told me. "I could not wait to get loose of that. Chapel Hill was the perfect place."

Bill got involved with the Cradle when he partnered with Dave Robert and Marcia Wilson. Marcia was from the eastern shore of Maryland and used some of her inheritance money to open the club. She based the Cradle on Caffé Lena in Saratoga Springs, New York. Marcia invested enough money to put down a deposit and buy a beer license and a cooler.

The partners kept the Cradle open by working in restaurants. "We were such poor businesspeople that we never made any money," Bill remembered. "We were always in trouble with tax people—bounced checks all the time and this kind of stuff—so we'd wait on tables." In the early days the Cradle mostly booked bluegrass bands. Acoustic music worked best in such an intimate space.

Soon, Bill began cooking at a French restaurant on Rosemary Street called La Residence. This also suited him. "I grew up where the dinner table was important," he said. "I guess it occurred to me

1

that you could transfer that importance to a profession. I've always enjoyed the idea of being an impresario of people's good times. When I owned the Cat's Cradle, it was the same thing: I loved the idea that even though someone who came out might end up as an accountant, one night I had them dancing on tables. It's just the devil in me, I guess."

Marcia Wilson died in a car wreck in the mid-1970s. "We owe her a great deal," Bill said. "I think of her often. She was a very kind person, an extremely generous person, and she had a beautiful voice. Knew all kinds of things about all kinds of music. She did us all a great favor. She was the foundress."

Later, Bill became much better known as a chef, but in his life food and music have always intertwined. "The one reason I stayed in Chapel Hill all these years was not the restaurants," he said. "It was the music. There are lots of people working in restaurants who are musicians. I love that. They have that work hard/play hard attitude that you need in a kitchen, too. They always tend to be smart people—and maybe argumentative and difficult, which creative people often are. It's all the same pack of dogs to me, the cooks and the musicians."

In the late 1970s, Cradle partner Dave Robert (known locally as DR) founded Moonlight Records, an indie label that released albums by North Carolina rock pioneers Arrogance and singer-songwriter Mike Cross. In the 1980s, Moonlight put out more local music by The Blazers, X-teens, and the Fabulous Knobs, reflecting a shift to punk and new wave. (It's worth noting that North Carolina musicians Don Dixon and Mitch Easter coproduced an X-teens spec record in 1982 prior to teaming up on R.E.M.'s debut album *Murmur* the following year.)

The Cat's Cradle moved to a slightly larger space on Rosemary Street in the early 1980s. It was in there that I, a sophomore at UNC, saw Flat Duo Jets perform in 1985. They were a two-piece, but the energy coming from them was indescribable. A teenaged Dexter Romweber fronted the band. He played a distorted black-and-white 1960s

Sears Silvertone 1448 electric guitar with a blue and white rope for a strap. The drummer, Chris "Crow" Smith, put a cinder block in front of his bass drum to keep it from walking across the floor as he stomped on the pedal. Dex wasn't so much front man as demented evangelist, who could move seamlessly from baritone croon to inarticulate shriek. Crow played head down, his torso bouncing like a piston. Until that moment, I'd never witnessed people my age being such confident authors of their own art.

Current Cat's Cradle owner and Chapel Hill native Frank Heath used some of his own inheritance money to buy the club from DR and Bill Smith in 1986. Frank is tall and trim, with shoulder-length hair and a faint smile. The only difference between now Frank and eighties Frank is that his hair has gone gray. Frank's not a big talker and appears free from any kind of conceit.

Frank would never have gotten involved with the Cradle without being "drug in by the community around me." He had been reading about cool bands coming through town like The Replacements and Hüsker Dü, gone to see live shows at the Cradle and The Brewery in Raleigh with a friend who worked at Schoolkids Records, and was convinced to buy the club by Richard Fox, then-chief engineer at WXYC, UNC's college radio station. (Fox had already been engineering live recordings and broadcasts from the Cradle.) The local bands Frank saw that made him excited about running a club were Let's Active, Flat Duo Jets, the Bad Checks, and Southern Culture on the Skids. But it was a band from Georgia that made him think he could make a go of it.

"R.E.M. jump-started everything in my mind," Frank told me. "It was easy to fall into that little swirl." That swirl—made up of a burgeoning local scene as well as an increasingly robust national touring circuit—was thanks in large part to R.E.M. They helped make Chapel Hill a stop for touring indie bands on their way up and down the eastern seaboard. College radio stations, including WXYC, began playing this indie music insistently, as well as a raft of great stuff coming from England. For those of us coming of age, R.E.M. was the first significant Southern band who weren't Lynyrd Skynyrd or Molly Hatchet. They were cool and smart, and they set an example to follow.

Because there was so much good music being made locally, by the mid-eighties Chapel Hill became known as the next Athens. Around this time, Flat Duo Jets had moved to that other little Southern college town for six months to get something cooking and were immediately included in the 1986 documentary *Athens, GA: Inside/Out,* to our good-natured irritation.

By this time the Cradle had moved again, to what is sometimes referred to as the "shoebox" location on West Franklin Street. Touring bands that cut their teeth in the smaller Cradle, like the hardcore punk band Black Flag, brought in more fans to fill out the larger venue—by this time, the club could hold 250 people.

Frank kept the lights on by having better-known area musicians play for two or three nights in a row. "I got to know all the bands really well," he said. "It felt comfortable booking local bands to play once or twice a semester if they wanted to. Things built that way." This approach made sense: Frank could utilize Chapel Hill talents like Snatches of Pink, a swaggering rock band with Dexter's sister Sara Romweber on drums (who had quit Let's Active in '84), or the sunny pop of Satellite Boyfriend to help work around touring bands' schedules. These groups also made ideal opening acts: There was so much musical variety around town that Frank could put a good bill together, since these were the days when touring bands didn't bring their own opener.

"At the time, I could just go and track Dexter down on the street and say, 'Hey, do you want to play October fourteenth?'" Frank remembered. "And he'd say, 'Yeah.' There wasn't as much long-range planning."

One Chapel Hill outfit who could easily sell out the new Cradle was the Pressure Boys, formed by high schoolers in the earliest years of the decade. Inspired by English bands like The Specials and English Beat (with an assist from West Coasters Oingo Boingo), the Pressure Boys were one of the few local bands (along with Raleigh's The Connells) who could fill a room. They were completely original and artistically self-contained, with a tight horn section, smart arrangements, and taut energy.

The Pressure Boys' first EP, 1983's *Jump! Jump! Jump!*, was produced by Let's Active's Mitch Easter. Mitch couldn't do the second one, *Rangledoon*, because Let's Active had just been signed and were going out on the road with R.E.M., so Arrogance's Don Dixon produced instead.

The Pressure Boys' last album wouldn't have been made without Frank Heath. "This was back when a huge paying gig was $500," front man John Plymale told me. "You know, a hundred and eighty people in the room was a huge fucking gig." The band wanted to make a full length at Steve Gronback's TGS Studio in Chapel Hill, an expensive proposition—especially because they never had any money. John had been friends with Frank since high school, so he was dispatched to ask for a loan. The two met at a local watering hole, Tijuana Fats restaurant on Rosemary Street, where Frank cut the band a check for $10,000 on the spot.

"Nothing was signed. He didn't ask for a percentage," John remembered. "He just asked if we could pay it back as soon as we could. It probably took us a year. It was so generous and trusting of him to do that with a bunch of guys who clearly could have gone south any second. So, that spoke a lot to me about what he believed in." *Krandlebanum Monumentus* was released in 1987.

The shoebox Cradle closed in August 1988, the same month the Pressure Boys broke up. And that, dear reader, is where our story begins.

I want to take you to a particular bend in the ever-flowing stream of time and say, "Look what came from this place. Listen to this." Chapel Hill, a seemingly average college town in the mid-South, produced an incredible amount of music between 1989 and 1999—music distinguished by its diversity and restless creativity. It caught the ears of national media and major record labels as well as the imagination of the public and made an indelible mark on American culture.

I use the term "Chapel Hill" advisedly. It began to be used in the eighties as a catch-all term inclusive of distinct scenes in other cities and thus became something of a trope. This book is more narrowly focused on Chapel Hill's music community, but Raleigh, Durham, and Greensboro all contributed mightily, as you will see. Excluding them would be as futile as trying to divide the wind.

The town of Chapel Hill was founded in 1793, a bit to the north and in the middle of the great horizontal state of North Carolina. It's modestly sized, a little over twenty-one square miles. The village of Carrboro borders the west side of town. The much larger city of Durham lies to the northeast. The state capital of Raleigh is almost thirty miles east of Chapel Hill and a little south. Together, Raleigh, Durham, and Chapel Hill make up what is known as The Triangle, with Carrboro being its fourth corner.

Chapel Hill was always a college town. The University of North Carolina, the first public university in the country, began enrolling students in 1795. By the late 1980s, Chapel Hill's population was more or less half students and half townies, making UNC (like its neighbors Duke, NC State, and UNC-Greensboro, just to name a few in the area) a giant youth factory, cranking out smart, curious, and creative young people. UNC's student headcount for the 1990–1991 school year was 23,852.

In 1900, author Mary Oates Spratt Van Landingham gave a talk in Charlotte on the "native literature" of North Carolina. After noting that the state is bound to the north by Virginia and to the south by South Carolina, Van Landingham quipped, "Where there are mountains of conceit, there are apt to be valleys of humility." This is more than just an accurate description of our comparative unpretentiousness: a sense of isolation has always informed and inspired North Carolina's aesthetic.

North Carolina has produced extraordinary music of every description: from Charlie Poole standardizing the bluegrass form in the 1920s to the creation of an entire diaspora of Black jazz, funk, and R & B musicians (a partial list includes Thelonious Monk, John Coltrane, Nina Simone, Maceo Parker, and Roberta Flack) as well as our state's most famous son, James Taylor. Carrboro gave us the gentle fingerpicked blues of Elizabeth Cotten. Blind Boy Fuller was from

Wadesboro. Lesley Riddle, a Black man who helped create country music by gathering songs with A. P. Carter and inspiring Maybelle Carter's guitar technique, lived in the small mountain town of Burnsville. Old-time guitar genius Doc Watson came up in Deep Gap. Triad pop architects Let's Active and The dBs helped establish a regional indie scene in the eighties. By the last decade of the twentieth century, musicians from the state continued the tradition by creating multivarious musical forms, scoring Top 20 hits, and selling millions of records.

In terms of how music was created and consumed, there is little to differentiate this near century of expression. Even in the 1990s, North Carolina musicians were relatively isolated, at least culturally. Outside of a few big Top 40 radio stations in population-dense Raleigh and Charlotte, there wasn't a lot of mainstream music to be heard. Those of us interested in scarce recordings (like, for me, vanishingly unavailable Velvet Underground records) could spend years looking for them. Local groups would gather to carpool to Minor Threat shows up in DC or haunt the import section at Schoolkids Records on Franklin Street to find the latest 4AD release.

While it's true that R.E.M. helped define the college radio market, it should be remembered that WXYC, UNC's open-formatted college FM radio station, only operated at four hundred watts—hardly enough power to be heard in Durham. (The Replacements' 1985 song "Left of the Dial" refers, literally, to the little frequency band at the lower end of the FM broadcast spectrum—located on the left-hand side of the dial—where college stations usually clustered.) In this sense, those of us whose tastes lay outside of the mainstream were an underserved community. The most viable option was to *make* the music we wanted to hear. A prevalent do-it-yourself sensibility, courtesy of the recent punk movement, gave us permission.

I see a few parallels between biological and cultural evolution, and one is particularly relevant here: geographic isolation facilitates new forms. Whereas every musician in this book incorporated outside influences into their creative approach, much of the sound we made was shaped by the community we lived in and identifiably our own.

In that time and place, music was often consumed publicly. We gathered at the Cat's Cradle or The Brewery or Local 506 to socialize and support each other—and not just musicians. Coworkers came out. People who worked at the Hardback Cafe or Nice Price Books did too, as did WXYC DJs and grad students and busboys. You could spend money buying the record of a band you were interested in (assuming a copy was even available), but it was cheaper to go see them play. More than that, it was important to see who else was at the show and hear what *they* thought about it. In other words, Chapel Hill created a scenius.

I should define this homely but precise term "scenius." In the mid-1960s, a young English art student named Brian Eno attended an exhibition of Russian avant-garde art. "It was a show at the Barbican, which is a big gallery in London," Eno remembered years later. "I'd always been interested in that period of painting and I thought I knew a lot about it. I went to this exhibition and I must have seen seventy paintings of painters I'd never heard of before. Good paintings. Seventy Russian paintings that I, who had studied Russian painting, had never heard of."

This fact not only confused Eno, it also gave rise to an idea. "I looked at this and I thought, 'There was a whole scene of people who were supporting each other, looking at each other's work, copying from each other, stealing ideas, contributing ideas,'" he said. "I knew the big names, but I suddenly realized that they weren't that much more important than all of the other people in the scene. The whole scene was important."

Eno immediately coined a term for such a community: "scenius." According to him, it stands "for the intelligence and the intuition of a whole cultural scene. It is the communal form of the concept of genius."

Until recently, the concept of communal genius didn't really exist. Traditionally, our culture has valued individuals as the sole engines of accomplishment. Scottish essayist and philosopher Thomas Carlyle is largely credited with originating the "Great Man Theory" in the nineteenth century. "The history of the world," Carlyle wrote, "is but the biography of great men." Brian Eno, when he walked into the Barbican exhibition, was expecting to see paintings by the "big names": Kandinsky, Chagall, Malevich. Those talented artists were certainly represented, but so were dozens of others of comparable ability.

Eno immediately understood there was another force at work, one that would turn the Great Man Theory on its head—or rather, flat on its back. Vertical structures are about power, after all. Horizontal ones are about community. This book is further proof of that idea.

To me, the nineties Chapel Hill music scene embodied the kind of scenius Brian Eno described. Instead of exclusively showcasing the bands most associated with the alt-rock Chapel Hill "sound" of the mid-nineties—they're amazing and in here too—I want to give you a sense of what was broadly going on musically and show you the fertile soil from which all this wondrous music sprang. Because this kind of community is very much like a garden: there are the beautiful flowers, of course, which command most people's attention, but for those flowers to grow there must also be rich dirt, pollinators, earthworms, and the right amounts of rain, shade, light, and decay.

By the same token, a successful creative community must have not only its stars but also its own climate of mutual support, including venues of expression and inspiration, lesser known but no less import-ant artistic collaborators, social connectors, affordability, collective identity, permeable social boundaries, and friendly competition. And, just as in any healthy biome, diversity is strength. Chapel Hill in the 1990s embodied all of these qualities.

The importance of this kind of community is so obvious that it's easily overlooked. Before music can be heard by the record label that will decide on its potential profitability, before it might land on the desk of the music critic who will make a subjective value judgment on it, and well before it ever reaches your ears with the potential to change your life, it must first be created. No matter how talented or inspired the artist who might bring that music forth is, if they don't feel supported or encouraged by the people around them, they might not do it at all. If they are very fortunate, they will find themselves in an environment like the one you're about to visit.

I think of scenius as a living entity that travels through space and time. We've seen it before: Berlin's art, architecture, and music during the Weimar Republic; the multidisciplinary artistic flowering of the Harlem Renaissance in the 1920s and '30s; and the justifiably famous outlaw country and punk scenes from Austin, Texas, in the 1970s and Washington, DC, in the 1980s. The magic combination of common elements that make a scenius come to life was available to us and can be to you, whoever and wherever you are. Ours looked and sounded a certain way. The next one will be remarkably different but no less marvelous.

1989

THE CAT'S CRADLE REOPENED AROUND VALENTINE'S DAY. ITS NEW location occupied the expansive middle floor of the former Bell South telephone building at 206 West Franklin Street, halfway to Carrboro but still proximal to UNC. Frank Heath remembers the rent for the much larger space was $5,000 a month, "a ton of money at the time." Still, it was a propitious move.

"I think that was a particular moment when more people were starting to enjoy local and live music," Frank told me. He could fill the old 120-seat Cradle by booking bands like Love Tractor from Athens, Charlotte's Fetchin' Bones, or Chapel Hill's Dillon Fence. "And then when we moved, they were suddenly selling five or six hundred tickets," Frank remembered. "I think it was probably a moment when the timing was right."

April was the best month the Cradle ever had. NRBQ played, as did Fishbone. It also marked the club's twentieth anniversary. To celebrate, Frank and his partner decided to resurrect the Pressure Boys. Their strategy was twofold: send a plane ticket to drummer Rob Ladd (who had since moved to Los Angeles) and call every former band member individually and get them to commit to doing the show if the other guys would. Everyone said yes, assuming somebody else would say no.

Rob doesn't remember the reunion gig fondly. "We were tired of each other," he said. "We loved playing and we loved the people who came to hang out and see us play, but all of us had mentally moved on." John Plymale had done so literally, into a new band called the Sex Police. "It had only been six months since the Pressure Boys last played," John told me, "but it felt like ten years."

So, the Pressure Boys played their last-last show at the new Cradle, and, as Frank predicted, it was huge. The end of their era is the beginning of ours. It's hard to overestimate the effect that Triad bands like The dBs and Let's Active had on the Chapel Hill music scene, but perhaps more than any other, the Pressure Boys—individually if not collectively—would continue to have a major influence on Chapel Hill music after their demise.

The Pressure Boys' bass player Jack Campbell opened Poindexter Records in 1985. Jack had gotten a job in 1982 at Schoolkids Records on Hillsborough Street in Raleigh and was soon running the store's inventory. "I seriously loved working there so much that I went around with a tape measure and measured out how to build the record bins," he said. Jack got together with a friend, borrowed some money, and opened Poindexter on Ninth Street in Durham. He soon hired a young music fan named Jay Faires. Jay was in business school at Duke getting his MBA and worked at Poindexter's on the weekends to keep his sanity.

"I started working at Poindexter and two things happened," Jay remembered. "Jack said, 'I'm in this band called the Pressure Boys. Will you come see 'em, and then will you be the record label and put out *Krandlebanum Monumentus?*' We got it to forty-three on the *College Music Journal* charts and I was fucking hooked." Jay took over the Pressure Boys' management and booking.

Jack and Jay nerded out on indie labels, the store's bread and butter. "Obviously we had to have the stuff on Warner Brothers and Columbia and all the majors that were selling," Jack said, "but we really tried to stock a lot of the more indie products. We were always watching for the ones that would send out promo materials and seemed to have a good business model."

For his part, Jay was obsessed with English labels, particularly Ivo Watts-Russell's 4AD. "Alternative music was successful there and cracked the mainstream way before it cracked the US market," he said. "How the fuck was Ivo selling a half million copies of Dead Can Dance records across Europe? It's amazing that he was doing it, but it was the same thing with Martin Mills and what he built with Beggars Banquet."

Lane Wurster was a newly arrived graduate student in UNC's Communication Studies program. A runner back at Wake Forest, Lane was getting into more creative stuff. He landed the lead role in a play and started making flyers for bands he liked.

Lane got a job as floor manager at Crook's Corner, a Southern restaurant bordering Carrboro at the very end of West Franklin Street. After hours, he'd walk down to Kinko's copy store and make posters. "They were basically ransom notes in terms of my approach to typography," Lane said. "I would buy a used book that had all these old fonts. It was so crude. I would cut them out, wax the backs of 'em, line them up as straight as I could, and form band names out of them." One of the bands Lane worked with was The Veldt.

The Veldt formed around identical twin brothers Danny and Daniel Chavis, who grew up in Raleigh and hung out with people from the hardcore and punk scene, befriending the band members of Corrosion of Conformity and Angels of Epistemology. At the same time, Danny and Daniel were heavily influenced by British bands like Cocteau Twins and Echo & the Bunnymen.

"I remember one day in the tenth grade, I bought Siouxsie and the Banshees' *Hyæna*, The Jam's double album *Snap*, The Dead Girls' single by Orchestral Manoeuvers in the Dark, and The Cure's *The Top*," Daniel told me. "All in one day. I went home and was floored." The Chavis brothers formed a hardcore band called Psycho Daisies, which ultimately morphed into The Veldt.

The Veldt based their sound on *The Top*. "It was a good combination of songs, it sounded morose and sad, and we liked it," Daniel said. "The Cure wore cool suits. That album was everything we wanted to be."

I saw The Veldt soon after they formed at a late-night house party in Chapel Hill. It was jarring because they were so tight and completely flash—not things local bands were particularly good at. Each member of The Veldt was in a suit, playing evocative, soulful dance music. It felt more like a TV performance than a drunken house party on McCauley Street. Clearly, this group was destined for bigger things.

"I really enjoyed doing stuff for The Veldt," Lane said. "They had it all. I went down this rabbit hole of trying to help them get dialed in to their aesthetic." At some point the band asked Lane to manage them, or something to that effect. Things aren't always completely nailed down with The Veldt. Maybe Lane was more of a publicist, but in any case, he felt strongly affiliated.

"I put together a press kit and was able to get them in the Duke *Chronicle* and UNC's *The Daily Tar Heel* and just did what I could," Lane remembered. "I went to fraternities and put up posters and flyers. One night, I walked up to them at a show and Danny or Daniel said, 'Hey, I want you to meet our manager, Jay Faires.' I was like, 'Oh. I thought *I* was your manager!' There were probably a dozen people who managed or thought they were managing The Veldt during those early days."

By the time Jay Faires came into the picture, The Veldt had established a following in the Southeast and were also playing lucrative frat parties. Capitol and Elektra Records started a bidding war. "An A&R guy from I.R.S. Records called and said, 'It's funny—you're a Black band, but you sound white,'" Daniel remembered. "That was the beginning of the end, right there. We were very naive. We didn't think that way."

The Veldt signed a contract with Capitol Records on Jay Faires's back porch. In September 1988, the band flew to England to record their debut album, *Marigolds*. Robin Guthrie, the guitarist from Cocteau Twins, agreed to produce. It was very much dream-come-true stuff, until drummer Marvin Levy got kicked out of the country for having drumsticks in his bag but no work visa. He was sent home on the same plane he came in on. Guthrie programmed a drum machine to replace Marvin's parts.

By this time, The Veldt's friends in Chapel Hill's Zen Frisbee had "wormed their way into Frank Heath's heart," according to drummer Chuck Garrison. "We were getting a lot of opening gigs at the Cradle," Chuck told me. "I think Frank liked that we were available on short notice."

Different iterations of Zen Frisbee had been performing since Chuck was sixteen, when he met guitarist Kevin Dixon in 1984. Eventually, Kevin's elfin brother Laird joined on guitar as well.

"I grew up in Chapel Hill, a very nice town with nice people," Chuck said. "Well educated. You never saw a bar fight. You never saw what you see in almost every other town. This place is just anointed. It was calm and special. Everyone was very polite and nice all the time. Getting out and seeing the world later, I started to slowly realize the rest of the world wasn't like that. There were very few assholes in town, and when there were they were shunned."

Chuck named Zen Frisbee. Once, when they were literal children, Chuck and Kevin were playing Frisbee on UNC campus. "There's something Zen about playing Frisbee," Kevin had mused. "That's the name of our band," Chuck said.

An early version of Zen Frisbee made a big impression on Chapel Hill native Dave Brylawski when he saw them during his second week as a student at UNC in 1986. "I remember they played the *Masterpiece Theatre* theme," Dave said. "That blew me away. There's Chapel Hill right there: somebody doing a shambolic but groovy *Masterpiece Theatre* theme. I was like, 'What the fuck.' That was transformative."

By 1989, Kevin Dixon was living in The Shack—a literal shack, out in the woods, up on a hill off Smith Level Road as it meanders south of town. The Shack had no phone and no running water. It did have electricity, which meant the band could practice there. At first the rent was thirty bucks a month, but at some point Kevin stopped paying even that.

Zen Frisbee was generally available and dirt cheap. Sometimes Frank didn't even pay them at all, like the night he asked them to open for Butthole Surfers. "We were a last-minute addition because whoever was supposed to do it couldn't," Chuck remembered. "Frank couldn't pay us, but he said that Public Enemy was playing the next day. None of us had tickets because we didn't have any money." An arrangement was made.

Zen Frisbee was an exhilarating, sometimes problematic, combination of profligate squalor, petty vindictiveness, and committed performance art. "We had to one-up whatever band we were playing with, but by poking fun at ourselves at the same time," Laird said. "That is one of the things I liked about Zen Frisbee—we didn't take ourselves that seriously, to our detriment."

An early gig opening for GWAR provided a great opportunity for Zen Frisbee–styled one-upmanship. GWAR was a heavy metal band from Richmond, renowned for their grotesque costumes and props. Their debut album was named *Hell-O*.

"We got a bunch of baby dolls from various PTAs and thrift stores and stuff," Laird remembered, "popped off their heads, and stuffed them full of peanut butter." The mutilated baby dolls were then hung up high behind the stage curtain, where the audience wouldn't see. A large Hulk head was placed on the front of the stage. "At one point, the all-powerful Hulk head commanded his minions to come down and all the baby heads were lowered as if they were attacking us," Kevin explained. Kevin and lead singer Brian Walker then produced Wonder Bread and steak knives and threw peanut butter sandwiches out into the audience. "That was our counter to GWAR's theatrics," Laird remembered. The headliners weren't amused, muttering "art fags" as they took the stage.

After getting kicked out of England on the way to record The Veldt's major label debut, Marvin Levy started practicing drums every day on the unused top floor of the Cat's Cradle building. According to Marvin, some of the Butthole Surfers wrote racist profanity on the upstairs wall after their show that night as a joke, knowing that Public Enemy would see it the next day. Marvin saw it instead and told Frank. The offending graffiti was removed. The next day, Flavor Flav came upstairs after hearing Marvin playing and hung out. "I'm so glad I got that red spray-painted over," Marvin said.

The mixes for *Marigolds* came back from England on little red advance cassettes. "I gave out seventy," Marvin remembered. "People loved it. It was this Ocean Blue–type Brit pop—not heavy. Washy but straight-up pop songs that were all under four minutes. More ethereal than commercial. Atmosphere rather than direct grooves."

Poindexter Records employee and MBA student Jay Faires wrote up a business model for a record label based on the new CD technology and cofounded Mammoth Records in 1989. "The beginning of Mammoth coincided with the record industry growing from 5 to 7 percent every year," Jay said. "All of a sudden CDs came in. People would buy a hundred CDs at a time. They were replacing their entire vinyl collection. Now you had a business that went from mature 5 percent growth to 100 percent year-over-year growth, four to seven years in a row.

"There were labels before Mammoth who were known as more indie, but they never paid royalties or their tour support checks bounced," Jay said. "So, the ethos of Mammoth when we started was, 'We'll take care of the business so you can take care of the art.'"

Mammoth's first location was a little office at 5 West Hargett Street in downtown Raleigh, which Jay shared with his partner, The Connells' manager Ed Morgan. Steve Balcom, then program director at WXYC, started working at Mammoth full time from a three-day-a-week intern gig. "I think Jay was paying me a little bit of money," Steve said. "I remember my last semester of my senior year of college traveling to San Francisco, going on the road with a new signing, and doing all this stuff while I was in college. I somehow got through school and then started at Mammoth. That early period was special. It was three or four of us in an office with a couple of interns."

One of those interns was Greg Humphreys, the front man for Dillon Fence. "Mammoth was built around the Pressure Boys' manager and The Connells' managers coming together, because they were the two big local acts at that time," Greg said. "They were the bands that my peers used to go see at the Cat's Cradle, and they were original. They weren't doing covers. They were rock stars, and they were doing what I wanted to do."

Dillon Fence had formed a couple years earlier. Greg was about to graduate. "We had built up a following and were playing on the weekends," he said. "I was really interested in trying to make a go of it as a full-time thing." Dillon Fence saw another local band called The Popes self-release an EP and service it to college radio and figured they needed to do the same. Their eponymous EP was released on NOCAR Records in 1989. The band hired John Plymale, late of the Pressure Boys, to produce. The sessions were held at Steve Gronback's TGS Studios in Chapel Hill.

Dillon Fence opens with a hit, "Something for You." Of course, I don't mean a hit in terms of sales, I mean a hit in terms of writing and performance—something so many of us were trying to do, regardless of how we chose to express it musically. The song's undeniably hooky vocal chorus floats over clinically funky guitar rhythms. "Something for You" went over big at frat parties and in the regional clubs.

Lane Wurster made the cover art for *Dillon Fence*. One day, Jay Faires called him into the Mammoth office. Lane brought his press kit for The Veldt. "Jay said, 'You seem like this hungry publicist,'" Lane recounted. "I didn't really feel like I was that. He's like, 'We should talk. I think there will definitely be some stuff that we can do together.'"

Another early Mammoth intern was Andrew Peterson. Andrew was a DJ at WXYC and thought of Steve Balcom as a mentor. "He would regularly say, 'Hey, check out this record. I think it's right up your alley,'" Andrew remembered. "He had me absolutely zeroed in. If Steve told me about a band that he thought I should check out, invariably I would love it."

Andrew was doing college radio for Mammoth, promoting bands on its roster like The Downsiders and Blake Babies and learning about the *College Music Journal* charts. He annoyed Jay because he kept wanting to talk to radio programmers about local bands he liked that weren't signed to Mammoth.

"I was impressed by Jay," Andrew said. "He certainly gave me a great opportunity just on Steve's word. I was wishing that he would focus more on local music, but he was obviously looking at a national brand. There were a lot of bands around Chapel Hill saying, 'Hey, you've got all this money and this ability to promote at a big level. Why aren't you looking at us?'"

One of the local bands Andrew wanted to promote was the acoustic duo Nikki Meets the Hibachi. He saw them play at the Carolina Coffee Shop next door to Schoolkids Records on Franklin Street and approached them. "You guys are great," Andrew said. "What are you doing to get out there?"

"Well, nothing," they told him. "We just like playing music together." Like Jay, Andrew started booking and then managing a few local bands he liked. He helped Nikki Meets the Hibachi make an EP and sent it to college radio stations reporting in the Southeast. Within a few weeks, it appeared on the regional charts.

Another one of Andrew's favorite local bands was Zen Frisbee, whom he first heard by playing one of their demos on WXYC. "One of the band members called the station and requested it," Andrew said. "I hadn't found it yet, so I hadn't played it. So, they called back and jokingly threatened me: 'We know where you are! You need to play this song or we're going to come find you!' So, I played this song called 'All the Angels Live in Potsdam' and it was like, 'I've never heard anything like this! These guys are incredible!'"

Andrew did not offer to manage Zen Frisbee because they intimidated him. "They were wild and had this larger-than-life charisma," he remembered. "I didn't feel comfortable approaching them. We're all the same age, but I felt like I was so much younger and just not worthy of going up and saying, 'Hi, how are you? I really like your music.'"

Zen Frisbee also made an early impression on UNC student Laura Ballance right after she'd moved to Chapel Hill. "I loved them," she said. Early on, Laura encountered guitarist Kevin Dixon and singer Brian Walker on Franklin Street outside of Hector's, a janky late-night food joint. "One of them gave me one of those Zen Frisbee newsletter/comic book things and I was just like, 'What the hell is this? Yes, I'm going to this show!'" Laura told me. "They were great. They were hilarious and weird."

Kevin, a mop-topped fellow who can really hold a grudge, created the Zen Frisbee newsletter with Brian. It was illustrated with Kevin's idiosyncratic cartoon drawings. (Kevin also worked at a copy store—a Chapel Hill tradition in a town where show promotion relied on printed flyers—so he took advantage and printed up Zen Frisbee newsletters on the company dime.)

"We thought it would be a funny idea if we had a little newsletter that came out with each show," Kevin remembered. "It was a mix of bragging about how great we were and all our adventures and then putting down every other band in Chapel Hill."

I don't want to give the impression that Zen Frisbee's pettiness was somehow unique. In a way, they deserve props for memorializing the kind of shit talk that many of us did in private, in the era before anyone had an electronic spy in their pocket.

At the time she was given the Zen Frisbee newsletter, Laura Ballance was a frowning goth girl with dreadlocks who worked at Pepper's Pizza, a furiously busy place downtown staffed by punk kids. Pepper's was right off campus, across the street from Schoolkids Records, and next door to the Record Bar. "It was hard work, and it was shitty, and it would stay open late until the bars were closing and then all the drunk frat boys would come in, and I hated them," Laura said. "The guys would always put me on the register, because they didn't want to talk to the frat boys. And of course, they used to harass me."

Laura ended up living in a crowded duplex with me at 34B McMasters Street. Phil Collins from Satellite Boyfriend also lived there, as did Cheryl Parker (a WXYC DJ who was heavily involved in the scene), a Schoolkids Records employee named Amy, Sue Hunter (another XYC jock who had a Budweiser bass because her dad worked for the company), and I can't remember who else. This is around the time Mac McCaughan finished his junior year at Columbia up in New York and came back home to Chapel Hill. Mac started appearing at our house to teach Sue how to play bass. He was showing an obvious interest in Laura as well and taught both of them a Guns N' Roses song. I remember Mac as a skinny kid who wore Converse high-tops.

I probably wouldn't have had a career in music were it not for Phil Collins—the Satellite Boyfriend guy, not the other one. He taught me how to play the riff from R.E.M.'s "Driver 8" and showed me barre chords. Satellite Boyfriend inspired me to form bands myself. Mac was also a fan.

"You guys are awesome," Mac remembers telling Phil. "'Why aren't you going out there?' Phil was writing incredible songs. I thought they could be like The dBs or the Soft Boys or something."

"We didn't have that mindset at all," Phil told me. "What we should have done is put out records, like Dillon Fence and The Popes. Just done it—put out a single or seven inch when it was fresh, but we never did that. When we did put out an album for the first time, it was a hodgepodge of demos recorded at four different studios."

Mac had been in several local bands already, including Wwax and Slushpuppies. Both of those groups appeared along with blackgirls, Egg, and Angels of Epistemology in a 1987 box set called *Evil I Do Not/To Nod I Live*, the brainchild of Wwax's bassist Wayne Taylor. (Zen Frisbee was supposed to be the sixth band featured and even recorded songs for the project. "We did not have the funds to contribute," drummer Chuck Garrison said, "so we didn't get included.")

Dana Kletter was in blackgirls. "The box set was really crucial to creating something that married the hardcore scene in Raleigh with the burgeoning music scene in Chapel Hill," she said. "Every band was a Raleigh sort of band. It was very much our collective—everything from the concept, the art, the bands that were on there. There was a strong community in Raleigh. I think Mac came out of that collective experience."

The *Evil I Do Not/To Nod I Live* release was foundational for Mac in other ways. Each band had their own seven-inch single in the box set, because they knew that seven-inch singles fit in a quarter-inch tape box. Barefoot Press, a new business in Raleigh, printed the booklets. Tannis Root, also based in Raleigh, helped silk-screen the boxes. All five bands played a release show at the Cradle and another one at The Brewery in Raleigh. Both performances drew large crowds. This was new for Mac, whose previous experience had been opening for touring bands.

"My impression of how it worked was that people didn't really go out just to see local bands, unless you were the Pressure Boys or someone that was already big," Mac told me. "These were all weird bands in the box set. There was nothing commercial about any of it. None of us had ever headlined our own show that drew that many people. The fact that we could create this situation where people were reading about this in *The Spectator* and then coming to the shows was a real eye-opening moment."

As is the way of things, most of the bands that appeared on *Evil I Do Not/To Nod I Live* soon broke up. Mac described his two takeaways from the experience. "One was that you could do it—you can make this physical thing and sell it," he remembered. "The other was that it's a valuable documentation of art that people are making around here. Because in a minute they're not gonna exist, and what do you have—a copy of some tape that someone dubbed for you?

Maybe you just saw them live and don't have any record of what they even sounded like."

Blackgirls, a trio consisting of piano, acoustic guitar, and violin once described as "menacing folk punk," were still a going concern. "Mammoth signed The Sidewinders, who were from Arizona," Dana said. "Then they signed A Picture Made, guys from Kansas that we knew from The Connells. Jay Faires came to a show at The Brewery and told me, 'I want you to be the first band from North Carolina that we sign.' The Mammoth offices were right around the corner from my house. There was this shitty gold-orange carpet on the floor and coffee cups everywhere. I walked in there and it seemed just like home! It was very informal. There was no offer of a contract or anything."

In 1989, entertainment lawyer Rosemary Carroll, married to punk poet Jim Carroll and yet to represent Kurt Cobain, was very much interested in blackgirls. "My first memory of Mammoth Records is talking with Dana," Rosemary told me. "I talked with her a lot before I started representing them and certainly while I represented them. I have a vague recollection of her telling me that Mammoth Records wanted to sign them. I think I said, 'What's a marmot record?' because I'd never heard of them." The other thing Dana told Rosemary was that producer Joe Boyd was flying into North Carolina to meet with the band. Rosemary promptly said she was flying in, too.

In the 1960s, Joe Boyd produced Pink Floyd, Nick Drake, and Fairport Convention. More recently, he'd worked with Billy Bragg and R.E.M. "I read a review of a single by blackgirls in a US magazine and it sounded interesting, so I ordered it by mail," Joe remembered. "I think the order went straight to Dana and she may have included a note saying, 'Are you the Joe Boyd who produced . . . ?' I was impressed by her voice and by the song, so I got in touch eventually by phone." The two talked for hours.

"Joe Boyd was a legend to me," Rosemary said. "I also thought it would be good for the blackgirls to have someone there who was unambiguously on their side, because record company people in general are really skilled at pretending they're on the artist's side. They're so good at it, they could really fool you. I knew that Joe Boyd would be more on the artist's side than the record company would be, that's for sure, but I'm sure he had his own agenda.

"I don't think I had any expectations about Jay Faires," Rosemary continued. "He was a record company guy. I knew a lot of record company guys and he didn't seem any better or worse than any of them." This came as news to Jay when I told him, as he and Rosemary had already been comanaging Fetchin' Bones.

A deal was struck in which Joe would produce a blackgirls album, Mammoth Records would foot the bill, and Joe's label Hannibal Records would get the rights outside of North America.

Dana thinks Joe's interest sealed the deal with Mammoth as well as helped secure a publishing deal with Bug Music. "I'm sure that was a boon for Mammoth, to have this venerable dude produce a record for their label," Dana said. "We were the last band to not have to sign over our publishing to Jay."

By the summer of 1989, Mac McCaughan and Laura Ballance were dating and in a short-lived group named Metal Pitcher. They soon enlisted Zen Frisbee's Chuck Garrison to form a new band. Chuck was Mac's old roommate, knew Laura through mutual friends, and lived three doors down from our duplex on McMasters Street.

"They just came over and said, 'Hey, do you want to be in a band with us?'" Chuck remembered. "I was like, 'Sure, why not?' You know, I didn't have anything else to do. At that point, I don't think I'd ever been in more than one real band at a time. It was summer and I had plenty of time."

Now Chuck was in two real bands. The new one with Mac and Laura was called Chunk, because Chuck's name in the phone book was misspelled as "Chunk" Garrison. Chunk recruited another guitarist by the name of Jack McCook and started practicing in Chuck's little cinder block house.

As a high school kid, Mac was a huge Pressure Boys fan. But he also took inspiration from a legendary Raleigh punk band. "The Pressure Boys were happening at a time where either you were gonna sign to a major or you were gonna stop being in a band," Mac said. "Now, the flip side of that was Corrosion of Conformity. They were like, 'We're just going to make insanely great records for different labels, tour incessantly, and become known as the greatest live hardcore band.'"

While up at Columbia, Mac went to see COC play a Sunday matinee at CBGB. The show was sold out, which shocked him. "'We love this band,'" Mac remembers thinking, "'but how does everyone else know about this?' Punk celebrities like Thurston Moore from Sonic Youth were there to see Corrosion, because they were that good."

Mac and Laura drove across the country at the beginning of the summer to take some friends to the West Coast. Mac's parents' van caught fire an hour outside of Farmington, New Mexico, so they rented a car to finish the trip. A friend of Mac's from college showed them the offices of a label some of her high school friends started called SubPop Records. Mac and Laura were already fans and had a couple SubPop singles.

On the way home, they saw a merge sign on the highway and found the name of the label they'd been talking about starting. The first few Merge Records releases were cassettes of bands that Mac had already been in. Then they moved to seven-inch singles. By year's end, the first Chunk single was released on Merge. It was recorded in Raleigh at Duck Kee Studios.

"We discovered Duck Kee from people in Raleigh bands," Mac said. "It was great because it was not intimidating. It was in this guy's house, but he knew how to make it sound good. He had a sixteen-track tape machine. It was a very comfortable and inexpensive place to learn how to record your band."

Jerry Kee was, and is, the owner of Duck Kee Studios. Jerry moved down to North Carolina after seeing an episode of *120 Minutes* on MTV in 1986 that featured Flat Duo Jets, Dexter's brother Joe

Romweber's band UV Prom, and The Connells. According to the show, Chapel Hill was going to be the next Athens, Georgia, home of The B-52s and R.E.M. Jerry moved because of that buzz and also the fact that a friend at NC State would let him couch surf until he found a place of his own.

Jerry loved the community. He joined bands and recorded them. His friend Matt Matthews introduced him to people and spread his demo tapes around. Soon Jerry was recording other bands. "It was an easy thing to do," he said. "I loved recording and a lot of people wanted a cheap place to record. It just snowballed."

By the time Chunk walked into Duck Kee to record their first single, Jerry had known Mac for a few years already, having recorded Wwax and Slushpuppies. At the time, Duck Kee was in Jerry's house on Bickett Boulevard near downtown Raleigh. It had been open for about three years. Jerry partnered with Matt, The Connells' soundman, to open the place. The Connells were working on their new album *Fun and Games*, which Matt was helping produce. The band gave Matt and Jerry a sixteen-track tape machine to record demos. This was quite a sophisticated piece of gear, making Duck Kee one of only a few professional studios in The Triangle.

The first Chunk seven inch was the fourth Merge Records single. It featured two originals and one Shangri-Las cover. Mac's song "My Noise" is a manifesto. The band's aesthetic elements are already in place: chugging guitars, feedback breakdowns, and Mac's double-tracked vocal yelp. The song's loud/quiet/loud arrangement recalls the Pixies, and the dissonance is a little industrial, but "My Noise" is not mimicry. It's a hit.

> It rides beside me, it has no choice
> It's my life and it's my voice
> It is stupid and it's my noise

These Merge Records singles were the start of a cottage industry, something Mac and Laura seemed born to do. Their role models were labels like Dischord and Teen-Beat Records in DC and K Records and Amphetamine Reptile from Washington state. "These labels all had an aesthetic and a DIY feeling about them that we were really into," Mac said. "You felt like someone made this with their hands. These are all people who are in bands and putting out the records. We really liked that aspect of it, because it felt transparent, as opposed to 'there's the bands and then there's the overarching record company.'"

Merge used United Record Press in Nashville, the same plant that manufactured the *Evil I Do Not/To Nod I Live* box set. Around this time, both Mac and Laura were working at Kinko's, which came in handy for designing record sleeves. "We would photocopy things," Laura remembered. "Move them around, tape them down. Use the rub-off letters. I still love that shit. You can't replicate that with a computer."

The sleeves were printed at Barefoot Press, where Mac's old bandmate Wayne Taylor worked. The vinyl and labels were then shipped to the house on McMasters, where whoever's band was involved would be summoned. "We'd sit around and drink beer and stuff plastic sleeves," Laura said.

"Nobody else seemed to be doing it that we were aware of in Chapel Hill, and there were all these cool bands that would come into existence and then fade away," Laura remembered. The benefits were twofold: First, good music was being documented. Second, bands could use these recordings to help secure gigs.

"We would release anything," Laura said. "It didn't matter how bad it sounded. It was all as cheap as possible and lo-fi. It reflected what was actually happening. We weren't trying to do anything that was polished or shiny. It was really about the fun of doing it. It's art, but people are also buying it, which makes you feel validated." There was still a financial hurdle: Each single cost up to $700 to record and manufacture. Bands cofunded their own release.

There were no Merge Records contracts. "It was like, 'We'll give you some of these seven inches and please sell them,'" Laura said.

"'Because we need your help to sell them at your shows.' But that was it. People were just excited to have something coming out physically. We weren't making money. If we were making money, it might have been $100 on the entire pressing and that would help fund the next thing."

In the fall, Jay Faires asked Lane Wurster for ad ideas to help launch Mammoth Records. Lane asked Jay how he perceived the label. "I think it's ironic that we're this small label with a big name," Jay told him. "The only thing I don't want anybody to associate us with is an extinct prehistoric creature. That would send the wrong message." Lane went home for Thanksgiving and came back with the opposite of this brief, an image of a woolly mammoth skeleton with the tagline "Music Like There's No Tomorrow."

"We didn't know what was coming next," Lane explained. "We had Public Enemy and the Pixies. It was a weird time. We were making fun of the Rolling Stones and The Who and these dime-store bands that were still touring. Jay and I started to have fun with this idea of, 'Why not go out in a blaze of glory? There's something cool about extinction.'"

Mammoth's roster was already getting national attention. MTV's *News at Night* sent a crew down to Chapel Hill to profile blackgirls. The host of the segment, Tim Sommer, had heard about the North Carolina scene since befriending R.E.M. after their first few shows in New York. "They used to say that a lot of people thought they were from Chapel Hill," Tim remembered. "R.E.M. and their manager Jefferson Holt instilled in me the idea that Chapel Hill is a pretty magical place for original alternative music."

A few years later, R.E.M. singer Michael Stipe recommended Flat Duo Jets to Tim. "The first time I ever saw Dexter was in 1986," Tim remembered, "when Michael Stipe said, 'You've got to see Elvis.' He didn't even call him Dexter. He kept on calling him Elvis."

Soon after, Tim's band Hugo Largo came and played the shoebox Cradle shortly after Frank Heath acquired it. "I instantly sensed that

Chapel Hill and The Triangle was a pretty amazing place," he said. "I think the first time we played there, the blackgirls opened for us. They were very special. You weren't even finding bands like that in New York in 1986. There was a level of knowledge and intelligence and wit and originality to the listeners and musicians in Chapel Hill that was immediately evident.

"By the time I came back in 1989 to do that MTV report, I had a sense that what was going on in Chapel Hill was arguably the most interesting, original alternative music scene on the East Coast, maybe in the entire country," Tim said. "It was more interesting to me than New York, let's put it that way." He decided it was worth the expense of bringing an MTV crew down to do a shoot.

The first blackgirls record Mammoth Records released was called *Procedure*, named after a song they'd put on *Evil I Do Not/To Nod I Live*. "It was so homey for that first album," Dana Kletter told me. "Everybody at Mammoth was funny and familiar, so I didn't feel like I was doing anything strange or emotionally dangerous. They put up a wall of pictures that were from people just querying them. It seemed like a mom-and-pop shop. It was so informal; it felt as if we were finding old friends. We were collaborating with people we knew."

UNC student Dave Brylawski, who'd had his Saul-on-the-road-to-Damascus moment seeing Zen Frisbee cover PBS's *Masterpiece Theatre* theme, had been teaching himself how to write and record music by messing around on his guitar and a four-track machine in his apartment. "My personal journey went from being an outsider looking at people playing music and really wanting to understand how you do that, and really longing for that, to figuring out piece by piece how to do it," Dave said.

In 1988, Dave recorded his own cassette tape of original songs called *Saturnine* and sent a copy to *Option* magazine. "It was glossy and you could buy it in a bookstore," Dave remembered. "It was a real magazine and they reviewed cassettes." *Option* reviewed *Saturnine*, as did *Tape Op* magazine. Dave started getting orders.

"What people like Mac McCaughan were doing musically . . . you might as well go to school and become a surgeon," Dave said. "I just didn't understand how they did that. Figuring it out quietly in my bedroom was the catalyst for all of it."

Back in Raleigh, Mammoth Records was on its hustle. Jay Faires scored a win by securing a deal with RCA Records for $100,000. In it, RCA and Mammoth would co-release The Sidewinders' new album. The Sidewinders were a Mammoth band from Tucson, Arizona. "Three weeks after we made that record, we sold it to RCA for thirty-three times what we made it for," Jay said. "We were like, 'Oh, we can do this.'"

Lane Wurster, assuming the role of Mammoth's art director, found himself on a parallel learning curve. "I did the layout for the Blake Babies' *Earwig* record," he said, "and sent off a color slide for the poster. I told them, 'Send us back a proof to sign off on.'" When asked, Jay told Lane he hadn't seen the proof. Then three weeks later, a stack of a thousand black-and-white Blake Babies posters showed up. "Why did you print a black-and-white poster?" Jay demanded. The printing company had sent a black-and-white proof to the Mammoth office and Jay signed off on it. Regardless, he made Lane eat half the cost.

"I thought, 'Okay, this guy's a businessman,'" Lane remembered. "Jay was like that. He was up-front about Mammoth having investors. A lot of the reason Mammoth made it through those early years was because of investors. They weren't selling enough records to pay the bills. They had seed money, and when they sold The Sidewinders to RCA, there was probably some cash there. But if you look at the sales for those first couple of years, I don't think they would have made it through."

Back in The Shack, where Zen Frisbee's Kevin Dixon lived, there was no running water and thus no indoor bathroom, only an outhouse out back. Using it was a fraught proposition. "You had to sit very carefully," Kevin said, "because it was entirely possible to fall into this cesspit and you would have a hard time getting out.

It was probably eight feet deep and dug straight down like a grave. One grisly night I shone a flashlight into the pit to gross myself out. The entire surface of the fecal matter was covered with these fat maggot things. It was a vision of Hell: Just a squirming, writhing mass of shit and decay. Then I felt depressed about living out there."

1990

THE BIG NEWS IN JANUARY WAS THE LONG-AWAITED RELEASE OF Flat Duo Jets' self-titled debut, which had languished in the can for almost a year. The band had signed with R.E.M. manager Jefferson Holt's Dog Gone Records label back in '88. *Flat Duo Jets* was recorded in early 1989 live to two-track tape and then put on the back burner because of label issues.

Dick Hodgin's M-80 Management was representing Flat Duo Jets. Dick had been in the business since the seventies. His brutal honesty had earned him the nickname "Dream Assassin." M-80 was also managing Pressure Boys alum Jack Campbell's new band Johnny Quest. In addition, Dick cofounded the North Carolina Music Showcase.

Dick promoted Flat Duo Jets tirelessly. "I wanted to bring them into the mainstream, which was somewhat difficult," he said, "because at that time they weren't a mainstream act. They were considered more of a wild, off-the-chain thing."

The previous year, running sound for Fetchin' Bones at a Capitol Records showcase up in New York, Dick ran into David Letterman's bandleader Paul Shaffer "stealing food and beer out of the deli tray" in the band's greenroom. The two got to talking.

Dick played Paul some *Flat Duo Jets* on his Walkman as they drank beer and shot the shit. Paul was impressed. "I loved the Flat Duo Jets," he told me recently. "Very much old rock and roll inspired."

Dog Gone Records' publicist Jocelyn LaBelle was also a Flat Duo Jets convert. To promote the album, she got the band good gigs in New York: two at CBGB and one at the Lone Star Cafe. Tom Petty came out to the latter. The *New York Times* called Flat Duo Jets a "dangerous band" and credited front man Dexter Romweber as having "the chesty bravado of Elvis Presley."

Tim Sommer returned to Chapel Hill in January with an MTV *News at Night* crew to profile several more local acts. A reporter for the Durham *Herald-Sun* met him at the Cat's Cradle. Tim came back to feature not only blackgirls again but also The Veldt and Snatches of Pink, a Stonesy trio with Dexter's sister and former Let's Active drummer Sara Romweber.

While Tim was waiting at the Cradle bar for the crew to set up the lights for that night's filmed performance, club owner Frank Heath walked up. "You might remember me from when Hugo Largo played here," Frank told him. "Oh yeah," Tim responded. "You were always great to us."

MTV filmed blackgirls, Dillon Fence, and The Veldt performing on the Cradle stage. A Flat Duo Jets segment that Tim Sommer's crew had recorded late the previous year aired that night. In it, Dexter declared, "I think we're gonna be the next Stones."

It's worth mentioning that two of the featured groups—blackgirls and The Veldt—didn't originate from Chapel Hill at all but were instead formed in the Raleigh punk and hardcore community. Regardless, the Chapel-Hill-as-North-Carolina trope was already inescapable.

The Veldt's lead singer Daniel Chavis didn't feel great about the MTV shoot. "My voice was blown," he said. "I was tired. People from our label were there." Daniel drove back to Raleigh with the band's manager and Mammoth Records president Jay Faires. A call came through on Jay's car phone. It was someone from Capitol Records. The Veldt were getting dropped. Their A&R person at the label had been fired and her replacement didn't consider the band "viable."

This story is typical of the major label music industry of the last century. "A&R" stands for "artists and repertoire." A&R people got bands signed and were the interface between them and the record label. An A&R rep could talk a good game about how great their label was, but more importantly they were the bands' inside champions. In an industry known for its high turnover rate, A&R people had perhaps the shortest tenure. If you were signed to a label—especially a faceless major like Capitol Records—and your A&R rep got fired, you were likely screwed. Without an advocate, the best you could hope for was an album release with no promotion. Otherwise, any recorded material would stay in the vaults and you'd get dropped.

"When the business was run by A&R people," Tim Sommer said, "it was run by small-mindedness." At the time, major label A&R wasn't looking for bands in North Carolina, however sophisticated they might be, because the entire state was considered a backwater. If bands like The Veldt or blackgirls had been based in New York or Los Angeles, they would have had no issue being signed to a major. The problem was, of course, that both were products of a very specific North Carolina community.

As their manager, Jay Faires made sure there was a severance fee in The Veldt's Capitol Records' contract for just this contingency. "That was the only good thing he did for us," Daniel said. Jay had his own takeaway.

"I saw that the value of an indie label was that it allowed you to build your own culture versus the label telling you what you should be," Jay recalled prophetically.

Chunk recorded their debut album over January 18 and 19 at Duck Kee Studios while Mac McCaughan was on vacation from Columbia. Chuck Garrison was also still in school at UNC. "It happened really quickly," Chuck remembered. "Mac had all the songs lined up and he had a vision. He knew what he wanted to do, which was admirable. I had no idea what I wanted to do with my life. I was adrift. He was goal-oriented, which it turns out is very helpful when you're trying to plan your life and stuff like that."

Merge couldn't afford to put out more than singles, so Mac was already in talks with label people about releasing the Chunk full length. "I knew Gerard Cosloy from living in New York," Mac said. "I mean, I knew who he was. I was a fan of records he was putting out on Homestead Records: Sonic Youth, Green River, Dinosaur Jr. This was the label for stuff I was into at the time." Mac would see Gerard out at shows in the city. He was friendly.

Chunk were in talks with Homestead to release a Merge singles compilation and maybe the Chunk record. Things got serious enough that Dutch East India Trading, Homestead's parent company, sent over proposed contracts. "I was very hyped on this idea, because I loved Homestead," Mac remembered. "Even though the deals that they were giving bands were notoriously terrible. They would own the recordings forever. Just usual record company stuff."

Mac's right: this was music industry business as usual and still is. Most label deals exchanged ownership for an advance. They would pay a band to record an album, which the label would then own. Many deals were structured so that the label would also own *any* recordings an artist made, including demos.

"In our mind, we were like, 'Hey, we're not really in the music business. We're in the indie record business,'" Mac said. "We thought it'd be different."

While Mac was still into the idea of being on Homestead Records, the lawyer who read the Dutch East contracts advised the band to take a pass. Mac continued badgering Gerard, calling from pay phones on campus to see where the deal was at. At the time of recording, Chunk wasn't sure who was going to put the record out. "Let's just make an album," Mac thought, "and figure out what to do with it."

In February, Dexter Romweber told UNC student newspaper *The Daily Tar Heel* that some days he loved *Flat Duo Jets* and some days he hated it, but he and drummer Crow were ready to go out and promote it. "We are about to play the game," Dex said decisively, before half-jokingly adding, "If something doesn't happen this time, I'm gonna die."

That the Flat Duo Jets even had a record deal distinguished them. The ability to issue their own singles also made Chunk a rarity. "Back then, it was a big deal for you to self-release a record," Glenn Boothe remembered. "A lot of times bands recorded demos that went unreleased. Putting out a record was a big step." Glenn succeeded Mammoth Records' Steve Balcom as program director at WXYC. One of the first things Glenn did was focus on local music because he was, as he put it, "infatuated with the scene."

Glenn initiated a compilation project called *Demolisten*, putting out cassette tapes featuring local music. Then he created a show on WXYC called *The Backyard Barbecue*, which he cohosted with Steve and Frank Heath. The three would play new local music and discuss what was happening around town.

"Glenn and Steve both had such a great conception of presenting something as a package, as something that you really need to check out," Frank said. "They were good at making a big production out of a rollout. So, it wasn't just me putting on shows. It was, 'Here's the show and this is why it matters.'"

Poindexter Records employee Kelley Cox became manager after owner Jack Campbell went out on the road with Johnny Quest. "We turned that thing into a total indie rock emporium," Kelley said. "Jack would come in and say, 'Why aren't there any Grateful Dead records?' But we had the entire SST and Homestead collection and all the SubPop singles." Glenn also worked at Poindexter.

Kelley had been thinking about starting an indie label of his own. "It was obvious that there were a lot of young local bands that were good," he remembered, "and it was clear to me that Merge and Mammoth couldn't handle it all. There was as much Raleigh going on in the early days of Merge as Chapel Hill and you had to have a friendly relationship with them to get on their label." On the other hand, Mammoth was mostly signing bands from out of town. A new indie label would have many good options to choose from.

Kelley talked to Glenn about the kind of music he was interested in. "To me," Kelley said, "punk was about doing it your way. Things didn't have to be so serious." Glenn suggested a young Greensboro band called Bicycle Face.

Bicycle Face guitarist Mitch McGirt grew up down east in Kinston and sported an unironic mullet. ("It was cool where I came from," he said.) Bassist Brian Huskey, having recently been dissuaded from having a career in TV and film—by one of his professors, no less— was playing music with his college roommate Chris Longworth. According to Brian, Mitch showed up with his "too high shorts" and Bicycle Face was formed. Chris played on trash cans because they'd heard that's what the Velvet Underground's Maureen Tucker started on.

"Brian and I were not cool, ever," Mitch said. "We were insuffer- able dorks. But Longworth was like having Stu Sutcliffe in the band. He was always way ahead of everybody else. I think that's how we got most of our gigs: 'Okay, the drummer's pretty cool.'"

Bicycle Face gigged around Greensboro before coming to Chapel Hill. Brian noticed similarities between the two towns. "I didn't get the feeling that people were doing it to be seen doing it," he said, "but people were doing it because they were just excited to do it. It was one of the first times I was like, 'Oh, there doesn't have to be an end goal.'"

"We were a geeky little band from Greensboro," Mitch said. "We played in the dorm basement and we played wherever we could get a gig. Then we got a record deal." Kelley signed Bicycle Face to his new label, Moist Records. Superchunk's guitarist Jack McCook designed the label's melty-lettered logo.

"I liked that Bicycle Face played very primitive rock that was catchy, quirky, and poppy," Kelley said. "Brian and Mitch were stand-up comedians, each of them completely different from the other. Brian was more verbally funny. Plus, I thought their songs were good. They were Minutemen-ish but wittier."

One day at Poindexter, Kelley was wondering out loud to Glenn about who to team up with as a distributor for Moist. Glenn recommended Andrew Peterson. Andrew's experience interning for Mammoth, promoting the Nikki Meets the Hibachi single, and his own admitted "youth, inexperience, and idealism" made him think he could make a go of it. Consequently, he started Baited Breath Productions. "This is the only guy you should meet," Glenn told Kelley. "You can really complement one another."

The comparative success of the Nikki Meets the Hibachi single had gotten Andrew a bit of local attention. "I had a few other bands approach me and say, 'Hey—we've got a record, we financed it, we're going to press it. Will you do whatever you did with them for us?'" he said. "I thought, 'I should make a record label.' Then Glenn introduced me to Kelley, who was thinking about doing the same thing. Neither one of us had any money or experience, but we both had a lot of enthusiasm."

One of the bands Andrew wanted to sign was Zen Frisbee. By now, UNC student Dave Brylawski was an XYC DJ. He remembers the band bringing newly recorded songs into the station. "They put that first demo on cart so you could play them on the air," Dave said. (Fidelipacs, better known as "carts," were strange little eight-track-tape-looking broadcast cartridges that had been around since the late fifties. Carts usually had about five minutes of tape and could be magnetically erased, so XYC's stash was reused constantly.)

"That was when Zen Frisbee was first being played on the radio and I would play them," Dave said. "There was that song 'Freeburn,' but it also had these really intricate, fingerpicky, layered things that were just amazing. For a while they *were* the Chapel Hill band."

Glenn had figured out another way to promote local music that also involved Kelley, who had just become comanager of a little club across the street from campus. One of Kelley's friends had been approached by a "good old boy with tobacco money" who wanted to open a dance club on the east side of town, near where Laura Ballance had been given a Zen Frisbee newsletter. The deal was that Kelley and his friend would run the club the way they saw fit.

Initially a dance club (Kelley told me it was the owner's way of coming out), Club Zen started booking local bands because of Glenn Boothe. The two decided to hold a WXYC Night every weekend and picked the bands to play. "It started in the spring of 1990," Glenn remembered. "The cover was two dollars and most of that went to the soundman because he brought the PA."

The new lineup of my band debuted at Club Zen. The core of the group, formed in 1986 while we were still UNC students, was always John Ensslin and me. We used to hang out at John's apartment on Bim Street in Carrboro and smoke weed out of a blue mermaid-shaped pipe with a broken tail. One day John was playing the James Bond *Goldfinger* soundtrack. He pointed to a song on the back cover called "Teasing the Korean."

"That would be a cool band name," John said.

"No, it fucking wouldn't," I said, rewriting history, because I don't think I actually said that.

When we started, I was a sloppy drummer and John was no musician at all. "At UNC, I was either going to major in theater or painting," he said. "I went to a party where there were a bunch of drama people. At the party, somebody played '1999' by Prince. Big hit at the time. I looked, and everybody in the room was mock holding a microphone and singing as if they were Prince. I said, 'I don't want to be in this environment. These people are show-offs!'" John started socializing with musicians instead. But to him, the hippest crowd in town were the local gutter punks.

"There were these kids hanging out in front of Hector's with their eyeliner and teased hair and dirty clothes and Rimbaud paperbacks," John said. "They were so much cooler than I would ever be and they were all fifteen. They weren't even old enough to go to any clubs, but they knew the cool music. They liked Flat Duo Jets."

Like Zen Frisbee, Teasing the Korean went through several iterations, finally coalescing around guitarists Timothy Roven and Lyndon "Dave" Jernigan as well as the best bass player in town, Jeff Taylor. Tim was a big fan of The Cure. Jeff loved The Smiths and Black Sabbath. Dave was way into Sonic Youth. John listened to proto-industrial oddballs like Virgin Prunes and Jim Foetus. I brought the Small Faces influence. In a scene full of iconoclasts, Teasing the Korean was a sore thumb. The new lineup's first show was at Club Zen. "Everybody was up close," John said. "We did well. I don't know if we made any money, but there were a lot of people there. It was somewhat auspicious."

Another early Club Zen WXYC Night featured DJ Dave Brylawski's new band. Dave had been jamming with his childhood friend Steve Popson and college buddies Ash Bowie and Eddie Watkins. "We played a couple parties and covered Pink Floyd's 'Interstellar Overdrive,'" Dave remembered. "It was that primitive." The band felt like outsiders in a scene dominated by polished pop acts like Dillon Fence, The Connells, and Pressure Boys.

Ash had gone to Spain for a year and returned a guitar prodigy. "I don't know what kind of crossroads deal he made," Dave mused, "but he came back fully formed." Ash and Dave were musical omnivores, listening to everything from Let's Active to Sonic Youth to Middle Eastern music. Drummer Eddie Watkins introduced them to prog bands like King Crimson and early Genesis. "Eddie was the most sophisticated one of us," Dave said. "He dressed very well and had sophisticated musical tastes." The group chose a name: Rum Tar Lust.

After almost two years of jamming and playing desultory house parties, Rum Tar Lust decided that their club debut would be the WXYC Night at Club Zen. Unusually, the show was booked as a double bill. The opener was another new local outfit called Metal Flake Mother.

Dave had known Metal Flake Mother front man Ben Clarke since childhood. The two had lived across the street from each other. "Ben had a mohawk in the sixth or seventh grade," Dave said. "That's another Chapel Hill thing that keeps coming back to me: a hybrid normality mixed with real art damage."

Ben played music from a very young age and was a guitar obsessive. As a teenager, he was in a local punk band called A Number of Things. (Marvin Levy, who would go on to drum for The Veldt, played bass.) The group took its name from a Robert Louis Stevenson poem called "Happy Thought."

> The world is so full of a number of things
> I'm sure we all should be as happy as kings

"Hollywood" Randy Ward wasn't in A Number of Things, but he was in Metal Flake Mother. Randy and Ben were best friends who had played music together since they were twelve. As a young man, Randy used to visit Zen Frisbee's Kevin Dixon every week to watch reruns of *Fantasy Island*.

"It was always kind of a drag when Randy came over, because he'd deliberately break things," Kevin remembered. "If you had one of those shitty portable tape decks in your room, he would just casually stomp on it and break it. Then he would invent these weird instruments with parts of the electronics that he broke at your house. So, there was a bit of a trade-off."

By 1990, Ben and Randy had written a batch of original songs and decided to form a band. Randy brought in a very gentle unicorn person named Quince Marcum to play bass. In turn, Quince introduced them to a lemur-eyed Mississippi transplant named Jimbo Mathus.

The two had met when Jimbo was working on riverboats. "Thirty days on and thirty days off," Quince remembered, "and using the thirty days off to try and figure out where he wanted to live. He showed up in Chapel Hill." Quince and Jimbo became good friends and ended up living together in a house on Airport Road.

One day, Quince was at the Hardback Cafe when Randy walked in. "I'd met him before when he was a goat spider creature crawling around town," Quince recalled. "He had really long dreadlocks and I thought he looked like a goat spider."

Randy walked up to Quince's table. "I understand you play bass," he said.

"I didn't really play bass," Quince told me, "but a friend had given me a bass, saying, 'You need to play a musical instrument.' So, I'd had a bass for a few months and messed around a tiny bit with it and didn't play well. Ben and Randy loved that I wasn't a good bass player. It was better for their purposes."

Quince, Ben, and Randy played together for the first time with a drummer that Ben and Randy didn't like. Quince went home and told Jimbo about it.

"I play drums," Jimbo said.

"You play drums?"

"No, but I just got this free drum kit. I can do that." Quince thinks Jimbo might have found the drums in a dumpster, but he could have been speaking metaphorically.

The next practice took place at Quince and Jimbo's house. Jimbo played standing up because he couldn't make the hi-hat cymbal work sitting down. Musically, things fell into place very quickly. Ben sang lead, played rhythm guitar, and wrote much of the material. Jimbo proved to be a minimalist drummer, solid timekeeper, and great singer and songwriter in his own right. Randy played lead unlike anyone else, wringing oblique melodies out of the chord changes. Quince held the whole thing together, musically and temperamentally.

"Randy and I would work on songs together for a while before we would bring it to the four of us," Ben said, "and the stuff he would come up with always would make a good song great. He was really good at helping arrange things, and with his guitar there was this constant second melody going the whole time."

"When we talk about being cool or having style or having good instincts," Quince said, "the thing that Randy had was that he was close to the truth. Randy's stuff was good because it was right. It wasn't a parody. It was exactly right. When someone said they wanted to be like Randy, they just wanted to be right as often as he was."

Metal Flake Mother's first show was an opening slot at the Cat's Cradle. They played six songs. My best friend and bandmate John Ensslin was there and gave me a detailed description. "They came out of the gate like fucking unreal," John remembered. "Talk about stage charisma. Ben's persona and physicality was almost like Sergeant Carter from *Gomer Pyle, U.S.M.C.* He looked like somebody's wrestling coach. He wore a Ban-Lon shirt. He made the mic stand short, so he had to bend over it. It made him look big.

"Then you had Randy, the grooviest lizard you've ever met," John continued. "He was so laid-back. He had the whipped-curl hair, he had the whole thing. Quince had this ability to play something that everybody could work off of when they were sprinting in different directions. There was a diabolical drummer, Jimbo, who looked like a creepy elf—and he sang too. His voice was maybe the best." To my ears, Jimbo sounded like Dexter Romweber with less fire in his belly. He became Chapel Hill's Levon Helm.

"I felt like I'd suddenly fallen into a pile of geniuses," Quince said.

Metal Flake Mother's fourth show was the Club Zen gig with Dave Brylawski's band Rum Tar Lust. "For some reason, they booked us after Metal Flake Mother," Dave said. "I don't know why. They came out of the gate fully formed—so tight and intricate. You were looking at this level of musicianship that you were never going to reach. And then we got up there and cleared the room! All the Metal Flake Mother people dipped. They should have, because we were not very good."

A demoralized Rum Tar Lust held an emergency meeting out on the street, gathered around somebody's car. The agenda was whether the band should break up after their first official gig. "The four of us were like, 'Okay, we're going to change our name and try again,'" Dave said. "And we did." He remembers people staying away from the band's next couple Club Zen gigs because the first one was so bad. In the meantime, Rum Tar Lust changed its name to Polvo.

After the Club Zen show, Kelley Cox and Andrew Peterson approached the opening act. "We saw Metal Flake Mother and immediately went up to them and said, 'Hey, we're this new label and we want to record you,'" Andrew remembered. "I think they were all like, 'We're just starting?'"

It's not surprising that Quince and Randy had had a fateful chance meeting at the Hardback Cafe. There were few places in Chapel Hill more suited to these kinds of interactions. Grant Kornberg founded the Hardback Cafe & Bookstore with partner Tom Cook in 1984. According to Grant, their goal was to open a place "where we'd like to hang out." The idea was to create an integrated bookstore and café. The Hardback was based on places like Kramer Books in Washington, DC.

The two owners wanted to make money, of course—maybe even open in other locations—but profit wasn't their primary motive. "We felt if we opened a culturally rich business that was user friendly, that the money would follow," Grant said. "And we were wrong! We were wrong all ten years."

In other ways the Hardback Cafe was a resounding success. It very quickly became an indispensable Chapel Hill social hub. Frequented by professors, poets, and painters, the Hardback hosted events, showcased bands, and generally operated as an oasis. Famed fiction writer Harlan Ellison once wrote a short story in front of the floor-to-ceiling windows facing North Columbia Street to raise money for a progressive political candidate. It was a mob scene.

More than most other places in town, the Hardback had a familial vibe. "That was probably accidental," Grant said. "It was organic and I deserve absolutely no credit. Tom and I put some stuff into place and were able to get a group of people who really liked working there and who cared a lot about the business."

One of those people was bartender Alvis Dunn, at the time a grad student finishing up his master's degree in Latin American history at UNC. "There was a lot of art that happened in the Hardback that still wouldn't be recognized as art," Alvis told me. "Stacking the bar glasses artistically or pouring a glass of wine beautifully. It was a thing that people took the opportunity to bring their soul into."

There was a concerted effort at the Hardback to hire musicians. "It was easy, because people in bands wanted short shift jobs," Alvis said. "All of the shifts were at least four hours long." Alvis often took it upon himself to go wake up a dishwasher and drive them to their shift "because they'd been up late playing music, or watching people play music, or participating in music in some way."

Oftentimes Hardback employees saw customers just sit and stare up at the ceiling fans. "We used to call it Thinking of String," Alvis said. "Like they were trying to unravel a gnarly ball of string in their mind. That was a great thing that was happening, like when they were staring at the milk in their iced coffee as it filtered through and created all kinds of art. It didn't matter that it wasn't captured."

Kirk Ross worked at Copytron, across from the Hardback Cafe on North Columbia Street. He had worked his way up the copy store chain, having been sent to sales school at Xerox Document University. Accordingly, he was put in charge of "course packs": photocopied collections of scholarly journals and other readings for classes at UNC. It was a lucrative business.

Kirk would open Copytron early every morning. Then he'd walk across the street, into the Hardback's back door, and meet house manager Jamie McPhail while she was getting the bar ready. The two would sit and drink coffee together.

"We checked in on people with each other," Kirk said. "Jamie and I have always done that. If somebody was losing it, we'd give each other a heads-up. Because it happens: young people get challenged in this world. Mostly we just talked about regular stuff, like what the hell happened the night before."

Grant Kornberg described Jamie McPhail as "a wonderful human being who killed herself for the Hardback Cafe." She's also a dedicated music fan. "I think for most bands it was not about any sort of success," Jamie said. "One of the reasons why Chapel Hill was such a great place was because there wasn't that desire to be famous. That wasn't what was fueling people. It was easy to just live without having to work too hard. It was cheap. I don't think they wanted the headache of the next level."

"Back then it wasn't about making money," Laura Ballance told me. "This is the thing that has freaked me out for a long time about musicians now, as they get into it. They think they're doing it to make money. When we started Merge, nobody had any misconception that they were gonna make a living off being in a fucking band. It was entirely for fun and to entertain yourself and maybe your friends. You would definitely be having a day job." Neither Laura nor Mac McCaughan paid themselves from Merge Records. Any money the label might make was rolled into the next project.

"I think our favorite place to play was the Hardback," Metal Flake Mother's Ben Clarke said. "Just a nice, small place that would get packed."

The MTV *News at Night* feature on The Veldt aired in March. "The Veldt were a band who deserved to be enormous," host Tim Sommer told me. "An African American Cocteau Twins? My God." On the broadcast, after mentioning that two of the band's biggest supporters were Cocteau Twins' Robin Guthrie and Living Color's Vernon Reid, Sommer said, "A lot of people are going to be surprised by The Veldt, one of the most promising bands on the active North Carolina scene. After all, few interracial groups are strongly influenced by the high-drama, very white British pop of The Cure, New Order, the Cocteau Twins, and Echo & the Bunnymen."

Around this time, Mac got a call from Homestead Records' Gerard Cosloy. "Look," Gerard said, "I know you have proposals from Dutch East, but I'm leaving, and I don't know who's going to be running Homestead. I'm starting a new label with Chris Lombardi, and I want to sign Chunk." An agreement was struck whereby Merge would still be allowed to put out singles and Gerard's new label, Matador Records, would release albums.

"Gerard and Chris were people who were starting an independent label and recognized what was cool about it," Mac said. "So, they didn't want to take away the thing that *we* were doing that was cool, which was putting out our own singles. At the same time, we didn't have the money or the resources to put out a full-length album."

There was a slight hitch. "The label said, 'There's another band called Chunk here in New York,'" Mac remembered. "'We don't know if you've ever heard them, but they're a Knitting Factory–type percussion ensemble.' We thought, 'Maybe they won't mind because musically it's very different?' It turns out they did mind! In coordination with signing to Matador we changed our name to Superchunk." The new name was apparently Mac's mom's idea.

As soon as school was over, Superchunk hit the road, touring the South and Midwest with two other young bands, Geek and Seaweed. None of the groups had released anything but seven-inch singles. "By the time we went on tour, we knew that we were going to be on Matador and Seaweed knew that they were going to be on SubPop," Mac said. "And so, we would have arguments about which label was cooler." Jack McCook pulled out of Superchunk prior to the tour and was temporarily replaced by guitarist Jim Wilbur.

In part because of Superchunk's busy schedule, Chuck Garrison quit Zen Frisbee in June. "I had gotten frustrated with those guys, because I felt like they were real fuck-ups," Chuck said. "And to be fair to me, they are! I wanted us to do more. I had to go out on the road for a long time and that was conflicting with what Zen Frisbee wanted to do. So, I quit the band. It was dramatic. I remember Kevin Dixon was mad at me, which is weird. Kevin and I have known each other for a very long time. He's not often mad, really, at anyone. I guess if he was gonna be mad at anyone, it was probably going to be me."

Superchunk released a new seven inch in June. The A-side is an anthemic snipe job called "Slack Motherfucker." Mac said he wrote it about a Kinko's coworker. "You haven't moved from that spot all night since you asked for a light, you little smokestack," he spits out.

You've wasted my time
I'd like to see you try and give it back

I'm working, but I'm not working for you
Slack motherfucker

By now WXYC program director Glenn Boothe was about to
move to New York. The new Superchunk single sparked some intense
discussions at the station between Glenn and his successor, Randy
Bullock. "Thurston Moore and maybe Kim Gordon came by the station on a promotional tour the Friday before Sonic Youth's *Goo* came
out," Glenn remembered. "We had just gotten a copy of the 'Slack
Motherfucker' seven inch that week, if not that day." Thurston, doing
a guest DJ slot, asked to play it.

It happened to be Glenn's last day in Chapel Hill. "There was a
big debate as to whether the station could play the song," he said,
because doing so would have risked being fined by the Federal Communications Commission. He remembers letting Sonic Youth only
spin the B-side, "Night Creatures."

One day in early July, Dog Gone Records' publicist Jocelyn
LaBelle got a call from the people at *Late Night with David Letterman*. The band that had been booked for an upcoming Friday night
slot just canceled. "We're looking at three different bands," the *Letterman* people told her. "What have you got?"

"Flat Duo Jets," Jocelyn quickly responded. When she told Dick
Hodgin that the group might have a shot at *Letterman*, he said, "Tell
them that Paul Shaffer knows who the fuck Dexter is." Two hours
later, the Flat Duo Jets were booked for July 13.

There was a three-band bill at the Fallout Shelter in Raleigh on
July 13: Finger, Metal Flake Mother, and Superchunk. The Fallout
Shelter was a little dance club in the basement of 2 S. West Street
in Raleigh. It tended to focus on industrial and goth music but also
booked local bands. This gig was one of Superchunk's first shows
there.

Kelley Cox was at the Fallout Shelter show and loved seeing Metal
Flake Mother again. "They were a super young band that was nothing like a super young band," he said. "They looked like rock stars,

not that I was looking for that. Their songs were fully developed. They were the real deal. You knew it when they walked up, and you knew it when they started playing."

Sara Bell was also at that show. Her former band Angels of Epistemology had appeared on 1987's *Evil I Do Not/To Nod I Live* box set. In 1989, Sara moved to Finland to learn Russian. In 1990, while she was still there—and to her surprise—Merge Records' Laura Ballance mailed her an Angels of Epistemology seven inch, even though the band had broken up the year before. It turns out Glenn Boothe made that happen too. "I'm listening to WXYC one night," Glenn said, "and one of the DJs plays a song by Angels of Epistemology I've never heard." After discovering a cache of unreleased Angels recordings, Glenn put up the money for Merge to release a seven inch.

According to Sara, when she moved back to Raleigh in 1990, "everything had completely changed."

Back in the Fallout Shelter on the night of July 13, headliners Superchunk took the stage. In the middle of one of their songs, the bartender made a signal with his hand and turned up the volume on the TV: David Letterman had just introduced Flat Duo Jets. Superchunk stopped playing as the crowd turned their backs to watch. Chuck Garrison remembers Mac McCaughan being "visibly irritated."

"We all knew it was coming," Chuck said. "I wanted to wait and play until after it had happened, but for some reason we didn't."

"I remember feeling like there was this understanding," Sara remembered. "'Our people are on national television. These are our friends. Of *course* everything's going to stop and we're going to watch this.' But Superchunk was playing one of their very earliest shows and everybody turned around, because the stage was facing the TV. I remember Mac being like, 'What's everybody doing? Why is everybody looking away?'"

On the television, Griz "Tone" Mayer, Dexter, and Crow, all looking serious, walk out from backstage to their instruments—Tone on stand-up bass, Crow standing behind a snare drum and cymbal.

Dexter, dressed in white, fires off a machine-gun rhythm on his Silvertone, his amp making an echoey, guttural bark. Then they're off into "Wild, Wild Lover," a track off *Flat Duo Jets*. It's frantic and gloriously loose.

The *Letterman* house band is playing along too, mostly in a supporting role. There's a wonderful moment during Dexter's primitive, double-stop guitar solo where the house guitarist, a polished-looking guy in a sports jacket, flashes Dex a genuine smile. After another verse, Dex jabs a finger at Paul Shaffer and howls, "Rock!" Paul complies, playing like a demon.

It almost didn't happen that way. "They were rehearsing the song that afternoon," manager Dick Hodgin remembered, "and Dexter said, 'Paul, you got to do a solo.' You could see Paul was flattered. Paul did a solo and he was rocking it out like Jerry Lee Lewis." After a producer said the rehearsal ran overtime, Paul decided to cut his solo for the night's performance. That is, until Dexter commanded him to do otherwise.

Back in the Fallout Shelter, as David Letterman was shaking the Flat Duo Jets' hands, the bartender lowered the sound on the television, the crowd turned back around to face the stage, and Superchunk resumed. "I don't remember what our set was like, but I remember that moment," Mac said. "Dexter was a local legend."

"That's when I was all in," Kelley Cox remembered. "Maybe that's even the moment I decided to 'marry' Andrew Peterson and go in with him on a record label. I didn't have any doubt that something was brewing around here, that it was big, and that it mattered."

Metal Flake Mother made their first recordings in August. They were produced and engineered by a nineteen-year-old chain-smoker named Caleb Southern at Lloyd Street Studios in Carrboro. Caleb had grown up in Durham County. When he was thirteen, he could hear the Pressure Boys practicing in an old house down the dirt road where his family lived. Caleb formed a band in high school and attended UNC "to stay involved in the music scene."

Not long after the Cat's Cradle moved to the old Bell South building in 1989, Caleb walked over and talked to house soundman Tim Harper. "Do you ever need a sub?" he asked.

"Tim wrote my name and dorm phone number down on a shoebox next to the mixing board," Caleb said. "I was the third or fourth guy on the list. Then he called me." Caleb became Tim's replacement. Frank Heath paid him $20 for one band, $25 for two bands, and $30 for three.

Caleb was obsessed with record production. "It was obvious that there was a lot of energy and something going on," he said about the Chapel Hill music scene. "I was in the right place at the right time. There were a ton of really good ideas but a lack of ability to execute them. I felt like, 'Maybe that's what I'm supposed to do: figure out a way to get the band's big ideas on tape even though they're not quite pulling them off.' It was an opportunity, but often frustrating. Nothing was ever as good as I wanted it to be."

Caleb knew the guys over at Lloyd Street Studios, a small building near the railroad tracks in Carrboro that had started life as a rehearsal space before acquiring some cheap recording gear. "Everybody was making seven inches, so there was work to be had," he said. "My competition was Jerry Kee in Raleigh. I was like, 'I'm gonna do it my way' but wasn't very good. I was a terrible engineer for four years." Caleb's first production gig was the Moist Records Bicycle Face seven-inch session in June. His second session was Metal Flake Mother.

"I was really opinionated," Caleb remembered. "I wanted everything to sound like a clean guitar through a Fender Twin, which it wasn't. I didn't break Randy's guitar sound, but I broke Ben's a little."

To my ears, Caleb perfectly captured Metal Flake Mother's voluptuous guitar sounds. Without getting too technical here (mostly because I'm incapable), the best distortion comes from overdriven tube amps. When cranked up, they produce the melty aural equivalent of crispy bacon. As contradictory as it may seem, there's a reason why many of the enormous Led Zeppelin guitar sounds were recorded on a tiny little 5-watt Fender Champ. Ben and Randy played oddly shaped sixties Airline and Supro guitars as well as a gold-top Gibson Les Paul. Randy played through a Fender Super Reverb with a 4 × 10 cabinet, turned up to a satisfying snarl.

A month after Metal Flake Mother made their first recordings, Superchunk came out with their debut album. *Superchunk* was released by Matador Records on September 25. It clocks in at just over thirty-two minutes. "Slack Motherfucker" sits smack in the middle of the sequence. "My Noise" is the second track.

Greg Kot, music critic for the *Chicago Tribune*, gave *Superchunk* four stars and praised its pop sensibility over everything else. "The production is a big, sloppy mess," Kot noted, "but time and again these guys mold the mud into a great pop song."

To my mind, this pop sensibility is the defining element of anything that can be called a Chapel Hill sound, but even this ultimately fails. Almost without exception, every band in this book wrote pop songs. Hit songs. Catchy-as-fuck songs. The way each band chose to arrange those melodies and chord progressions was as diverse as the people writing the music. I guess a better term for it is folk music. We were folk musicians. Musical training helped but wasn't a requirement. Mac wrote much the same thing in a nineties essay for local culture weekly the *Independent*, which he doesn't have and I can't find.

At some point, Jay Faires and Mammoth Records partner Ed Morgan parted ways. Former intern Steve Balcom got kicked upstairs. "Jay was like, 'Do you wanna be the label manager?,' which is what Ed's role was," Steve remembered. "I was like, 'Sure.' This idea of a label general manager was pretty much my job from nine months into it until the end of it." Mammoth moved to Carrboro, which was easier for Jay and Steve, who both lived in Chapel Hill. The label's first Carrboro office was located upstairs in the old textile mill.

The Mammoth move didn't feel great to blackgirls' Dana Kletter. "That was the absolute opposite of what they'd been in Raleigh," she said. "Everyone sat far away from each other compared to the close cluster of desks in Raleigh. That was the weirdest feeling, walking into a different place. It felt as if the stakes had been raised by the new office. It felt more formal. It felt more corporate.

"All of us had come out of the punk rock, hardcore tradition," Dana said. "We all knew Ian MacKaye and the Dischord people. It was obvious that Jay had serious ambitions."

Polvo bounced back from their disastrous Club Zen debut as Rum Tar Lust. "We played in Raleigh," Dave Brylawski said, "and Erectus Monotone, Willard, and Picasso Trigger all showed up. And that was it. We got embraced by Raleigh, and that gave us the confidence to go back to Chapel Hill.

"There was a show that Glenn Boothe organized at The Spiral in New York for the New Music Seminar called the 'Tar Heel Toe Jam,'" Dave said. "I think Metal Flake Mother played. A bunch of Chapel Hill and Raleigh bands played. It was our first show in New York. Superchunk was around the corner playing CBGBs, so we all went over there. They'd sold out. So, we just massed outside CBGBs, drinking forties."

Chuck Garrison saw a little article in one of the New Music Seminar's pamphlets about how well North Carolina was being represented. The name of the piece was "Chapel Hill Rocks?"

Polvo self-released their first EP, *Can I Ride*, on their own Kitchen Puff label in the fall. Some of its seven songs were produced by Caleb Southern at Lloyd Street Studios in Carrboro, the rest by Jerry Kee at Duck Kee in Raleigh. The title track is a monolithic mix of Eastern modalities, cinematic rhythmic landscapes, and buried vocals. "I'll arrive," Ash Bowie sings, "though it takes me a while to get there." Eddie Watkins rushes the shit out of some sixteenth-note snare drum fills, but all it does is add kinetic urgency to the performance.

Around this time, Mac McCaughan caught a Polvo gig. "I remember seeing Polvo in a basement at a party in Raleigh," he said, "and thinking, 'This is awesome.' It sounded like Hüsker Dü, but there were all these crazy tunings. Everything was off-kilter until they would lock into some riff or really techie part. After all the weird, atonal guitar things, they would play something catchy and memorable."

Over at Merge Records, Mac and Laura Ballance were inspired by what some other independent labels were doing, in particular British ones like Factory Records and 4AD. Teen-Beat Records emulated Factory by giving everything—whether it was a tape or the label founder Mark Robinson's car—a matrix number. "It's like they were saying, 'Our label isn't just the record you're getting,'" Mac said. "'It's our whole life.'" Merge Records also used matrix numbers.

To this day, every Merge Records matrix number is accounted for except one, MRG011, which was supposed to have been released between the Breadwinner and Finger singles in November. It turns out that MRG011 had been reserved for Zen Frisbee.

"I'm not sure if we dropped the ball or they did," Kevin Dixon said. "We might not have even known they were saving us a spot until years later."

"I remember hearing whispers that Merge had a bookmarker for a single," Laird Dixon told me. "I thought that was just chatter amongst the Merge people."

"Yeah, we wanted to put out a Zen Frisbee seven inch," Laura recalled, "and I think they gave us something weird. It felt like they were playing a joke on us and we were like, 'No, we're not putting that out.'"

"My memory is that we agreed to do one," Mac said. "You know, they've gone through phases of existing and not existing. So, either they recorded one and then didn't like it and didn't want to put it out, or they broke up after we had already agreed to put out a single."

In fact, Zen Frisbee had recorded four perfectly serious songs at Duck Kee that would have been released as MRG011: "Russian Redeye," "Spaghetti Park (Mall)," and "Freeburn (I Want Rock!)." These are the songs Dave Brylawski remembers the band putting on cart at WXYC.

There are two probable reasons why the MRG011 matrix number remains unused. One is that Zen Frisbee, who'd already missed an opportunity for inclusion on the *Evil I Do Not/To Nod I Live* box set three years previously because of insufficient funds, couldn't come up with the money to help pay for the Merge release either. The other is that the band broke up after Chuck Garrison quit in June.

Zen Frisbee winked in and out of existence as a matter of course ("Brian Walker would quit every week," Kevin quipped). They'd already replaced their bass player a few times. At some point the band reformed around a new drummer.

"Brian and I were walking down Franklin Street one afternoon just wasting time," Laird said, "and this skinny, goofy-looking guy runs up to us and says, 'Hey! You guys play in that band Zen Frisbee, right?' God knows how he knew who we were. He introduced himself as Jimbo. We conscripted him."

"Metal Flake Mother was suddenly more popular than we were, so we were a little jealous and tried to steal their drummer," Kevin said. During the first Metal Flake Mother show at the Cradle, Frank Heath sidled up to Kevin, saying, "This is the first Chapel Hill band influenced by Zen Frisbee."

One night, the new Zen Frisbee lineup was booked to play the Cradle. Since no one had wheels, there was some question about how they'd get their gear down to the venue. All the band's equipment was in Laird and Brian's house on Basnight Lane, a few blocks west. Brian let an unhoused man named Mr. Freeze keep things in his broken-down car parked outside.

"Mr. Freeze was some crazy homeless guy who would go around town and collect junk everywhere and had shopping carts full of stuff," Kevin said. "So, you had this mountain of cool trash. It was fun to go through, especially after Halloween when he'd find all the weird, discarded parts of costumes."

Mr. Freeze not only stored things in Brian's car, he also slept there. "A census person came by at one point," Laird remembered. "We said, 'Oh, someone's living in the car,' and he was like, 'I don't know how to do this.' He ended up writing down Mr. Freeze's address as Brian's license plate number.

"It was Jimbo who had the brilliant idea of, 'Let's just load all of our amps, all the equipment—the drums, everything—into these shopping carts,'" Laird said. The band filmed themselves racing down the sidewalk to the Cat's Cradle. "It was really neat, because the front gate of the carts was perfectly level with the height of the stage," Laird remembered. "We opened up the tiny gate and slid our amps onstage."

"After the show, we all got rides back, but we left the shopping carts down at the Cradle," Kevin laughed. "They were Frank's problem then." Frank used them to transport cases of beer. When my band shot a video at the Cradle, we put the director in one and pushed him around like a camera dolly.

1991

On Saturday, January 26, Teasing the Korean played what became known as "the baby doll show" as part of another Glenn Boothe initiative, the WXYC Local Series. This time the venue was Cat's Cradle.

"I had gotten this doll," John Ensslin said. "Baby Shivers is what it was called. You could unscrew the head and put batteries in. It would shake till you picked it up and held it. But the way to get the most amusement out of the doll, of course, was to just set it on the table, watch it shake, and go, 'Yeah. That's for you!' I didn't get it thinking I would use it onstage. Then I thought, 'Oh, it's good.'

"I used the baby doll as a prop for maybe two numbers right at the get-go," John said. "Taking the stage with it perched on my shoulder, ass forward. Then I would either pay too much attention to the baby doll or not enough. Sometimes I would just hold the baby by the head like a sack of potatoes and sing.

"It worked beyond my wildest dreams," John remembered. "I've had plenty of props. I've done lots of schtick. Nothing was ever as successful as the baby doll show."

Baby Shivers *was* schtick, but John's abilities as a front man were not. By this time, he'd created an onstage persona that was unique in town. A small subset of bands from the area had amazing front men—the Bad Checks chief among them, also UV Prom and Zen Frisbee—but their numbers dwindled going into the nineties. John had the goods. He would command a stage, glaring at the audience like Sam the Eagle from *The Muppet Show*, walking like a marionette, or simply standing stock still. He fussed over outfits and makeup. He built a gestural language.

Robert Sledge played bass in a Greensboro band called Toxic Popsicle, who gigged with Teasing the Korean at a North Carolina Music Showcase in Wilmington. "It was as if Serge Gainsbourg and Nico had a kid named John Ensslin," Robert said. "His godfather is David Bowie. This is the mythology I was thinking in my head as soon as I saw Ensslin, who decided to sing a few lines in between puffs of smoke. It was like, 'That's the coolest motherfucker I've ever seen.'"

The Cradle was full that night, maybe even sold out. The noise of the crowd yelling for an encore followed John up into the second-floor greenroom after our last song. "It was a white room that was empty," John said. "And I remember going like, 'Wow, this is so great.' It felt like a one-off even then. I didn't feel like, 'We've made it and all the shows are gonna be like this.' I did not. But I felt like that one really worked. I knew that we were gonna do an encore, but I wanted to just hang in that space. Because that's a sweet spot, for sure. So, I was like, 'I'm just going to sit here and calm my breathing down.'"

Internal pressure had been building inside Dillon Fence to make a career of it or break up. Everything pointed toward the former: the band was doing huge numbers regionally and selling stacks of *Dillon Fence* out of the back of their van. Drummer Scott Carle joined right after the EP's release. "We kept building, it kept growing, a fire was lit, and it was insanity," Scott said. "We'd go to Virginia Tech and it would take us twenty minutes to get to the stage. It was like boxers entering the ring."

Teasing the Korean's opening gig for Dillon Fence at The Mad Monk in Wilmington is a good example. "It was a sold-out show," John said. "The crowd had been standing in line in the rain. We come out there and nobody pays any fucking attention to the band at all. Everybody's got their red solo cup full of beer and they're standing around talking like it's a party. I'm like, 'How're you doing?' Crickets.

"We do the whole act," John remembered. "I don't even know if they applauded between songs. It was weird, like we weren't even there. Dillon Fence comes out. Greg's like, 'How y'all doing?' The crowd made a sound like the ocean crashing back down on the Pharaoh or some shit." Despite this, no record labels had yet to make Dillon Fence any offers.

At some point, Mammoth Records got wise to the fact that there was easy money to be made. Greg Humphreys thinks Steve Balcom was responsible for their signing because he liked them and recognized their ambition. If anything, the Mammoth recording agreement was worse than what Superchunk had been sent by Dutch East India Trading.

"Looking back, we probably shouldn't have signed that contract," Greg said, "because it was not a very good offer. But at the time, we were under pressure to make something happen. That's one of those dynamics of the music business, where you've got these young and hungry acts that are like, 'Where do I sign? Because we want to move forward.'"

In addition to the Mammoth recording agreement, Dillon Fence also signed a copublishing deal. In it, they granted partial ownership of their songwriting intellectual property to Jay Faires's publishing company. "It always stuck in my craw that our lawyer didn't fight harder for us," Greg said, "and I asked him about it years later. He said something along the lines of, 'What was I supposed to do? They were the ones bringing me all the business.'"

"Early on, the Mammoth checks were all handwritten," Lane Wurster said. "I remember getting the checks and there would always be a tear in the top or the side of them. I said, 'Do you guys have a tear in your check?' and somebody told me, 'Yeah. Jay always tears them.' The logic was, if they were torn they couldn't be automatically processed by whatever the machines are that you could slide a check through. So, it all had to be processed by hand, which would allow for an extra day or two for the money to clear."

"That was the high-wire act of cash flow," Jay said when I asked.

Meanwhile, Kelley Cox and Andrew Peterson had joined forces and were running what was now collectively referred to as Moist/Baited Breath Records. The Moist side put out *Irrelevant*, Bicycle Face's seven inch. "WXYC program director Randy Bullock wrote a great review of the single," Mitch McGirt said, "then we played Cat's Cradle and had a great audience. For two weeks we were the kings of Chapel Hill. After that, it was like, 'Okay, we're done with these guys.'"

Mike Kenlan, a recent New Jersey transplant, was at that Bicycle Face show. "They were on fire," he said. "Mitch was down to about three strings, but absolutely captivating. Everybody's watching them and going crazy. My date was like, 'You know, I love that I can come see this guy play in his band, but I'm really glad he's not my neighbor.'"

Around the same time, Moist/Baited Breath released *Deem-On*, the Metal Flake Mother seven inch also produced by Caleb Southern. It immediately went into heavy rotation at WXYC. In addition, the label issued two local full lengths: one by Nikki Meets the Hibachi and one by UNC student Natalie Farr. Some records, like the Metal Flake Mother single, bore the Moist Records label. Others, like Natalie's, were released by Baited Breath Productions.

"I was hearing bands talking about how awful labels were to them," Andrew Peterson remembered. "I didn't realize that bands only got 12 percent of record sales. According to the numbers, they should have gotten a lot more than that. I thought, 'I'm gonna fix this.'

"Once the label had a couple of releases out, we were looking to sell one to three thousand copies of each new album," Andrew said. "That was the goal; to break even on it. If you could get records out there to radio and press, then the bands could go on the road. That was the R.E.M. model: You keep doing it and you go back. Eventually more and more people show up."

It was a gamble. Moist/Baited Breath didn't have the resources to promote the records they were releasing. "The goal was, 'Let's get this out there and start working on the next recording for the band,'" Andrew said. "And hopefully they'll get a break."

One day in February, Zen Frisbee was practicing with their new drummer Jimbo Mathus at the house on Basnight Lane when Randy Ward showed up. The band took a break. "Randy took Jimbo aside but not far enough," Laird Dixon remembered. "He said, 'Hey, we're going to go record the Metal Flake Mother record up in Boston with Caleb Southern.'"

Laird feels Randy made sure he was overheard on purpose. "I remember being incensed," he said. "It felt awful, but Randy could be that way."

Moist/Baited Breath was making a big bet on Metal Flake Mother by sending them into a proper studio with a producer for their full-length debut. Andrew and Kelley had a few thousand dollars saved up. Andrew's grandfather cosigned a loan for $30,000. "That was our budget to spread over several records," Andrew said. "We had a budget for Metal Flake Mother. I was absolutely convinced that they could be huge."

Huge, in Andrew's mind, was shifting thirty to fifty thousand copies, which is what bands like Sonic Youth and Hüsker Dü were doing. That would get the attention of major labels. It seemed perfectly reasonable that Metal Flake Mother could be sold to a major, not unlike the Sidewinders/RCA Records deal that Jay Faires pulled off while Andrew was interning at Mammoth.

"I would guess that Andrew was looking at Mammoth and I was looking at Merge," Kelley said. "You looked at everybody, because if somebody was getting records out there and getting paid for them, you paid attention to that."

"It didn't feel competitive with the bands," Laura Ballance said, "but seeing Moist/Baited Breath starting this label and watching the way they did it, I was just like, 'Huh?' It didn't make sense to me. They were spending a lot of money and acting like, already, that was a big thing. I was just like, 'Okay, well, you do you. We're just gonna do our little thing.' We had started earlier, but the way they were operating felt like they were a major label compared to Merge."

"I never thought anything about success with music," Metal Flake Mother's Quince Marcum admitted. "I didn't know anything about it. It seemed totally unreal to me. It was more about observing and holding space for Ben and Randy and Jimbo's feelings about that. I think Jimbo was the most traditionally ambitious. He always had an instinct for the hustle."

Andrew started looking for a producer. He was interested in the stuff that had been coming out of Boston, specifically records by the Pixies made at Fort Apache Studios. Andrew flew up there and was introduced to Lou Giordano. Lou had been the soundman for Hüsker Dü until 1988. By the time he met Andrew Peterson, Lou had produced a ton of records, including ones for King Missile, Mission of Burma, and The Lemonheads.

"Lou looked into the band and was very interested," Andrew said, but the label couldn't afford Fort Apache. "He said, 'Well, I've got this jazz studio in Stoughton and it's much less expensive,'" Andrew remembered. "'Maybe we could go there.'" Lou flew down to Chapel Hill. He and Caleb Southern selected and demoed songs that would go on the album, a process known as preproduction.

By this time, blackgirls were back in England making a second record for Mammoth with producer Joe Boyd. "Joe was paying us and doing everything in pounds currency, and Jay Faires looked at the exchange rate and got it wrong," Dana Kletter recalled with a chuckle. "He read the old *Wall Street Journal* instead of the new one and got a bad exchange rate, giving us a little more money. He was not happy about that. He really did ask for some of it back, and I really did say, 'Not on your life, motherfucker.'

"I didn't have any kind of face-off with Jay, but our attorney Rosemary Carroll did," Dana said. "It was because another band called themselves Black Girls. RCA Records were so afraid that we would sue them that they offered a shit ton of money for no reason; I guess to buy us off. Jay took a sizable amount. He took a big cut of it. Mammoth took most of it. Rosemary talked Jay into giving us a small percentage. She called me and told me that happened, but I was not part of that negotiation. I just got the check. I think that was the last time I talked to Jay." The second blackgirls' record for Mammoth was also their last. It was called *Happy*.

On Saturday, March 23, Metal Flake Mother opened for Teasing the Korean at the Cradle. *The Daily Tar Heel* wrote glowingly of the proceedings, taking time to mention the "legendary" baby doll gig before noting that "the magic from that show may have been missing, but the band still radiated its trademark sound." Oh, fickle fate. You can't bring Baby Shivers to *every* goddamned show.

A couple things about this date are of note to me at this great remove. One is that Metal Flake Mother opened for *us*, which seems a bit like an energetic reversal. The second is that TTK started the show with an acoustic set, with me on guitar, Tim Roven on violin, and Jeff Taylor on flute. This was a lovely, if aesthetically confusing, concession to my growing obsession with prewar jazz, a style I'd been Hoovering up since I saw a film of Cab Calloway from the early thirties on television back in 1988. I dedicated myself to learning how to compose in the style of menacing, old-school Harlem hot music. John called them "cabaret songs." The night of the baby doll show in January, we opened with an acoustic version of David Bowie's "Boys Keep Swinging." In March, we came out of the gate with Calloway's "Minnie the Moocher."

Moist/Baited Breath's other two big releases of 1991 were more grounded in potential success, largely because each band had an established local touring base.

The first was *Medallion* by Sex Police, released on April 5. The group had formed two years previously around former Pressure Boys front man John Plymale.

"We realized we needed a singer because I wanted to play guitar and not sing," John said. "We had two different practices with two different lead singers, and the first one was Randy Ward. We were thinking, 'Who would be a cool front man? Maybe Randy Ward! He'd be cool as shit.' Of course, this was before Metal Flake was starting to play."

Trumpeter Stacy Guess knew how to find Randy—way out on Borland Road in a house with no electricity or phone. "We went out and found his ass," John remembered, "and he said, 'Yeah, I'll come try that out.'" The ensemble decamped to the ground floor of the Eurosport sporting goods store between Chapel Hill and Durham to hold their one rehearsal.

Bassist Norwood Cheek had a few Plymale-described "funky white boy songs," and the instrumentalists started playing those. "Randy was amazing," John remembered. "He didn't really sing anything. He just ran around leaping and hopping off the counters, just wailing. He reminded me of a very acrobatic Scott Weiland. We tried to find Randy a few more times to come back. We went back to that house—it was like this half of a barn that was falling over. We never could find him again."

The Sex Police lineup was completed by trumpeter Je Widenhouse, trombonist Robert "Robo" Jones, and drummer Jody Maxwell (no relation), formerly of A Number of Things. John and Norwood traded vocal duties. Their first gig coincided with the Pressure Boys' one-off reunion show at the new Cat's Cradle in 1989. "That show was literally the weekend before the first Sex Police show opening for the Dead Milkmen at the Cradle," John said. "I remember being kind of bummed." By 1991, Sex Police were playing 150 shows a year and packing out the Cradle, raking in as much as $4,000 on a Friday night.

Norwood's song "Elevator"—an infectious funk fest with punchy horn stabs—was the single from *Medallion*. Its music video was shot in the Cradle and directed by Peyton Reed, a college buddy of Norwood's. Peyton had moved out to Los Angeles and was doing some behind-the-scenes stuff for movies like *Back to the Future* and *Forrest Gump*. He'd also done a couple music videos, including one for The Connells. "Man, that was so much fun," Norwood remembered thinking about the shoot. "I want to do that as much as playing music." He doesn't think Moist/Baited Breath ever even paid Peyton.

"It was weird," Norwood said about the record company. "They were such a local, homegrown label. It didn't feel like, 'Oh, the guys from New York are here.' It felt like you were just hanging out with some friends who were music fans. Those guys were nice and loved the band. There was never a meeting where I'm like, 'You guys aren't publicizing this.' It never occurred to me, because releasing the music was exciting and recording was exciting. Playing live was what I loved."

On Wednesday, April 10, The Veldt opened for Cocteau Twins at the Cameo Theater in Miami, Florida, during the *Heaven or Las Vegas* tour. This was around the time that Capitol Records should have released *Marigolds*. Instead, The Veldt had no label and no album but plenty of work.

"We were going from the soundboard to the stage, up a series of steps and landings," Marvin Levy told *Indy Week* magazine in 2016. On one of the landings, someone said, "Why the fuck is a Black band opening up for the Cocteau Twins?"

At the beginning of The Veldt's set, Daniel Chavis walked up to the mic. "Ladies and gentlemen," he said, "before the show, we were asked why a Black band is opening for the Cocteau Twins. You're just about to see." After the last note of the last song, Daniel approached the mic again. *"That's* why we're opening for Cocteau Twins." The band got a standing ovation.

"In Chapel Hill, we never talked about that shit," Danny Chavis said. "We never had that shit happen to us. We never talked about color; we were always just us—no matter who we were playing with. Then the outside world came in and fucked it up. That's one of the sad things about life, that people can't leave well enough alone."

The other big Moist/Baited Breath CD release in 1991 was by another legendary local live act, Southern Culture on the Skids, also known as SCOTS. The label had already issued a seven-inch single by the band. "They were huge in town," Andrew Peterson said, "but they hadn't really achieved any sort of national recognition yet. We were like, 'What's wrong with people? Why isn't everybody listening to this band?' That initial seven inch, we pretty much sold it out."

Too Much Pork for Just One Fork, released on May 5, was Southern Culture on the Skids' second full length, after a homegrown 1985 debut. The band recorded with Caleb Southern over two days at Lloyd Street Studios.

The libidinous slink of "8 Piece Box" embodies SCOTS' vibe. Rick Miller's guitar percolates through a tremolo amp, punctuated with Dave Hartman's snare drum thwacks. "I started on a thigh and then I got me a breast," Rick sings, "My mouth got so full I had to save the rest."

> *Yeah I'm snackin' all night, it's all right, all right*
> *Got an 8 piece box*

"We'd been touring a lot," Rick said. "We'd been all living in one house, hunkering down getting our shit together. Touring, booking ourselves, all that kind of stuff. But when that Moist Records thing happened, we quit our day jobs. We've never had another job since."

"That record did really well," Andrew said. "They were an incredibly hardworking band who would get out there and play to whoever would listen and just spent the years building up an audience. They did it the right way."

Shawn Rogers was a young Moist/Baited Breath intern. "Southern Culture ended up really floating the label for a long time," he said, "because they would sell so many CDs on the road. They'd get the CDs from the label and then come back and hand 'em a bunch of cash. I'd be like, 'Okay, now we can pay rent!'"

Shawn started with Moist/Baited Breath back at the beginning. He was in college at the time, DJing at WXYC. Shawn's roommate was in a band with Kelley Cox and Mike Kenlan called Three Hour Head. Shawn's other roommate Eric Bachmann was in another band with Kelley called Reem. Kelley was also in a group with Mike and Eric called Cupcake UK. Shawn would hang out at various band practices.

Kelley was friendly, bought Shawn beer, and turned him on to a bunch of SubPop singles. Shawn fully immersed himself in local music. "I was going to more shows, selling merch at the Cat's Cradle, and just starting to get to know more people in the scene, for lack of a better word," he said. "I guess community is probably a better word."

One day, Kelley told Shawn that he was starting a label with this guy Andrew Peterson. "The first thing I did was help stuff the Bicycle Face seven inches," Shawn remembered. "I enjoyed hanging out with Kelley and Andrew. I would go there and just help them do whatever they physically needed doing—stuffing envelopes, that sort of thing. Now people would call it an internship. I wasn't supposed to be there at any particular time. I just enjoyed their company. We'd listen to records and just do this stuff."

Shawn's music industry trajectory went from stuffing seven-inch plastic sleeves to working college radio. "Kelley and Andrew were like, 'We need a radio person. We can't afford to hire an indie, so you do it,'" he said. The first record he promoted was *Too Much Pork for Just One Fork*. "My position kept getting better," Shawn mused, "but I don't remember being paid anything. Maybe a few hundred dollars. I was a waiter at Chili's."

Although it seemed like Andrew's initial business plan of releasing records by successful touring bands was working, he soon learned what the actual indie label killer was. "We borrowed $30,000 and that seemed like a huge amount at the time," Andrew said. "But in promoting records nationally, that's nothing. So, we burned through that quickly and were reliant on the distributors to pay us. It became clear that distribution was the big cog in all of this. Distributors liked to not pay you for records. If you gave them new records, you could get them to pay what they owed for the old one. So, we had to develop a schedule: if we wanted to get paid every couple months, that meant we needed to release a record every eight weeks."

A few blocks west in Carrboro, Mammoth Records had just neatly solved this problem. "The early part of my job was dealing with the distributors," Steve Balcom said. "I was sending records to Cargo in California, I was sending records to Touch and Go, sending boxes of records to ten or fifteen distributors. The records would come into our office. We would put labels on them. I would have to create invoices. It was difficult to do business that way, but that's how most independent labels did it."

"When you were selling your records to different distributors, no one really wanted to pay you," former distribution executive Mark Lipsitz said. "They didn't know if somebody was gonna buy records from distributor one and return them to distributor two. It was a nightmare for indie record labels to get paid." At the time, Mark was working for Important Record Distributors, who, like everyone else, would buy records from labels on consignment and compete to sell them to stores. Mark had just been promoted from salesman to record buyer. The first label he was assigned was Mammoth Records.

"At the time, the business was competitive," Mark said. "All the distributors had the same records to sell. Mammoth had a strong roster. They had Dash Rip Rock, blackgirls, and Blake Babies. I went to my boss and said, 'These are great releases, they have a good plan, and they're worth taking a chance on, but I don't think we can compete with the other distributors. We're gonna be selling the same stuff.' He said, 'Make a deal and get a better price.' It was the first time anyone had ever done something like this in the independent business. I went to Mammoth and said, 'I'll buy seven thousand of your records if you give me a special price,' and they were like, 'Damn straight we'll give you a special price!'"

The deal was an absolute game changer for everyone. "We said to Mammoth, 'If you give us this exclusive, we will pay you like clockwork,'" Mark remembered. "'You will set your watch by the time you get a check.' Mammoth didn't give us a huge discount, but it made enough of a difference that we could pass that on to our customers and sell more records. It was good business."

"All of a sudden, it's like, 'Okay, we have this one distributor,' and by that point we had manufacturing in line," Steve said. "So, we just had our manufacturer ship the goods directly to the distributor. That saved us so much time and energy."

There was an additional upside for Mammoth in its deal with Important, because "it meant we had a distributor that would pay more attention to us," Steve said. "We were more of a priority." There was a consequent bump in sales.

Merge Records was also dealing with multiple distributors. "I would mail them a copy of the seven inch, they would listen to it, and I would call them and say, 'How many of these do you want?'" Laura Ballance remembered. "'I'll take twenty.' I would put twenty in a box and send it to them. It was always consignment. Then they would pay us. Mostly, it was fine. Cargo Distribution went down, and they owed us money. They're the only ones who screwed us."

"Distribution was the holdup," Mac McCaughan said. "If you were Twin/Tone or even a bigger indie, it was hard to get your records into Sam Goody or whatever. You could still sell a lot of records at independent record stores, because there was a ton of them. The excuse that bands like The Replacements gave for why they signed to major labels was, 'Warner's is going to have our records everywhere, not just in the cool stores.'

"When we were starting, that was the landscape," Mac remembered. "Our goal was never to get big. Our goal was just to make records and play music. The only examples we had of bands that had tried to get big were bad ones. The Replacements started making records I didn't like as soon as they signed to a major label."

Around this time, Flat Duo Jets' second album, *Go Go Harlem Baby,* was released on Sky Records, which had acquired their label Dog Gone Records. The album was produced by Jim Dickinson, who was responsible for records by Ry Cooder, Big Star, The Replacements, and Jason & the Scorchers, among others.

Go Go Harlem Baby was mostly recorded over three days at the new Easley McCain Recording studio in Memphis. "Tone had quit the band, so there was no bass," manager Dick Hodgin said. "Dexter said, 'I'm just going to do it without the bass player.'" This was how Flat Duo Jets started anyway, with just guitar and drums.

Jim Dickinson did the right thing by setting up a couple mics and letting the band rip. The album's intimate cover of the Andrew Sisters' "Apple Blossom Time" is disarming. It's just Dex singing and playing barrelhouse upright piano. For someone capable of being such a wild man, he has a lovely voice. Up in Detroit, a teenage kid named Jack White dropped the needle on the Duo Jets' apocalyptic cover of "Frog Went a Courtin'" and was given new raiment. Jack later gave Flat Duo Jets proper credit for inspiring his own band, the White Stripes.

"The biggest thing on Dex is that we never had what you would call a commercial single," Dick said. "That's tough when you look at a band with a cult following like Flat Duo Jets. Back then, that's what you had to have to break through."

The first Zen Frisbee EP, *Jack*, was issued in May on a new local indie label called Jettison Records. It contained the four songs originally recorded at Duck Kee Studios for Merge. Todd Goss founded Jettison by accident in 1990. "Merge had been going on for about a year," Todd said. "Mac was puttin' out shit he liked. Blue Chair, Mind Sirens, and Scuppernong were my favorite bands back then and nobody was putting their records out. Brian Butler told me I was gonna put the Mind Sirens record out because he couldn't get anybody else to do it."

Since he admittedly had no idea what he was doing, Todd called Mac McCaughan. "He gave me the names of all the pressing plants and mastering places," Todd said. "He helped me out, and I believe he helped Kelley Cox out over at Moist as well as the D-Tox guys in Greensboro."

"I'm glad somebody's putting these records out," Mac told Todd. "These bands need to get documented."

One of the bands Todd most wanted to document was Zen Frisbee. He knew about the MRG011 tapes and a friend had given him some money to cover the expense of releasing them. "That record had been sitting in the can for about a year," Todd remembered. "I just went to Mac one day and said, 'I got somebody to pay for this Zen Frisbee record. Do you care if I put it out?' He said, 'No, I want that to come out. Go ahead.'"

Todd got the original Zen Frisbee tapes from Duck Kee and remixed the songs with Caleb Southern and Ugly Americans' bassist Chris Eubank. This mixing session was the beginning of what Caleb described as his most cherished producer–band relationship. *Jack's* matrix number was JET-005.

The Zen Frisbee sound is exemplified on songs like "Freeburn (I Want Rock {pt.II, v.II})": Kevin and Laird Dixon's driving, intertwined guitars underpinning Brian Walker's languid-yet-menacing double-tracked vocal. He comes across like a bored, inconvenienced occult priest.

In August, Metal Flake Mother drove north to a studio called The Outpost in Stoughton, Massachusetts, to record their first album with Lou Giordano and Caleb Southern. "We gave them their per diems to take with them when they headed up to Boston," Moist/Baited Breath Records' Andrew Peterson said. "It wasn't a huge amount. We may have given them $300 that was supposed to last the first week. Then we were going to wire them the rest. On day two they called us and said, 'Hey, can we get the rest of it?' I guess they had gone shopping and bought some instruments and some shoes. They said, 'We don't have any money left.'"

Andrew had formed a bit of a paternal relationship with Metal Flake Mother. "It was frequently my job to figure out where they were and what they were doing," he said. "So, I would make a lot of visits to Ben and Randy's apartment. If they weren't there, they were usually in our office. That was because we had bought this big coffeemaker and had an endless supply of coffee. So, they would come in and attempt to spend the entire day sitting in our office drinking coffee and smoking Lucky Strikes. And while that was fun, it wasn't terribly conducive for the rest of us to do any work!"

"While we were making the record, working every day for three weeks, Lou kept saying, 'I can't keep going like this without getting paid,'" Ben Clarke said. "We didn't have any money. We were eating canned shit we bought at the gas station. But the money came through and we finished it. I think Moist was doing everything they could to make it happen and they were having trouble getting the money. They got it eventually."

Caleb Southern, working on the Metal Flake Mother album as second engineer, found himself on a steep learning curve. From producer Lou Giordano, Caleb learned how to do things like punch in overdubs on the tape machine and make a lead vocal comp. "When we did 'Tongue Long' and Ben got up there and sang it," Caleb remembered, "I saw this excitement in Lou's eyes. Ben got the take and Lou looked at me and said, 'That's it!' It was a first take—no edits, no nothing.

"I said, 'Yeah, I think it could be better,'" Caleb continued. Lou looked at me and said, 'Shut up, Caleb! Sometimes when they just do it, they do it and you know it, and you gotta keep it.' That really impressed me. I didn't want to believe it, but that's true. It was a great take.

"Lou Giordano was a mentor to me," Caleb said. "I went up there with a nineteen-year-old's arrogance. Luckily, I checked my ego, figured out that I could learn something from this guy, and it changed everything. Most producers teach themselves and don't talk to each other. It's a lone wolf career. I moved up a notch from seeing how he did things properly."

Lou helped shape Metal Flake Mother's songs, such as making room for a Randy Ward guitar solo on "Wingtip Lizards." Randy played something astonishing, then looked up at Caleb. "Was that good enough?" he asked.

"It was weird," Caleb remembered. "He seemed almost insecure about some of these things. 'Randy, that was great, man! That's perfect!' They came into their own in that studio."

Ron Liberti, who'd seen Teasing the Korean's baby doll show during a visit back in January, moved to Chapel Hill in August. In 1989, he and his friend David Alworth, better known as Dave IT, came down to visit Mike Kenlan, another New Jersey pal who had already moved to town.

"Mike was living on Carr Street, upstairs from John Ensslin," Ron said. "It was still winter and shitty up north, but it was one of those spring days down here. Dave and I were like, 'Look at this fucking place.' Mudhoney was playing up at the Cradle; there were a lot of shows all over. Mike was living in a house with a wraparound porch for what I was paying to live above a liquor store in Montclair. So, there was something that happened in my head."

Back in New Jersey, Ron was in a band with Dave IT called Love Onion. After he came home from his Chapel Hill visit in 1989, Ron saw Superchunk play at Maxwell's in Hoboken. "I remember thinking, 'Look at these fuckers!' because we were still dressed in all black," he said. "They looked like hot, dirty Muppets. I remember Chuck had this stripy sweater with the elbows blasted out, Mac had his long hair, and fuckin' Laura Ballance. And the music was just right there, like Buzzcocks. Right in my wheelhouse. I made a note in my head, like, 'This band is fantastic!' Then I realized they were from Chapel Hill and was like, 'Fuck, man. There really is something going on down there.'"

After moving, Ron quickly got hired at the Hardback Cafe. "Jamie McPhail gave me a job and Alvis Dunn taught me how to be a bartender," Ron remembered. "He said, 'You like music. You wanna start booking some shows here?' It just all fell into place. It changed the trajectory of my life."

Ron dropped into the Chapel Hill groove. Alvis took him to last call over at Tijuana Fats, a few blocks up on Rosemary Street, where he saw the back-of-house staff from almost every restaurant in town hanging out at the bar. He came to see how supportive the scene was.

"Up north, it wasn't as much 'Oh look, we're in this together. Who cares what your band sounds like?'" Ron said. "I loved Chapel Hill for how inclusive it was. When I first moved down, I got hassle from people back in New Jersey: 'Why the fuck are you moving down there with fucking rednecks?' I was like, 'This place gives me the time and the space to do whatever I want.'

"I think a lot of people felt the same," Ron continued. "It was affordable, there were all these places to play, there were all these people to play with. You could do whatever you want here, as opposed to up there where you could do what *we* want you to—other bands wouldn't share gear with you, you didn't want to play with a band that didn't sound too much like you. And everything was so spread out, where down in Chapel Hill it was all right here."

On September 24, a band named Nirvana released a record called *Nevermind*. They weren't from North Carolina. I only mention it because of the album's future narrative relevance. Nirvana played the Cradle on October 4 while touring in support of *Nevermind*.

At one point, Kurt Cobain's guitar amp started feeding back. "I think it was a Fender Twin," Kelley Cox said. "He took it and just slammed it onstage until it stopped. Then he went up to the mic and asked, 'Is there a music store in town?'"

"They destroyed all their equipment because they got famous and were going to buy new stuff the next day," former Cradle soundman Tim Harper said. "Kurt Cobain was on the side of the stage selling his amplifiers for five or ten bucks just to get rid of 'em."

In October, Mammoth released a Dillon Fence EP, *Christmas*. It was recorded at TGS Studios in Chapel Hill. This time, Steve Gronback produced. Teasing the Korean guitarist and Greg Humphreys's housemate Tim Roven played violin on the title track. It's a little sad, like any good holiday song.

So it's Christmas
So it's Christmas

Happy holidays
Why can't I feel something?

To help keep the station afloat, WXYC conceived a two-night benefit show called the "Madonna Showdown," a name that was almost immediately shortened to "Madonnathon." Taking place over the weekend of October 19 and 20 at the Cat's Cradle, the Madonnathon featured eight curated local bands. It was mostly put together by a DJ named Carrie McLaren.

"WXYC was home," Carrie said. "The studio was open 24/7—including holidays and school breaks—so you could drop by any time of day and peruse the archives, listen to records, make mix tapes, or just hang with whoever happened to be there. It was our clubhouse. It didn't revolve around drinking. It was a social club for a not particularly social group."

Fellow XYC jock Sue Hunter (whom Mac McCaughan taught bass along with Laura Ballance) was a huge Madonna fan. Sue played Madonna on WXYC and had her posters on the wall. "The WXYC DJs were overwhelmingly male," Carrie said. "I thought the Madonnathon would be a way to raise this question of gender and have a feminine theme. I wasn't a Madonna fan. I thought it would be funny for everybody to do a Madonna cover."

Superchunk, Polvo, Finger, Zen Frisbee, and Bicycle Face were booked for Saturday, while Metal Flake Mother, Erectus Monotone, and Vanilla Trainwreck performed Sunday night. There is a bootleg recording out there somewhere of Polvo's extended rendition of "Borderline." It meanders along unrecognizably until the chorus, which the band collectively sings with a jet-engine shriek, really drawing a bright line under the "feels like I'm going to lose my mind" lyric.

Polvo was getting a lot of attention. Superchunk had taken them on tour up the East Coast and they'd just released a two-song single produced by Caleb Southern. Teasing the Korean's John Ensslin saw the band again after their Club Zen debut as Rum Tar Lust. "As far as having a vibe, having a look, having a persona onstage, Ash Bowie was unbelievable," John said. "He'd have on a Hawaiian shirt and be hitting these weird things on guitar. It was like Miles Davis: this completely impassive, totem-like appearance and vibe. They were discordant and inscrutable enough to separate the men from the boys."

Moist/Baited Breath's Andrew Peterson was at Madonnathon. "This was right when Metal Flake was hitting their stride," he said. There was a reason for this. "When Metal Flake Mother got back from that recording session with Lou Giordano, they played a show at the Cradle," Caleb remembered. "It was like, 'Wow, this is amazing!' Then I realized what they were doing—they were covering the album they had just made." ("We're gonna do a Metal Flake Mother song," Ben Clarke would announce when the band was about to perform something from those sessions.)

"Every other band had played a Madonna song, then Metal Flake closed out the night," Andrew remembered. "They brought the guys from Bicycle Face up onstage with them and said, 'You know, we're disappointed in all these other bands. WXYC gave us very clear instructions that we were supposed to pay tribute to Godzilla.' Then they broke into Blue Öyster Cult's 'Godzilla.' It was epic."

By now, Superchunk belonged to the world: they played nearly every night of the New Music Seminar in New York that summer and had just wrapped up a tour with Mudhoney. One day, British Knights, who had done a shoe commercial with MC Hammer the year before, requested to license a Superchunk song. "Someone from Chapel Hill that Mac knew worked at the agency," Laura Ballance said. "He told Mac they would record something in our style if we said no." The band created a Superchunk-ish track for the ad apparently called "Tasty Shoes, Tasty Shoes."

In mid-October, Superchunk had just played a release party at the Cradle for their second Matador full length, *No Pocky for Kitty*, when Mac McCaughan and now-permanent guitarist Jim Wilbur walked over to Chuck Garrison's house on Pritchard Avenue and kicked him out of the band.

"By that point, I was already trying to figure out when I was going to quit," Chuck said. "But I didn't have the wherewithal to do that on my own back then. So, it got figured out for me. I wanted to be in *our* band. I didn't want to be in Mac's band."

Mammoth Records' art director Lane Wurster's brother Jon was brought in as Chuck's replacement. Jon originally moved down to Winston-Salem to join a band called the Right Profile in 1986. By August he'd relocated to Chapel Hill. "We went on a tour in the summer of '91 out to LA to get a record deal," Jon told music journalist Emil Amos. "It was the worst experience ever. I came back here with four dollars. I stopped by my brother's office and he said, 'Hey, Mac from Superchunk called,' and I was just like, 'Please, *please* need a drummer!'"

Jon was working as a window washer for a company called Classic Glass. One of their accounts was Schoolkids Records on Franklin Street. Soon, Mac McCaughan stopped by Schoolkids one day when Jon was working. The two talked in the store. "They had a tour with Mudhoney coming up," Jon said, "and they weren't sure if it was going to work with Chuck anymore. Mac said, 'You know, we'll see how this goes. But if it doesn't go, would you be interested?' He gave me a cassette of *No Pocky*. I have a vivid memory of listening to it over and over again while I was washing windows."

By the night of Superchunk's Madonnathon performance, Jon was in and Chuck was out. The band was billed as "Super-duper-chunk," because former guitarist Jack McCook sat in as well. They opened with Metallica's "Enter Sandman."

Matador Records officially released *No Pocky for Kitty* eleven days later, on October 30. Recorded in Chicago by an uncredited Steve Albini, the record never lets up. It's clean and punchy and, regardless of the occasional lyrical vitriol, joyfully enthusiastic. "Hit the gas straight on," Mac's buried voice sings on the album opener.

Run through the lights, run through the tree
Skip steps one and three

Back at the Hardback Cafe, Ron Liberti was blossoming. "I was twenty-two when I moved here," Ron said. "I met people who were five or ten years older than me, like Jamie McPhail and Kirk Ross. I'm like, 'Oh, wait a second. They're doing what they love to do.' My old man told me, 'Whatever you do, you should like what you do, because you're going to be doing it all the time.' It really started to click: 'Oh, I could do this.' I was able to slide in with my poster work and the band stuff."

Ron was a fine arts major in college. He started making show posters almost immediately. He also formed a punk band, Pipe, with his New Jersey buddies Dave IT and Mike Kenlan. Chuck Garrison played drums, which in Ron's mind gave the outfit a lot of local credibility.

After getting canned from Superchunk, Chuck wasn't sure what he was going to do. He considered moving up to New York. "Then I was approached one night by Mike, who I knew from the band Small," Chuck said. "He was like, 'Hey, we're looking to put something together and wondered if you're interested.' I thought, 'Fuck it, why not? These guys are from New Jersey. I've always got along with people from New Jersey.' I thought Mike was asking me to join Small, but when I showed up for practice, it was him and Ron and Dave IT. So, I got onto Pipe. Not long after that, Small needed a drummer. I kind of slid into that." Pipe's first show was in November.

By year's end, Metal Flake Mother's success seemed assured. The *Deem-On* seven inch was a local sensation and made it onto the *CMJ* singles chart. Their live shows were getting better and better. They had a well-produced debut album in the can. But there was one unresolvable issue.

"Randy Ward and I got clean and started playing music together again," Ben Clarke said, "but Randy decided he didn't want to continue with that. I tried going that route, living with what it was like with Randy being on drugs again in the band. I couldn't do it. So, I sat down with Randy and said, 'I just can't be in this environment with you.'

"He was my best friend," Ben said. "I knew him through the worst of things. We went through a lot of that stuff together as eighteen-, nineteen-year-old kids and then we went through getting clean. He was my ally, going to all these clubs and having to deal with being around insobriety. That already felt bad, then I was the only one. I knew he was headed downhill. And he was."

Ben called a band meeting at Quince Marcum and Jimbo Mathus's house on Airport Road on Friday, December 13. Moist/ Baited Breath's Andrew Peterson also attended. "I didn't know what was going to happen," Quince said. "I guess Andrew knew what was going to happen. It was basically Ben announcing that he couldn't be in the band anymore. He said eventually he'd start using drugs again if Randy was using drugs, so he just couldn't do it."

"I had a real heart-to-heart with Randy when he left the band," Andrew remembered. "I think he was more honest with me then than he ever was any other time. One of the things he said to me was, 'I think you're a nice guy, but I don't trust you. I think your goal is to make money off what we're doing.'

"It's interesting," Andrew reflected, "because ultimately I guess he wasn't wrong. I wasn't attempting to *lose* money by putting out records, but I thought my earnestness was readily apparent. He essentially said, 'I'm happy to talk to you about this, but you're not going to influence my decision one way or another, because you're not understanding where I'm coming from.' He was probably right."

Kelley Cox wasn't at the meeting but has often thought of it since. "I tried to turn Metal Flake Mother into something they weren't," he told me. "I didn't understand that it wasn't in their best interest to be on their own on the road. I just thought, 'Everybody wants to be on the road, and we all want to make this record. Everybody needs to hear this and love it, and you gotta go on tour to do that.'"

Randy was mostly quiet during the meeting. At one point, Andrew turned to him and asked, "Randy, what do you think?" and Randy replied, "Well, I think they should get a new guitar player."

"At that point, I remember saying, 'No. Fuck that,'" Quince said. "'If it's not the four of us, it's not a band. I'm gonna leave town and go traveling somewhere.' In the passive way I emphasized it, it was my one argument with Ben. It was, 'Don't think you can do this and the band is just going to somehow be the band. No fucking way. You want to make this decision? I get it. But that's it and you should know that.'"

1992

K EN MOSHER MOVED TO CHAPEL HILL IN JANUARY 1989. HE FOL-
lowed his fiancée from Missouri, where he had worked for the
Democratic Party. Ken was always very musical but didn't consider
himself a musician. "Because," he said, "to be a musician in St. Louis
meant you had to be in a cover band." Ken knew nothing about the
Chapel Hill music scene. He enrolled in Philosophy of Law classes at
UNC-Greensboro.

On the night of January 4, Ken went to the Hardback Cafe. A local
band was playing, and as Ken remembers, "They were terrible. And
the next band was terrible. When I say that, it's not that they weren't
my cup of tea—I didn't think they were good enough to be playing!
My first thought was, 'Oh my God. I might be able to do this here.'

"At the time, I was a perfectionist," Ken said. "I really felt like I had
no objective. Then I go and see something that was so beautiful and
off the cuff. It was what I would embrace and become."

One of the bands Ken saw that night was called Evil Wiener. Its
founder, Bill McCormick, was the drummer for Mind Sirens. Evil
Wiener was a side project Bill started with another local drummer,
Groves Willer. "It was gonna be Groves and I switching off between

guitar and drums," Bill said. "I lived with Chuck Garrison at the time and he started playing with us. We had this thing called the 'guitar player hat.' Whoever was playing guitar at the time had to wear a certain hat. When Chuck came in and started playing drums, I remember being stressed out because we only had one hat and now there were two people playing guitar!"

"Bill had a vision," Chuck said. "It was kind of wacky, but he knew what he wanted. I didn't take that dream seriously at the time, but it turned into something pretty fun."

Bill had ambitions to be a professional drummer. He practiced his rudiments and played to a metronome. He wanted to be in a band that toured and put out records. At the same time, Bill was writing original songs on guitar and recording them on a four track at home, but not performing them. That changed when he attended a show in Greensboro.

"The band that really inspired me to get up in front of people with a guitar was Chew Toy," Bill said. "I could see how Ken would say it was awful seeing Evil Wiener play, because I had a similar reaction to Chew Toy: It was awful in a great way. They were just up there going for it. It was cathartic to see that. It felt like we were all levitating.

"There were a lot of bands at the time—I'm thinking specifically of Galaxie 500 and Beat Happening—that put out records that had wrong notes," Bill said. "The singing was off-key. I was buying those records. Zen Frisbee were also always wavering on the line between horrible and great. The first time I saw them, Kevin and Laird Dixon were standing across from each other kicking each other's guitars, while Chuck was spinning a chandelier with his drumstick. It sounded completely weird and was visually amazing. But Chew Toy influenced me to get a real band together and start playing live."

Chew Toy formed in Greensboro in August 1991. Christina Pelech and her friends Stacie Smith and Amy Wilkinson were working in a bookstore called News and Novels.

"At some point, the three of us decided to form a band," Christina remembered. "Based on I don't know what, because none of us could play any instruments or had any kind of musical background at all. Going to see music was a huge part of our lives. We saw people who were just getting up onstage and doing it. It felt like, 'Well, this is possible.'"

One of the bands who got up and did it was Greensboro's Bicycle Face. "There was such freedom," Christina remembered about seeing them perform. "They obviously didn't care what other people thought." Friends pitched in and bought Stacie an $80 child's drum kit. Bicycle Face's Mitch McGirt introduced them to a new member, Karen Mann, who knew a few chords on guitar and owned a bass. "We started practicing in somebody's bedroom," Karen said.

Chew Toy debuted at a house party and immediately started playing out in clubs. Bill McCormick must have seen the band soon after they formed. Teasing the Korean's John Ensslin was another early Chew Toy convert.

"They were interviewed for a Greensboro zine," John said. "And in it, Christina said they were a combination of glamor and slovenliness. On the basis of that, I reached out and said, 'Hey, you want to open for us?' An all-girl band named Chew Toy? Slovenly? Come on. They had a song called 'Crazy Train Kept A-Rollin,' which was all about Russian literature. They had another song about somebody leaving an artificial leg on the subway."

Chew Toy was the real deal. For them, all apparent liabilities—diffidence, limited technical ability, lack of polish—were practical assets. They were more authentically themselves than almost any other band around except Flat Duo Jets and Bicycle Face.

The four women also had a different intraband dynamic. "Men would sometimes be present at our practices," Christina told me. "More than one of them said, 'This is nothing like when men practice music together.' With us, there was a lot of, 'Oh my gosh, you're so great!' 'That's amazing!' 'How did you come up with that?' An absolute outpouring of support at all times because we were friends. We were sisters. There was never any question that if someone left the band, the band was over."

The members of Chew Toy saw Bicycle Face and formed a band. Bill McCormick saw Chew Toy and was inspired not only to form Evil Wiener but also to adopt an entirely new musical ethos. "Don't just make a cassette," he said. "Play a show. Get some friends together and get up there and do it. There's nothing stopping you from stepping out on the stage. Even if you can't play your instrument at all, you can still get out onstage and something is gonna happen." To me, this isn't just a T-ball trophy attitude. It speaks to the heart of authentic creative expression as opposed to skillful mimicry.

One mild night in the New Year, perfectionist Ken Mosher wandered into a chaotic Evil Wiener show at the Hardback Cafe. Afterward, Ken went home, got out his four-track tape recorder, and began whacking some original songs together.

On January 11, Nirvana performed for the first time on *Saturday Night Live*. By this point, *Nevermind* was number one on the Billboard 200 and selling three hundred thousand copies a week. Jimbo Mathus and I watched it over at my little brick house in Carrboro. I remember Kurt Cobain's guitar sounding thin as a mosquito. Afterward, I turned to Jimbo and said, "Well, that's the end of grunge." Subcultures, after all, can't survive mainstreaming. What I couldn't quite wrap my head around was that college radio had just gone Top 40.

Joe Fleisher, working at A&M Records in Los Angeles, saw an immediate industry shift. "The bluntest way to convey it is that, overnight, Nirvana wiped all factory-farmed rock off the planet," Joe said. "When *Nevermind* was released, there was still a Sunset Strip hair band scene and people were still signing them. After it broke, there was a cultural cleansing in rock that was jarring. I would drive home from my A&R job on the Strip and there would be guys who looked just like Mötley Crüe. It seemed like a day later they were all gone and replaced by guys wearing flannel shirts.

"The effect that had on the major label record industry was so pronounced that they were unable to catch up," Joe said. "So, there was a mad rush to alternative music. A lot of them didn't know what that meant. 'There's a guy down the hall who does college rock promotion, but we've never spoken to him. He's got goddamned Pixies and Mekons records!' No one listened to that guy, and now that guy was super important. 'How do we cram something like that on the air?' In the span of a few months, alternative radio went from something that nobody cared about, which maybe had forty or fifty stations nationwide, to a primary format that could cross you to Top 40. That was unexpected, and it was solely owing to *Nevermind*."

"*Saturday Night Live* had commercials for Teen Spirit deodorant immediately before and after Nirvana played 'Smells Like Teen Spirit,'" Raleigh's *News & Observer* music critic David Menconi remembered. "Suddenly, I started getting a lot of phone calls from record companies. 'Who should we be looking at down there?' I was having a hard time picturing Polvo on Columbia Records. It seemed like a foreign language they were speaking.

"This is really a different world down here that has nothing to do with what's appearing on MTV," David told them. "Yeah, there are a lot of young, loud bands that play fast, but that's not all there is here. None of them really sound anything like Nirvana."

On January 28, *Marigolds* by The Veldt was co-released by Poly-Gram subsidiary Stardog Records and Mammoth Records. This was *not* the 1988 album of the same name produced by Cocteau Twins' Robin Guthrie, because Capitol continued to own those shelved master recordings after dropping the band two years previously. Instead, this *Marigolds* was a nine-song EP recorded at Raleigh's JAG Studios in 1990, using money The Veldt earned from the Jesus and Mary Chain tour.

In the meantime, The Veldt signed with Mammoth Records for two reasons: one, Jay Faires reportedly told them that no other labels were interested; and two, they wanted to get something out there sooner than later.

The ultimate effect of the Mammoth signing meant that tensions between The Veldt and their former manager-turned-label boss only intensified. Things came to a head when Daniel Chavis went up to New York in 1991 to meet with Roger Kramer, Living Color's manager. "Roger said there were many labels who were interested in signing us," Marvin Levy told me. "Jay was keeping it from us. Daniel came back with that information." There were lawsuits and countersuits. Finally, PolyGram functionally bought The Veldt's contract from Mammoth and co-released *Marigolds*.

Although the *Marigolds* EP contains some of the same songs that were on the shelved Capitol album, everything had been rerecorded. It was produced by musical polymath Lincoln Fong, who also played bass. By this time, Fong had produced Lush, A. R. Kane, and the Gun Club. "We added more of the sonic boom that we wanted," Marvin said, "more of the 808s, a little bit more guitars."

Back in 1988, producer Robin Guthrie rejected the idea of hip-hop drum sounds on The Veldt's record. "I put on Cocteau Twins and my life was never the same," Danny Chavis said. "I thought, 'What if you had a beat like Run-DMC's "Sucker MC's" and that guitar sound?' Then, when I met Robin, he didn't really understand it. I said I wanted to put that beat underneath it and he said, 'Isn't it funky already?'" Living Color's Vernon Reid offered to produce a couple songs for the original *Marigolds* album, another idea Guthrie scotched.

The *Marigolds* EP "was a shorter record, a louder record," Marvin said. "Not as lush, but more in your face. Looking back, I wish it had been better produced. The tempos were a little rushed, and it wasn't as spacey and spaced-out as I would have liked."

It's still a powerhouse. "CCCP," *Marigolds*'s opening track, soars. The chorus is hook city. Daniel's soulful, declarative vocals are well up in the mix—distinguishing the band from their European shoegaze counterparts. Marvin's drumming is crisp and propulsive. "A fine EP, *Marigolds* has plenty to offer in its twenty minutes," Andy

Kellman wrote in his review for AllMusic. "It sounds like the band is brimming with ideas, making one wonder why The Veldt weren't able to deliver another handful of songs to make a full album." I guess nobody told him about the shelved record.

Metal Flake Mother's debut *Beyond the Java Sea* was posthumously released by Baited Breath Productions in early February. Apparently named after a recent book on traditional art called *Beyond the Java Sea: Art of Indonesia's Outer Islands*, the album's title was clearly more of an homage to the bottomless coffee pot in the Moist/Baited Breath offices. Former Superchunk guitarist Jack McCook drew a midcentury-looking image of a steaming mug for the cover. Mammoth Records' art director Lane Wurster did the layout. Producer Lou Giordano insisted that the record was good enough to send to a mastering lab, so the label paid for that as well. Radio promotions guy Shawn Rogers put those expenses on his credit card, a decision he later came to regret.

"I think Lou deserves a lot of credit for how good that thing sounds," Ben Clarke said, "because we were so young. He listened to us the entire time. He made what we were thinking and what we were doing more than what it was when we were in preproduction. He had a vision for us. His heart was in it."

Moist/Baited Breath's Andrew Peterson calculated total recoupable costs for *Beyond the Java Sea*—including studio/engineer/producer fees, mastering, equipment rental, band per diems, art, photos, and related marketing materials—at $16,935.90.

Recoupable monies are those advanced to the artist by a record label or music publishing company who is then allowed to "recoup," or make back, that money out of record sales or song revenue before the artist starts seeing royalties. Many bands rightly assumed that there would never be any money on the back end and looked only to advances as the sole form of potential income from a record or copublishing deal. "That CD cost a shitload of money," Ben said. "You'd think it was irresponsible for a young label to spend that much money on it."

Ben has a point, but *Beyond the Java Sea* documented one of the most incandescent and shortest-lived bands from that time and place. The only problem was that there wasn't anybody to go out on tour to support it, and touring—far more than good press or college radio airplay—was key to selling records. "In all, *Beyond the Java Sea* sold maybe five thousand copies," Andrew said, "which was our biggest success to date."

"There was this dark cloud over the office," Shawn remembered about Metal Flake Mother's breakup. "I'm sure Andrew must have felt some sort of financial dark cloud as well, but it was more like, 'Holy shit. This band is so great. Is there not some way that they can patch this up?' But, you know, bands have feelings! You can't just fix shit."

The label promoted *Beyond the Java Sea* anyway. The reviews were glowing. Grant Alden was managing editor and typesetter for *The Rocket*, a Seattle-based music magazine. "Somewhere in there I started writing a singles column," Grant said. "Part of it was because I was a collector geek and could get my hands on all these free singles. Part of it was an attempt to become familiar with what was going on in the broader world, so I could contextualize what was happening in Seattle."

Grant started getting singles from North Carolina. He was familiar with Merge but paid particular attention to what was being issued on Moist/Baited Breath. "I did not have the personal relationship with anybody at Merge that I had with Andrew Peterson," he said, "and that matters."

Grant had just started reviewing singles when he got a promotional copy of Metal Flake Mother's *Deem-On* seven inch. "I liked what they were doing," he said. "I could hear life in the music." That's also what he heard when he got his promo copy of *Beyond the Java Sea*. "In any kind of fair world," Grant wrote in March, "'Ballroom' and 'Fine Lady' would be instant hits. Since it's not a perfect world, you will be obliged to hunt for *Beyond the Java Sea*. How to persuade you it's worth the trouble? Try this . . . the last record I played constantly for days on end was called *Nevermind*."

On a more elevated track, Mammoth Records released Dillon Fence's debut, *Rosemary*, on February 11. "We hired Ron Saint Germain as producer," front man Greg Humphreys said. "It was a heady time."

"Ron Saint Germain was a big deal," Mammoth's Steve Balcom remembered. "He'd done Bad Brains, Living Color, and Soul Asylum at that point. We begged. He really liked the band. We had a $5,000 or $6,000 recording budget. He flew his plane down to Chapel Hill, came to our office, and said, 'I can do it for thirty.' Somehow, we found $30,000."

Dillon Fence were regional sensations. At the time, they'd been gigging with a band out of Columbia, South Carolina, called Hootie & the Blowfish. "The bands that were coming out of Chapel Hill—Johnny Quest and Dillon Fence—were the bands we wanted to be," Hootie's singer Darius Rucker told me. "Those are the bands that helped us get our start and break the North Carolina scene."

"I never got Hootie and we had Dillon Fence," Steve told me bluntly. Mammoth passed on the band.

Hootie were especially enamored with Dillon Fence. "They were the coolest and biggest band in the scene," Darius remembered. "We'd get a Dillon Fence date and when you showed up to the club there'd be a line five blocks long. Then you'd get in and realize that none of those people were getting into the show because the place was already packed." The two bands traded opening slots depending on whose state they were playing.

"There were high expectations for *Rosemary*," drummer Scott Carle said. "And when it dropped the sky caved in. I believe it sold thirty thousand copies in the first week." Dillon Fence hit the road to promote the record. Sometime before that, the *News & Observer's* David Menconi was at the Cat's Cradle and overheard a conversation between Greg and a friend.

"Superchunk was playing that night," David remembered, "and Greg was grousing about not being one of the cool kids in town. The person he was talking to said, 'Greg, look around. There's a hundred people here, maybe. If Dillon Fence was up there playing it would be sold out.'"

The success of Madonnathon the previous year inspired Moist/Baited Breath Records' Kelley Cox and Andrew Peterson to plan a local three-day summer music festival. "We wanted to showcase bands on our home turf," Andrew said. "We would do showcases in New York and at South by Southwest in Austin, but it wasn't the same. We wanted people to see Chapel Hill." During one of Metal Flake Mother's hyper-caffeinated visits to the office, Jimbo Mathus jokingly asked, "When are you gonna send us to the big record stardom convention?" That's when the festival got its name.

"The world was looking for the new Seattle," Kelley said. "Every band coming from Chapel Hill was hit with a Superchunk comparison. We were all sitting around thinking, 'What the fuck are you actually talking about? That band doesn't sound like Superchunk!'"

Grant Alden admits to partial responsibility for the "new Seattle" moniker. "I began writing about Chapel Hill as the next scene as a defensive measure," he said. "It was an attempt to create hype and a little bit of a practical joke. Not that I didn't believe in the music, because I did. But being on the ground in Seattle, I really felt that we needed some of the pressure taken off. I thought nobody was gonna pay attention to it.

"The Triangle had all those universities," Grant said. "It had a small number of clubs where people were fighting for space to get on those stages, it had bright people, it seemed to have label infrastructure between Moist/Baited Breath, Merge, and Mammoth, and I could hear life in the music. I didn't think it was there yet, but I thought it was enough that Chapel Hill could at least be the new Minneapolis."

Kelley and Shawn Rogers from Moist/Baited Breath met with Cat's Cradle owner Frank Heath as well as Mammoth Records' Steve

Balcom and Lane Wurster downtown at the Carolina Coffee Shop to plan the Big Record Stardom Convention. "It was like, 'Okay, who are the bands that we want to play this? What are the potential venues? What is the overall vibe, and why is it happening?'" Shawn said. "The idea was, 'Let's have this really fun time for people who don't know what Chapel Hill is like, in an effort to show what's going on down here and how great the music community is.'"

"Every band got to play the Big Record Stardom Convention," Kelley said. "If they were legit, I found a slot. They didn't all play at the Cradle, but I had satellite gigs going all over the place. My band didn't play. I didn't think it was about me. I thought it was about, 'People need to hear these fuckin' bands.'"

"It grew bigger than our roster," Andrew said. "We couldn't put out all the bands. The other labels around town were releasing great music. It was like, 'We don't want to be selfish. Let's throw a big party.'"

While Dillon Fence was shifting a lot of records regionally, another Mammoth Records artist was breaking nationally. One of the label's early signings was a band from Boston called Blake Babies. They broke up in 1991. Mammoth released former member Juliana Hatfield's debut album, *Hey Babe*, in March. When early sales looked promising, the label took the opportunity to level up.

The first thing Mammoth had to do was resolve a dispute with their distributor, who by this time had rebranded themselves from Important to RED Distribution. RED had stopped making any payments to Mammoth.

"RED had given us a number of advances, but we had not recouped those advances," head of business affairs Chris Sawin remembered. "We were in a quandary, because that's where the money came from."

"We were three years into our deal with RED," Jay Faires said. "We went from Dash Rip Rock at ten thousand copies sold in one year with RED, to twenty thousand with the Blake Babies' *Sunburn* album, to fifty thousand with Juliana's *Hey Babe*. It was a three-year term and the term was over. They didn't own any of the label."

Jay hired gunslinger entertainment attorney Elliot Goldman, for-
mer head of BMG Music, to lead the showdown. Four Mammoth
Records reps and Elliot took cabs out to the RED offices in Queens.
Chris was there. "It was February of '92 and cold as shit," he recalled.
The distributor played hardball, saying they wanted to extend the
contract. Then Elliot spoke.

"Well, as a point of fact, you cannot do this," the Mammoth lawyer
said. "Let's pull up the contract. It says, 'In the event that Mammoth
Records fails to recoup, RED may withhold payments *or* extend the
deal.' You have already withheld payments. This does not say 'and/or,'
so you cannot, by the definition of the contract, extend the contract as
well."

"There was fucking silence in the room," Chris said. "We're all
sitting there thinking, 'Oh, my God. This guy's our hero.' And sure
enough, they knew it was checkmate."

Around the same time Merge Records negotiated their own distribution deal. "In '92, we started working with Touch and Go," Laura
Ballance said. "Corey Rusk was a very upstanding guy. Totally cool,
punk rock community-thinking person. He had noticed that we were
putting out these seven inches and tapes and was like, 'You guys are
doing cool stuff. I was wondering if you might want to do a manufacturing and distribution deal with Touch and Go. We'll pay for manufacturing and we'll distribute it. We'll keep 30 percent of the profits
and send you the other 70 percent.'"

"People like Steve Albini and Ian MacKaye were vouching for
Corey at Touch and Go," Mac McCaughan said. "We believed in
what they had been doing and they were saying that this person was
on the level. I don't think they'd fuck with this guy if he wasn't. We
were lucky to have the guidance of these people that we really looked
up to."

The proposed terms were agreeable. After signing the Touch and
Go deal, Merge began profit sharing with the bands on their roster:
50 percent after recoupment. The one thing that didn't change was

the fact that there were still no Merge Records contracts: all recording agreements were handshake deals.

By the spring, Teasing the Korean had had a record in the can for almost a year. It was recorded at a place called Turtle Tapes in Winston-Salem by former Cradle soundman Tim Harper, whom we dubbed "The Smiling Aunt Bea Buddha." Tim initially approached us to record some demos, which then became preproduction for an album, which then was just the album, which we subsequently took to Moist/Baited Breath, who said they'd put it out. Other record labels hadn't overtly rejected us; they simply didn't respond.

"We did it all in one weekend," John Ensslin said. "We slept on the floor in sleeping bags. Tim stayed up late and ate a lot of barbecue. I remember Dave Jernigan's amp would shock you whenever you turned it on or off and he was a little spooked by it. So, Tim would do it, saying, 'I kind of like it.'" With an actual record release on the horizon, we changed our name to What Peggy Wants, Peggy being the name of my parents' German shepherd. Moist/Baited Breath scheduled a May release.

"A starlit hill, far and still," John sings on "Come On Wallflower."

> *Ancient quaint and dainty horror*
> *Chlorophyll is dripping steel*
> *Sticky lipstick, sweet Jean Harlow*
> *Well, I'm free at last 'cause I've got no past*
> *Just these promises of black umbrellas*

I have a distinct memory of Jimbo Mathus and Ben Clarke coming into Crook's Corner where I tended bar late one afternoon in March, all smiles. "Do you wanna be in Metal Flake Mother?" they asked. The remaining three members had decided to re-form. Jimbo was moving up to guitar and the band needed a drummer.

"Basically, it was like, 'What do we do?'" Ben remembered. "Of course, I wanted to stay in the band. So, I talked to Jimbo and Quince about it. I guess I was optimistic. Jimbo was such a good songwriter and guitar player that I thought we could work it out."

"I went to Czechoslovakia at some point, which is what I said I was gonna do," Quince Marcum said. "I remember Jimbo, who I still thought of as my best friend, taking me aside and asking me, 'Would you consider playing bass again with us?' and me feeling that I was violating some sort of principle but then saying, 'Yes.'"

I also said yes. I remember Lane Wurster, Mammoth's art director and Crook's front of house manager, walking down the length of the bar in front of me afterward and saying excitedly, "Metal Flake Maxwell!"

On Thursday, April 16, What Peggy Wants and Metal Flake Mother played a double record release party at the Cradle, even though our album wasn't going to be released until May and Metal Flake's had been out for a couple months. *The Daily Tar Heel* did a full-page spread on it. "Maxwell was invited to stand in as the temporary drummer for fellow labelmates Metal Flake Mother when MFM does a month-long tour with newly acquired Virgin artists, Cracker," the article said. Cracker was former Camper Van Beethoven guitarist David Lowery's new band. "David was a friend," Andrew Peterson told me. "He really liked the CD and made the opener offer."

Pipe recorded their first EP, *Ball Peen*, on April 28. It was produced by Caleb Southern. By this time, Caleb had a studio of his own: Kraptone, located in the Cat's Cradle. "I saw the recording gear in the studio with Lou Giordano and I knew what this other world was," Caleb remembered. "Steve Gronback had the only real studio in The Triangle at the time with TGS, but I never worked there. I convinced Frank Heath to loan me some money and bought a Neotek mixing board and an Otari one-inch, sixteen-track tape machine." Caleb was given a space in the venue for his control room. He recorded bands on the Cradle stage after hours, using the club's microphones. "I had to start at three in the morning," Caleb said, "and somehow convince bands to show up and stay up all night long."

"Caleb had his calendar and he would bug me: 'Hey, can we do a session this night?'" Frank remembered. "I didn't really care. He worked sound for all our shows, so I couldn't really say no. He was keeping me from having to find a sound guy, which for the first ten years of my Cradle life was the most painful process. If you didn't have a sound guy, you didn't have a show.

"Caleb was a musician," Frank said, "so he understood all these people. But he also had this aesthetic that nobody could really touch and that a lot of people didn't understand. He was able to translate that by recording them. I remember all these bands listening to what he had done and saying, 'Wow!' It felt like a light bulb switched on when he was able to pull out the stuff that was cool about their music and guide them into making more of that." One of those bands was Pipe.

John Ensslin heard about Pipe long before he saw them, because their shows never lasted more than twenty minutes and John is not a punctual person. People thought John would like Pipe because they also had a front man. He finally caught an early performance at Rosie's Good Times, a sports bar off Rosemary Street.

"They had this big TV screen," John remembered. "Ron Liberti had a VCR and during their set he projected a montage of hockey fights he'd recorded. It was perfect. They were everything they were cracked up to be. Massive riffs. Ron had this puckish quality that really worked well, like Mickey Rooney in A *Midsummer Night's Dream*."

Ball Peen was released by Massachusetts's Sonic Bubblegum label. A six-song flamethrower of an EP, it clocks in at thirteen minutes and twelve seconds.

Guitarist Mike Kenlan's other band Small released their first EP, *Makes Me High*, in April. It had been recorded in November at Duck Kee with drummer Darren Hall, who Chuck Garrison later replaced. The guitar work between Mike and guitarist Eric Bachmann is somehow a cross between Big Star power pop and Sonic Youth dissonance.

Energetic but less amphetamine-tempoed than Pipe, the *Makes Me High* EP was released on the Matt label, named after Small's bass player Matt Walter.

In June, Jettison Records released a new Zen Frisbee single called *Dog City*, which contained "Action Slacks" b/w "A Kaunji Kaunji Christmas." Kevin Dixon printed all the Jettison single covers under the table at Kinko's because he had the midnight-to-eight shift. "Everybody came to me for their free printing," he noted. Kevin's *Dog City* cover illustration depicts a squalid yet whimsical street view of Chapel Hill.

The Dixon brothers' guitars are almost indistinguishable in the sinuous, magisterial opening riff of "Action Slacks." "Let's all have some fun," front man Brian Walker later deadpans in a way that makes you question the idea. By this time, Zen Frisbee included drummer Matt Murphy and a teenaged bassist named Andrew Maltbie. "That was the best lineup as far as I was concerned," Jettison Records' Todd Goss said, "and the easiest to record. We knocked that single out in two days, though it is production heavy."

Part of the reason this was possible is because Todd coproduced *Dog City* with Caleb Southern at Kraptone. "I really liked Laird's backing vocals," Caleb told me. "It was this magical thing. I would put these weird, rolling delays on 'em and double 'em. It wasn't even meant to sound like a voice. It was almost a keyboard sound." Caleb described his production approach at that time as "obsessive" and "single-minded."

"I wouldn't leave until we got things where I wanted," Caleb said. "At one point I drank too much, tripped, and knocked my whole studio over. I knocked my shit down and pulled all the soldered wires out. Somehow, I got it put back together in twenty minutes."

"Caleb was great and easy to work with," Kevin remembered. "Jerry Kee was amiable but sort of shy, whereas Caleb would actually have opinions. He'd also make you play a part more than once to get it right. You know, 'Play it with feeling this time.' He'd have little suggestions, like, 'Maybe we could throw in a keyboard here.' It was the first time that you felt like you're working with an actual producer who wanted to have an input, whose input was good, and that you trusted."

Sometimes, when Caleb needed to work on something by himself, Zen Frisbee would explore the empty upper and lower floors in the Cradle building. Down in the basement, they found a stack of old Bell South student welcome packs that contained phone books, shaving cream, and condoms. "I remember Andrew getting all the condoms out of these things," Kevin said. "I tried to give him a warning, like, 'Do these condoms have an expiration date? They're at least five years old.'"

Andrew scoffed. "I'm not gonna eat 'em," he said.

At some point, the band would remember that no one was doing overdubs. "We'd go check on Caleb and he'd be in the control room passed out asleep with these incredible cigarette ash towers," Kevin said. "Lit cigarettes in his hand right next to magnetic tape. We'd take the cigarette out of his hand, put a couple of pillows on the floor, and lay him down. 'Okay, I guess we're done.'"

"I didn't care about sleeping or eating or anything," Caleb said. "It was a compulsion. I had to be part of this. It felt like there was a thing that was bigger than me and bigger than any of the bands, and it was depending on me to do my part."

When Frank Heath came into work the morning after a Zen Frisbee session, he found an empty Bass Ale keg, a pile of dollar bills on the bar, and Caleb in a corner playing the Galaga video game.

Naturally, there was a mix-up with the *Dog City* release. The records came in while Todd Goss was out on tour with Flat Duo Jets. Todd described his duties with the band as running sound, road managing, driving, accounting, and "babysitter for Crow." The delivery truck driver switched palettes, so Zen Frisbee found themselves with a thousand John Denver records pressed up for a special event. Meanwhile, down at the event in South Carolina, confused John Denver representatives found themselves being told by Brian Walker to go have some fun.

"I was straightening out the whole mess and cussing out John Denver's people who were holding the records hostage," Todd said, "while pumping a roll of quarters into a pay phone at a truck stop somewhere in Wisconsin."

Both the What Peggy Wants album, *Death of a Sailor*, and the Bicycle Face full length, *Trust and Obey*, were released on May 4. *Death of a Sailor* was the only joint Moist/Baited Breath release.

By this point, I was bartending four nights a week at Crook's, practicing with both Peggy and Metal Flake Mother, and playing locally with the former while going out on the road with the latter. The Cracker tour happened in May.

I really liked the guys in Metal Flake Mother. Ben Clarke was jittery and inscrutable but lovely. I admired him as a singer, songwriter, and guitarist. We'd talk about Django Reinhardt. I'd known Quince Marcum since college. He was, and is, a gentle soul. I always feel better after hanging out with Quince. Jimbo and I were becoming fast friends. We bonded over prewar jazz and blues. He was really into Charlie Patton, and I was really into Skip James. Jimbo was feral but charming, with a ready laugh. The Metal Flake Mother songs were fantastic, but I was in anguish.

What Peggy Wants felt like family. John and I had been best friends since I was seventeen and intuitively understood each other's aesthetic. I might have been sitting in with Metal Flake Mother, but I *was* in What Peggy Wants, even if we were no longer a vanguard band and frankly a little long in the tooth. It didn't help that people were advising me to quit Peggy and stay with Metal Flake. What I would have loved to quit was my restaurant gig, but that didn't seem realistic. I wanted to write a better song and play a better show. Turning pro was beyond consideration.

"We played a show with What Peggy Wants," Mitch McGirt said. "I think we had an attitude: 'Bicycle Face is a pure band.' We thought, 'These guys are so pretentious.' I was talking to John Ensslin before a gig. I was like, 'I like music that's real honest.' Without thinking, he said, 'I like music that's kind of like theater.' I thought, 'I love

David Bowie. I love all these bands that he likes, too. I'm full of shit because it's all just show business.' Then they cranked up and played and I was like, 'I love this band.'"

It didn't matter that the eye of capitalist Sauron had turned its gaze toward Chapel Hill. The summer of 1992 was a musical wonderland. Moist/Baited Breath's Shawn Rogers graduated in June with an economics degree and decided that a career in banking didn't sound like so much fun after all. "That entire year was like, 'Are you kidding me?'" he said. "The world is exploding with music that I love, and all this is going on in my backyard!"

Mammoth Records' Dan Gill felt the same way. "That time in Chapel Hill was incredible," he said. You could go see any local band. I had friends from New York and LA who would fly in for the weekend to just check out the music scene. There were so many great local bands. Some of them saw the light of day and some didn't, but the creativity that was going on in that small college town at that time is crazy when you think about it.

"I wish Mammoth had been signing more of the cooler bands, like what Merge was doing," Dan admitted. "We weren't signing the coolest things in the world. Some of them were."

I loved entering the warm, humid embrace of a summer night to see shows with John Ensslin and Lane Wurster after Crook's Corner closed. "I remember leaving in the middle of a shift to go see a band at Local 506 for thirty minutes and then coming back," Lane said. "It was late, so we weren't really serving anybody. I could walk down there and back super quickly and not miss a beat."

"Every night there was somewhere to go, pay two bucks, and see a fucking amazing band," John said. "You'd go and see a band or two and then after that there would be a house party where this other band was gonna be playing. You could see three or four bands a night every night of the week."

Evil Wiener's Bill McCormick was happy as a king. "There were three college radio stations that would play your music and interview you," he said. "You had all these publications, and occasionally television would get involved. I felt like I'd made it, honestly. I didn't really see the world outside of Chapel Hill. I just thought, 'I'll go do this interview for *Trash* magazine. Then I'll go to Pepper's Pizza and maybe Frank Heath will pick up my tab. Then I'm off to see the Polvo show—I'm sure I can get on the guest list.' Within that world, I felt happy and didn't really have ambitions outside of that."

Mammoth, however, was concerned with more worldly things. Juliana Hatfield's *Hey Babe* was doing numbers. Major labels were sniffing around. "We were still a small operation," Steve Balcom said. "We certainly weren't paying anywhere near major label advances for anything. But we had a team of people who really believed in these acts and were passionate about them. That's why the Atlantic deal came in."

Danny Goldberg was the new president of Atlantic Records and comanaging Nirvana. He considered it his mission to expand Atlantic's presence into indie rock. One of the first things he did was acquire half interest in Mammoth as well as a distribution deal. "I met with Jay Faires," Danny said. "It was a good meeting of the minds in terms of what he was looking for, which was about some funding and some major label promotional support to supplement what Mammoth could do. My memory is that it was an easy deal to make."

It didn't hurt that Danny was married to blackgirls' friend and attorney Rosemary Carroll, who also happened to represent Mammoth's rising star Juliana Hatfield. Just to close the circle, Rosemary's partner David Codikow represented Jay Faires in the Atlantic negotiations.

"I remember vaguely talking to both of them about the deal," Rosemary told me. "Talking to Danny, who was my husband, and David, who was my partner, and maybe back channeling it a bit to help my partner's client get a fair deal.

"By 'back channeling,' I mean I was telling my husband what David was asking for," Rosemary explained. "If he told me that it was fine, I knew that David could push harder, right? And if he told me that he was gonna walk away from the deal because David was asking for too much money, I would know that David had hit the sweet spot."

"It was a crazy time," Steve remembered. "These major labels were gobbling up indies, giving them resources, and helping them hold on to their artists. I'm sure we would have had a hard time holding on to Juliana if she didn't know she had that muscle from a major label behind her."

As a result of the Atlantic deal, Mammoth Records was neither fish nor fowl: It still looked like an indie label but was now inextricably in bed with a major. This duality was an accurate reflection of the dynamic between aspiring industry mogul Jay Faires and music lover Steve Balcom, who by this time had become label vice president.

"I've had a chance to work for other organizations since then and be part of different company cultures," Chris Sawin said. "The indie part, the part that remembers everybody's name and you can get on the phone—that's Steve. And the part that is constantly in hype mode, that is constantly pushing the narrative of 'We're all cutthroats if necessary'—that's Jay. It's like Mom and Dad."

Blackgirls' Dana Kletter saw the Mammoth/Atlantic deal as her opportunity to bounce. "I did not want to be on Mammoth anymore and I did not want to be in blackgirls anymore," she said. "We had broken up on tour. I was already on Joe Boyd's label for overseas stuff. I talked to him and he said, 'You know, we could just do this.' So, I called Rosemary. It didn't seem like I could get out of my Mammoth contract. They were not amenable to my leaving. My advice was to get on the phone and act like a crazy person and that's what I did: I was such a crazy, fucking New York loudmouth Jewish broad bitch."

Dana knew, at least intuitively, that blackgirls were too out there to flourish in a major label environment. "Women wouldn't be in all-women bands and be that fucking weird and concentrated for another seven or eight years," she said. "There was really no home or place for us there." Dana was released from her Mammoth contract.

"Dana called me up and was like, 'Hey, I'm starting this band and I want you to be in it,'" former Angels of Epistemology member Sara Bell remembered. "I really wanted to do that. I was either gonna go join the Red Cross or Dana's band. I was excited about it because I loved her. We studied Russian together at NC State. We would ride our bikes to school together." Dana also brought in Duck Kee Studios' Jerry Kee on drums as well as Motocaster's guitarist Bo Taylor. Sara played bass. They called their new band Dish.

"Dish was an astounding relief to me, because two of my best friends, Bo and Sara, were in it," Dana said. "Jerry had been the soundman for blackgirls and traveled with us. He recorded almost everything we put out. This was me in a band with my best friends. I think the most wonderful thing about it was that we got to hang out."

Two significant events happened in July. The first was the release of Polvo's debut *Cor-Crane Secret* on the thirteenth. The Touch and Go deal gave Merge Records the opportunity to release full-length albums. "We put out the Superchunk singles compilation *Tossing Seeds* and then Polvo," Laura Ballance said. "When we put out Polvo, I was like, 'Okay. Now I feel like a real record label because it's not our band. It's this other band.'"

Merge was experiencing other benefits from its distribution deal. "I remember getting paid from Touch and Go for the records we had sold," Mac said, "and it was way more money than we'd ever seen from Matador. It was easy to understand how they'd arrived at the amount we made, because it was a very transparent way of accounting. All philosophical things aside, we were clearly making more money dealing with Touch and Go."

Cor-Crane Secret was recorded at Duck Kee in early January. The production is clean and articulate; the music by turns dreamy, insistent, dissonant, and discursive. Like Zen Frisbee's Brian Walker, Ash Bowie was great at double-tracking seemingly off-the-cuff vocals. "The channel changer is sitting on the stereo," he sings.

I'll pick it up, I'll put it on your favorite show
I'll promise to watch if you promise not to go

Sonic Youth released their seventh record, *Dirty*, on July 21. This was also of provincial significance because there's a song on the album called "Chapel Hill." The lyric references Internationalist Books owner Bob Sheldon, who was shot and killed while closing the store on February 21, 1991. Bob opened the Internationalist in Chapel Hill in 1981. At the time of his murder, he had been very vocally opposed to the Iraq War. "Back in the days when the battles raged and we thought it was nothing," Thurston Moore sings.

A bookstore man meets the CIA and we know
Throw me a cord and I'll plug it in
Get the Cradle rocking . . . too bad the scene is dead

The Big Record Stardom Convention took place between August 5 and 8. "Kelley Cox was like, 'Hey, we're gonna have people from the bands picking up writers from the airport when they come in, so they can talk to them,'" Shawn Rogers said. "Either Duncan Campbell or Ritchie Williams from 81 Mulberry were going out to the airport and grabbing the writers that Kelley had arranged to come in and taking them to their hotel."

One of those writers was *The Rocket's* Grant Alden, who flew in from Seattle. He crashed at Andrew Peterson's place. "Michelle Roach from Sky Records was on one couch and I was on another," Grant said. "Her general manager took one look at the place and got a hotel. I think after the first night she joined him there. Andrew's house was kind of scary. There was a lot of mold in the shower. The thing is, I was incredibly nearsighted. It didn't bother me. I stayed at his house because nobody was paying for me to go out there."

"We treated A&R people like shit," Kelley remembered. "We didn't give them any backstage passes. We didn't put them up in anybody's houses. They had to fend for themselves. The price tag for them was higher than everybody else's."

David Menconi's editor at the News & Observer was married to M-80 Management's Dick Hodgin. She was confused about the Big Record Stardom Convention. "She kept pressing me," David remembered. "'Why are they doing this? What are they hoping to accomplish? Is it just for *Spin* to come in and say it's cool here?'"

David's conversations with Kelley and Andrew didn't help. "They had a lot of hippie talk that my editor rejected, being a hard-assed news woman," he said. "For her, every story was about 'follow the money.' Well, what if there wasn't any money? I never could really satisfy her as to articulating what the point was. Because every time I'd ask Kelley or Andrew, I'd get some pie-in-the-sky thing that I think, in retrospect, was sincere: 'We just want to show off what we've got here.'"

Forty-nine bands played the Big Record Stardom Convention. There were shows all over town, in every available venue. There were shows in people's backyards. There were kickball and basketball pickup games between writers and bands. "Just don't call it a scene!" it read at the top of Tannis Root's festival poster.

Small played the Cradle on Thursday the sixth right before What Peggy Wants, who were followed by Dillon Fence. "I don't remember a whole lot about the actual shows other than just being absolutely drenched in sweat," Mike Kenlan said. "They were packed. I had so many friends from New York and New Jersey come down for that. It was impossible to get around the room without having to stop and talk to five people."

"I remember joking around with Eric Bachmann backstage," Chuck Garrison said. "We were playing characters: 'I'm Big Dick from Big Dick Records. I'm gonna give y'all a wheelbarrow full of money!' We thought it was gonna be great. We were gonna be big and do the Chapel Hill Rocks tour."

I performed again with Metal Flake Mother on Friday night. I don't remember that show, but I have a distinct memory of a friendly stranger coming up to me right after soundcheck, standing onstage in front of the drum riser.

"My band is playing tonight," he said, "and I just wanted to tell you how much I love What Peggy Wants." He kind of went on about it. He told me his name was Eric Johnson and that his brand-new band Archers of Loaf was opening that night's bill. "I used to stalk your band," Eric told me recently. "I've only seen Superchunk more than What Peggy Wants."

"I was presenting songs to Small," Eric Bachmann said, "but couldn't get my ideas through the band. So, I started my own band. I met Eric Johnson on the bus going back to The Villages apartment and we started Archers."

Matt Gentling transferred down from Bates College in Maine and became the Archers' bass player. After some personnel changes, Mark Price became the drummer. "We were pretty much a pop band until Mark joined," Eric J said, "and then it got faster and louder and harder. I'm grateful for it, even though it was a little unnatural for me. I was more into new wave." Archers of Loaf's first show was at the Hardback Cafe in November 1991.

"That was the Archers' goal for the longest time," Shawn Rogers said. "'Can we just headline the Cat's Cradle?' Because that was our church. That's where we all congregated to see this wonderful art that was coming through town that we collectively appreciated without even talking to one another about it." It's funny to look back on things that at the time seemed unattainable but were always available. The Big Record Stardom Convention was the first of many Archers of Loaf shows at the Cradle. "The Archers were my favorite thing on earth," Frank Heath told me.

"It just felt so good to be playing that thing with other bands that you liked," Eric Bachmann said. "I didn't think anything was gonna come of it."

Back at the Big Record Stardom Convention, Bicycle Face took the Cradle stage after Archers of Loaf. Bassist Brian Huskey had an altogether weirder conversation with another musician before their set. "You know, my band moved here to make it," the guy told Brian. "We heard that Flaming Lips have a hot sound, so we might sound like them. We're gonna see what's popular here and do that."

Polvo played Saturday night, before Superchunk and Zen Frisbee. "My memory of that was coming off the Madonnathon where we had this great show," Dave Brylawski said, "to *not* having a great show at the Record Stardom Convention. That was the show that Archers of Loaf just slayed it. They came out really fired up, tight, loud, and powerful. Everyone was like, 'Holy shit.' They were basically right out of the box."

"I remember seeing Polvo," Copytron's Kirk Ross said. "What really impressed me was they played this whole Polvo-esque song. Then, at some point, Ash Bowie leaned into the mic and sang one word. And that was it. That was the only word in the song. I was like, 'I gotta write a song like that!'"

Spin magazine was at the Big Record Stardom Convention. The concluding paragraph in "Robbing the Cradle," its article on the festival that appeared in the December issue, began: "At 3:30 a.m., Polvo singer-guitarist Ash Bowie takes me to a Chapel Hill party that's just starting to rock. He looks troubled. 'Do you really think there's a Chapel Hill sound?' he asks quietly."

"I was two feet away when it happened," Todd Mormon told me. At the time, Todd was WXYC's station manager. "It wasn't a house party. It was right outside the door of Local 506. Marc Sloop walked up. He had overheard the question; he wasn't part of the conversation. I'll never forget it: he stuck a beer right in front of the *Spin* correspondent's face, loudly popped the top, and said, '*That's* the Chapel Hill sound.'" In that moment, local history was made.

"There's a lot that's blurry about the nineties," Marc told me when I asked him about this story. "It definitely sounds like something I would do."

Marc did a lot more than that. "He was such a lover of music," Todd said, "and it really showed. Chapel Hill was full of folks like that, who would go out to hear something different, see what's going on, or see their favorite band for the eighteenth time. Marc was so good-hearted, open, and accepting. He was the epitome of the supportive Chapel Hill audience."

"Marc sat in with me once," Evil Wiener's Bill McCormick remembered. "We were both bearded at the time. I shaved the right side of my face and he shaved the left side of his face. We stood next to each other onstage so that between us we had one full beard. Otherwise, we dressed like sorority girls. I wouldn't have had the nerve to do that on my own. I can't remember whose idea it was, but the fact that he was so sure about it got me to do that weird thing. It was the weirdest thing I'd ever done in front of people. I've had no qualms wearing costumes, being silly, and even cracking eggs on my head since that happened. Taking that deeper dive into weirdness really opened possibilities for me. I would've never done that without Marc."

"Going to shows was definitely my bread and butter," Marc told me. "That's what I lived for every night. I got to spend my twenties in the thick of it all. There was a sense of community here like I've never experienced anywhere else." I think Marc Sloop's beer can description of the nineties Chapel Hill sound is the definitive take.

"I always thought what Marc did to that *Spin* guy was hilarious and even a little poignant," Chuck Garrison said. "There *was* no Chapel Hill sound. What we had here was a supportive environment where all these bands could coexist, no one really hated each other, and they all sounded different. The thing that unified us all was recreational drug use and alcoholism."

Eric Bachmann left Small in November—sort of. "For the past six months, Eric had been clearly focused on Archers of Loaf," Mike Kenlan said. "We all knew that. We were like, 'Well, are you going to do this or not?' He wouldn't say anything but started being late for practice. It was getting to be kind of a drag.

"Eric called me up one day and said, 'Hey, can you meet me at the practice space?'" Mike remembered. "He told me, 'I have to leave the band. I just can't keep doing two bands.' You could tell he was emotional. *I* was emotional. It was tough. He's like, 'Please don't tell the other guys. I want to tell them.' I went home and waited an hour, then called Matt. 'Has Eric called you yet?' 'No.'" Small had a meeting and decided to let Eric go. "It was sad because we all loved Eric," Mike said. "He was a great bandmate and such an amazing talent. But at the same time, we knew it was coming."

Archers of Loaf recorded some demos with Caleb Southern and put a song called "Wrong" on cart at WXYC. Carrie McLaren, the DJ who organized Madonnathon, loved it. "I used to go jogging to that song," she said. The band was already drawing large crowds around town. Despite that, no one seemed in a hurry to sign them.

"When I started at XYC, you had to pass a test of music knowledge to be accepted," Carrie remembered. "Once you were in, it felt very inclusive and homey, but the tension between the in- and out-crowd was always there in the background. I think that's the case with the larger music scene as well. I wondered whether one reason Merge didn't initially want to release the Archers' first single is because they had started drawing a pretty fratty crowd. When huge crowds of unfamiliars showed up at the Cradle, the instinct of a lot of us was to be wary."

Carrie approached Eric Bachmann with an offer to release an Archers of Loaf single in the premiere issue of her new zine *Stay Free!* She had been a college rep for Sony, mostly because she needed the money, and was already making a zine called *SONY LAND*. It was a way of promoting but also gently mocking bands on the Sony roster like Pearl Jam and Spin Doctors. "I had no interest in any of those bands," Carrie said. "I thought it was a good opportunity."

Carrie worked (and sometimes slept) at Poindexter Records. She printed out stuff she wanted in the zine in the Poindexter office, cut them up, and took them to the Kinko's in Chapel Hill where Zen Frisbee's Kevin Dixon was working. Kevin would help her paste the zine together and print copies. *SONY LAND* also described itself as the "exclusive distributor of the Zen Frisbee newsletter!"

At the time, Carrie was cocreating another zine, *Trash*, with a guy named Dave Jimenez, who ran an esoteric little video rental store named Dave's Videodrome. When that situation got weird, she conceived *Stay Free!* and approached the Archers. The band rerecorded "Wrong" and a song called "South Carolina" with Caleb at Kraptone. "That was pretty awful sounding," Caleb confessed. "But I love the band and I loved the performance."

"What's funny is that by the time they recorded with Caleb, they were getting really popular locally and selling out places," Carrie said. "I don't think we want to do 'Wrong,'" Eric Bachmann told her. "We're so sick of that song."

"Yeah," Carrie responded. "Just because you're sick of playing it locally doesn't mean it's not a single."

Eric had originally brought "Wrong" to Small, but their first drummer Darren Hall thought it sounded so much like "Smells Like Teen Spirit" that he would only play that song's backbeat. "He and Eric butted heads over it," Mike Kenlan remembered. "Finally, Eric was like, 'Well, fuck it. I'll take it to my other band.'"

For the *Stay Free!* single, Eric wanted to release a new song, "Web in Front," but Carrie talked him out of it. "This is the first song where I really worked at it and crafted a song," Eric confided in Mike.

"It shows," Mike told me. "That's a really fucking good song."

Carrie didn't want to run a record label. She just wanted to document something she liked. "Looking at it like a marketing person," she said, "I thought, 'Nobody's heard of this band. We'll just put a little zine in there. That'll be a weird thing that will maybe get some attention.' We hand-colored the covers, we did one hundred covers where we glued pasta to the singles, and we put in a big dumb contest.

"I knew music writers," Carrie said. "If they didn't have anything to say about a band, they weren't going to write about them. So, if you shove all these novelties in the record, that'll give 'em something. But the fact is that the song was awesome."

The Archers single came out late in the year and was immediately well received. As a concession to the band, "Wrong" was relegated to the B-side. It's still a hit the second it starts, with a left-panned rhythm guitar playing staccato changes. A right-panned lead guitar chimes in with some bright high notes, then all hell breaks loose. "You've got it all wrong and you can't get it right," Eric Bachmann wails.

> *Why don't you come down from off of my back*
> *And won't you get yourself a job somewhere away from me?*

"When Carrie put that single out," Eric said, "that's when stuff started to happen for us." It was time to start taking things seriously.

"Eric was my roommate," Moist/Baited Breath's Shawn Rogers said. "He was like, 'We don't know anyone that has any music business experience. You seem to have some. You up for it?' I was like, 'Yeah, I'll be your manager.' I had no idea what that meant. So, I got Donald Passman's book *All You Need to Know About the Music Business,* studied that, and just started sending out demo tapes, basically. I started working with Archers and Picasso Trigger.

"They were cool bands, but they were just people we knew," Shawn said. "It was a really strange and wonderful time, because you would see so many different types of people at shows. There are real music fans here and I always loved that."

1993

MOIST/BAITED BREATH RECORDS WAS IN TROUBLE. ITS ROSTER was drifting away. The Sex Police issued their sophomore album, *Second String*, on their own Scuff Cakes label. Southern Culture on the Skids had bailed out, too. "They were having problems," Rick Miller said. "We played South by Southwest and were approached by Jim Reynolds at Safe House Records. We didn't think Moist was gonna make it." SCOTS's *For Lovers Only* was released on Safe House in 1992.

"We were over our heads, for sure," Andrew Peterson said. "It worked for a few months. We were getting records out there, getting paid, and getting bands back in the studio. But it came to a point where Dutch East India Trading, our primary distributor, owed us around $75,000 and wouldn't pay us a dime."

Andrew's partner Kelley Cox was also looking for an exit. He didn't like where the label was headed, and consequently was coming into the office less frequently. "It became a bit of borrowing from Peter to pay Paul," Shawn Rogers explained. "It was going to collapse eventually. My job at the end became, 'Hey, I can't answer this call. It's a bill collector. Can you take it?'"

Meantime, the national buzz was getting invasive. Chapel Hill was not just the subject of articles in music-oriented publications like *Billboard, Spin, Rolling Stone,* and *Alternative Press.* We were being told who we were in the *New York Times, US News & World Report, Time,* and *Entertainment Weekly.*

"*Details* sent this guy and he spent a lot of time in the Polvo house, drinking with us and hanging on," Dave Brylawski said. "Chapel Hill was amorphous enough that we thought, 'Oh, this guy wants to hang out and watch us smoke and drink? Sure.' He wound up halfway asking questions and then our responses all became quotes. We didn't like that. We didn't want someone trying to figure us out." The *Details* article was published in February. Titled "Chapel Hill-billies," it described the town as "Seattle on Prozac . . . part metal, part Saturday-morning-cartoon cuteness."

"When someone tried to come in and say, 'Chapel Hill's this and Chapel Hill's that, it's the next Seattle but it's slacker and they don't care about sounding good or being tight'—which wasn't true—you started to chafe," Dave said. "Because that's not the way you thought about it. There's some natural resistance to the process of being put in a box. It's like stealing your soul a little bit. At the same time, as a musician, that's part of the deal: You don't have control over how people perceive what you're doing."

Seventeen magazine came down to shoot a photo layout featuring several local bands. What Peggy Wants got in because Flat Duo Jets weren't available. Our guitarist Dave Jernigan had quit soon after the release of *Death of a Sailor,* so we were a four-piece. In our picture, everybody in the band is looking at the camera except me. I'm wearing a Cab Calloway T-shirt and staring off into the distance with an annoyed expression (to be fair, that *is* my resting face).

I wasn't irritated at still hanging out and creating music with the guys in Peggy. I was tired of playing better and better shows to fewer and fewer people. Also, at twenty-seven, I had the keen sense that I was aging out of rock and roll. "We're not allowed to have favorites," *Seventeen* wrote, "but we *luv* What Peggy Wants—the band for all tastes." None of it felt real.

"There's a killer in Seattle," John sings on a song we demoed but never released. "Screw the new Seattle."

Superchunk's third full length, *On the Mouth*, came out on February 10. Recorded the previous September, it was drummer Jon Wurster's first record with the band. The sixth track, "Swallow That," departs from the group's usual up-tempo slugfest, chugging over six minutes in a Polvo-adjacent sway. It's wonderfully dissonant and not apparently obligated to any specific key base.

Archers of Loaf recorded a seven inch with Caleb Southern at Kraptone on February 15. The lead track was "Web in Front," the song Eric Bachmann originally wanted for the *Stay Free!* single.

"Stuck a pin in your backbone," Eric sings in a Southern warble after five snare drum hits.

> *Spoke it down from there*
> *All I ever wanted was to be your spine*
> *Lost your friction and you slid for a mile*
> *Overdone, overdrive, overlive, override*

"I sent a cassette of the single out to Caroline Records and people like that," Archers' manager Shawn Rogers said. "If we're being completely honest, I didn't know that a band named Archers of Loaf was going to necessarily make the cool scene. I wasn't sure a label like Matador would sign them no matter how they felt about the music."

Mammoth Records' Lane Wurster had one of Shawn's Archers of Loaf cassettes in his Honda Civic. He played it for label boss Jay Faires. "It sounds like a Superchunk rip-off," Jay responded. "Why would we sign a band in the same town that sounds just like them?"

Alias Records approached Shawn about signing the Archers. Shawn wasn't super familiar with the label but liked a record they'd put out the previous year, Yo La Tengo's *May I Sing with Me*.

Alias also approached Small. "They talked a good game," Mike Kenlan said. "They took us out to dinner." Alias's lawyer was talking the label up to Small's bassist Matt Walter. "If you want to talk with any of our bands," he bragged, "they'll tell you how great we are." He gave Matt Ira Kaplan's number from Yo La Tengo. "It's the worst mistake you could make," Ira apparently told him.

Small was ambivalent about signing with Alias. "We were talking with the guys in the Archers and we're like, 'Well, what are you gonna do?'" Mike recalled.

"We don't know. What are you guys gonna do?"

"We'll sign with them if you sign."

"Yeah, okay. That sounds good. At least we won't be alone in this."

"We wanted to tour and didn't have any way of doing it," Archers guitarist Eric Johnson said. "Our eagerness really cost us. We were impatient. Had we been able to play for a year without a label, we might have been able to get something better."

"I was thinking, 'I'm not gonna do this forever,'" Eric Bachmann said. "'Let's just take it now, make a record, and tour some. That'll be cool.' I was working at the Carolina Coffee Shop and New Orleans Cookery and living above Marathon restaurant for $135 a month. I was *broke*, man."

Alias offered the Archers an advance of $5,000. "We said, 'Well, a van is going to cost more than that,'" Shawn remembered. "'Can you give us $6,789.52?' There was a used car place out past Allen & Son Bar-B-Que on 15-501 South. We found a silver van there that seemed like it was in decent shape and that's how much it cost. We signed a four-record deal."

Small signed with Alias as well, along with Picasso Trigger. "It bummed me out a little bit," Pipe's Ron Liberti said about Small's signing, "because they were our buddy band too." Both Mike and Chuck Garrison were doing double duty in Small *and* Pipe. It's easy to see how Ron might have felt left behind.

Soon afterward, Zen Frisbee, Archers of Loaf, and Bicycle Face set out on a ten-day package tour down south. It was the first time either Archers or Bike Face had ever left the state. The first show in Athens, Georgia, seemed to go okay. According to Bicycle Face's Mitch McGirt, only five gutter punks came to the gig in Tuscaloosa, Alabama, at a place called The Endzone. Everyone crashed at those kids' apartment, which had no furniture because they were probably squatting. Mitch slept in a closet. Then it was on to Tallahassee, Florida.

In a typically Chapel Hill egalitarian move, the bands rotated performance slots on the tour. "Bicycle Face would play first, second, or third based on the rotation," Mitch said. "I think we played first or second that night. I don't know what was wrong with this crowd. If Archers of Loaf couldn't get your juices flowing, then you got a fucking problem, okay? This crowd sucked."

As usual, Bicycle Face's solution was confrontation. "We were always trying to get a reaction. We didn't care if you loved us or hated us. I couldn't stand to see bored people out there."

"To be clear, they were fearless," Moist/Baited Breath's Kelley Cox said about them. "They weren't scared of saying stuff. Mitch, primarily. He didn't care."

"We were trying to amp the crowd up, goading them and saying dumb shit," Mitch recalled. "A couple of dumbasses up front said, 'Yeah, play some Jimmy Buffet.' I was like, 'Okay. I wrote this next song with Jimmy Buffet when he was blowin' cocaine up my asshole!'"

"Oh, man!" one dumbass exclaimed. "I'm gonna get my fuckin' pistol and shoot this motherfucker!"

Since no one was enjoying Tallahassee anymore—especially with the new possibility of physical violence—all three bands hopped in their respective vans (except Bike Face, who were touring in Brian Huskey's Honda hatchback) and took off for Gainesville, where Brian had an epiphany.

"Some people were gonna let us crash at their place," he said. "I remember pulling up and everybody getting out and fucking around in the parking lot for fifteen minutes before they all went off and found thrift stores and stuff. For whatever reason, that moment where I was looking around at all these musicians, all these weirdos, I both felt really *out* of place and then felt very *in* place."

I had a similar experience a couple years earlier, vibrating on trucker's speed and standing in a deserted parking lot in Wilmington,

North Carolina. After a few years of struggling with the idea that playing music was somehow illegitimate, that night I looked up at the empty bowl of the sky and was suddenly at peace. "It's okay," I felt in my head. "You can have this life."

"I think that tour predates any kind of serious ambition I had," Eric Bachmann said. "The way I was raised, it was like, 'You can't do this. It's just a hobby.' It's one thing if you're born into a situation where it's nurturing, but if you're coming from an insurance salesman and a PE teacher and you don't have any music industry skills or knowledge, it's a tough step to get there."

Pipe released a new seven inch in March, their first for Merge Records. The A-side, "Ashtray," is pure sonic assault. "I remember standing in my driveway!" Ron Liberti shrieks over cascading guitar and drum runs. Mike Kenlan's obtuse, heroic guitar solo sounds like Neil Young if he'd been in Poison.

Pipe recorded their single in a new Chapel Hill studio called the Yellow House. It was located on Rosemary Street, next to Internationalist Books and across from Mama Dip's Kitchen, a legendary Southern eatery. The Yellow House was run by former Pressure Boys guitarist Bryon Settle and an engineer named Mike Beard, often credited on records as "The Cheese Man."

The Yellow House served many functions. Pipe, the Chicken Wire Gang, and Spatula all rehearsed there. Someone had a painting studio in one room. Former Metal Flake Mother guitarist Randy Ward had an electronics studio in another. "I was in the rehearsal room one day," Ron said, "and I heard what I thought was Randy and somebody else playing. It was fifteen minutes of this beautiful two-part guitar instrumental. He came out and I said, 'Hey, Randy, who are you jamming with?' He's like, 'Oh, that's just me.' That was the most beautiful thing I've heard in my fucking life."

Ken Mosher, who'd been inspired by an Evil Wiener show at the Hardback a year previously, got a job at the French restaurant La Residence on Rosemary Street. Early Cat's Cradle partner Bill Smith was head chef. Randy Ward and Jimbo Mathus were two of the dishwashers. There was lingering tension between the former bandmates.

Ken and Jimbo became friends. "I talked to him about Metal Flake Mother," Ken said. "There was always something wrong. Most of my perspective of the band came from Jimbo, and I really didn't ask that many questions, but I got the feeling that Jimbo was sick of Randy's shenanigans. Ultimately, it felt like he wanted more credit for what was going on."

Ken was not only documenting his own "weird shit" at home, he had a side hustle of recording live shows by bands like the Emperors of Ice Cream at the Hardback. He demoed some new Metal Flake Mother songs in his house in Dogwood Acres on a cassette four-track tape machine. There was some vague idea that the tape could be used to get either a second record out of Moist/Baited Breath or possibly a new contract with Mammoth Records.

I stopped drumming for Metal Flake Mother sometime after the Big Record Stardom Convention. The first time Ken heard the band perform was when he played drums at Cat's Cradle for their last ever show. The new lineup had only rehearsed two or three times, and Ken had never played drums before. "I'm not kidding you," he told me, "the first time I hit the bass drum onstage and it came through the monitor I almost fell off the stool!"

"Ken was wonderful," Quince Marcum said. "He was ready to do anything. Matter-of-fact, down-to-earth, and eager at the same time. It reminded me of when Jimbo jumped in to join the band in the first place. Ken was like, 'Oh, this is a great chance. I will learn how to do this.'"

"We tried to find somebody to replace Randy," Ben Clarke said, "but it was so difficult. We brought in drummers so Jimbo could play guitar. We brought in guitar players so Jimbo could play drums. Randy was the one who made that band great. It was the way he created and thought that made my songs work in a particular way. After he left, the essence of the band was lost. Randy was the leader. That's the way it felt to me."

Metal Flake Mother disbanded for good. "Something about being in the band with Jimbo put some distance between us," Quince remembered. "When he decided to break up the band, I didn't have any insight. I did have that feeling of, like, 'You wanted me to stay and now you want to break up the band? Okay, we're just gonna do what you want.' I couldn't fault him for it, either."

"It's rare to get four guys together in the right place at the right time," Ben said. "I tried to find it over and over again afterwards. It's super frickin' rare. It was great to be a part of that."

Atlantic Records allowed Jay Faires to simultaneously have an office on Sunset Boulevard in Los Angeles and run Mammoth Records back in Carrboro. "At first it worked really well," Jay said. "They wanted me to have the office there to integrate Mammoth acts better into the Atlantic system. That was why I was on the West Coast with Danny Goldberg. I was supposed to oversee alternative and rock at Atlantic."

Doing this, Jay felt, gave Mammoth an advantage. "If we were gonna make our records work, I had to get inside and work the building," he said. "You can't really do that if you're not inside getting the dirt all day long."

Atlantic's strategy was to hire four or five other indie label executives like Jay and pit them against each other. "They each had pet projects, and you had to win over your coworkers at Atlantic," Lane Wurster said. "It was that *Survivor* mentality, where you try to form alliances. It was totally unfair to the artists, but there was so much music in the pipeline that you had to make deals to get things done. Suddenly, you're not the only gal at the ball."

"It was us versus every other record on that roster," Jay said. "Atlantic had a management philosophy of 'We're gonna put out lots of records and the one who's the hungriest is gonna rise to the top.' I always saw it as healthy competition. It crossed over into unhealthy at times, but that was the culture they built."

Merge Records released Polvo's second album, *Today's Active Life-styles*, on April 19. It was produced by Bob Weston, who was also in a band with Steve Albini. Polvo was getting national attention. *Spin* liked their new record, for whatever that's worth.

Listening to *Today's Active Lifestyles*, it feels like further expression in the guitar rock form doesn't seem possible. Majestic one minute and rubber-band boingy the next, riff-tastic heroics turning discursive as a Yes album—the band is sui generis. And right there, rolling with all the unpredictable time signature changes and skittering stops, is their unflappable drummer Eddie Watkins, whacking that snare drum like it owes him money.

Dillon Fence was also sidestepping a sophomore slump. "By the time our second album *Outside In* rolled around, we had already been a band for about six years," Greg Humphreys said. "We were trying to make a statement with our second album, since our first one had been our greatest hits from the previous five years. 'Okay, here is your first album. You have one year to write an album that's better.' That was a real intense time for us." The band recorded preproduction demos in Kraptone with Caleb Southern.

Outside In was produced by Lou Giordano and recorded at Fort Apache in Boston. "We talked to Lou all the time about the Metal Flake Mother record and how much we loved it," Scott Carle said. "We kinda worshiped it. He was very humble about it."

The strong Dillon Fence melodies are still there on *Outside In*, but Greg's vocals are more in competition with distorted guitars. The opening track, "Collapsis," is a catchy example. "Free fall away from the past," Greg sings in the middle of a mid-tempo swirl.

> *And from all the things that you believe*
> *Swallow your fear make it whole*
> *Let it fall into the atmosphere*

Dillon Fence hit the road again, opening for X, Lemonheads, and Weezer. "I'm not blaming Mammoth for this," Greg said, "but they didn't have that $250,000 to put behind our album to get it played on rock radio. We would go visit the stations, but they knew and we knew that we didn't have the push we needed to compete with the Stone Temple Pilots of the world."

This would have been bad enough if the music industry had been open to a band like Dillon Fence at the time. It was not—because of the intense pressure to find the next Nirvana. Bands that fit the mold, like Soundgarden and Pearl Jam, advanced. Others, like Dillon Fence, Hootie & the Blowfish, and Dave Matthews Band, languished.

(In addition to Hootie, Mammoth also passed on Dave Matthews. "Jay Faires was into Dave Matthews and he had me go see them at a fraternity party in Chapel Hill, which is not a great environment," Steve Balcom said. "I just remember standing there, going, 'I can't see this happening.'")

"Let me tell you, when Dillon Fence got their record deal, there was no doubt in my mind that they were gonna be the biggest band in the world," Hootie's Darius Rucker told me. "We heard their record before it came out and were like, 'Holy shit! Listen to this thing.' When it didn't pop the way we thought, we said, 'If they didn't make it, what the hell are *we* gonna do?'"

After a misfire major label deal, Hootie self-released an EP in 1993 called *Kootchypop*. One of the songs on it was a nod to their buddy band. "Dillon Fence was always using capos," guitarist Mark Bryan said, "and I noticed how chimey it made the guitar sound. I was writing music one day just after playing with Dillon Fence and thought, 'I'm gonna put a capo on to change things around a little bit.' I started strumming this song that had different changes but a similar rhythm to their song 'Sad Inheritance.' Darius hears that and he's like, 'Wow, this reminds me of a Dillon Fence song.' He started writing lyrics."

"When I wrote 'Put on a little Dylan, sittin' on a fence' for 'Only Wanna Be with You,' that's totally a shout-out to Dillon Fence," Darius said. "They were about to be a huge band. It was just a shout-out to my boys."

Hootie & the Blowfish had other North Carolina influences too. They were employing a touring strategy called the Johnny Quest Playbook, named after an approach M-80 Management's Dick Hodgin developed for former Pressure Boy Jack Campbell's band, which Dick managed along with Flat Duo Jets. "We would go into a college town, and I would call up the biggest frat house," Dick explained. "I'd say, 'Hey, man, I got this band Johnny Quest. We want to come play your house.'"

"We've heard of you," a typical fraternity brother would tell him. "How much do you cost?"

"'We'll come play for free,'" Dick would say. "'You get the sound system. You put the band up in a hotel and give them beer.' They'd be like, 'Fuck yeah!' Then we'd come down and smoke the joint."

After playing three different frat houses in the same town over the course of a month, Dick would then book Johnny Quest into the biggest local club. "That's how we sold out the Georgia Theater," he said. Hootie's manager Rusty Harmon was paying attention, partly because he interned at M-80 Management for a year. Rusty implemented the Johnny Quest Playbook with Hootie & the Blowfish.

Jack Campbell left Johnny Quest not long after their van flipped in Gaffney, South Carolina, in March. Drummer Steve Hill was racked up and couldn't play for six months. "Whatever led us to the point where we were in that aggro, nineties, white boy funk kind of bag," Jack said, "that was gonna be a fleeting thing." Jack turned his attention instead to opening a new Poindexter Records down in Wilmington.

One spring day driving around Carrboro, I saw Jimbo Mathus walking along the side of the road and picked him up. He was excited. "I'm starting a jazz band!" he told me. I knew exactly what he meant.

By this time, Jimbo was living in a decrepit farmhouse north of town with his new love, Katharine Whalen. Katharine had been a dishwasher at the Hardback and was now waiting tables at the Flying

Burrito. Jimbo made wooden marionettes and sketched fanciful characters; Katharine painted. The two of them would visit my house in Carrboro and dance with me and my girlfriend to Fats Waller records. Jimbo was as much into that kind of old-school jazz as I was.

"I grew up playing mandolin in my dad's band," Jimbo told a magazine writer back when I was drumming with Metal Flake Mother. "I really don't listen to pop music. I like bluegrass, 1930s jazz, and Robert Johnson."

"Jimbo knew he wanted a new band," Ken Mosher recalled. "He didn't know what exactly it was gonna be like at first. In my mind, it was going to be a rock band like Metal Flake Mother. I remember going over there and playing acoustic versions of some of those songs that I recorded, like Jimbo's 'Ghost in the Friendly Barber Shop.'"

At some point, biomedical engineer and stand-up bass player Don Raleigh showed up at a rehearsal with Ken and Jimbo. "We can do any style of music," Ken remembered thinking. "We can do pop music with weird instruments." Ken saw a cantankerous drummer named Chris Phillips at a party and asked him to drop by a practice. Chris had been in the teenage hardcore/punk band Subculture back in Winston-Salem.

Things really gelled when Katharine started singing. Jimbo was already teaching her how to play banjo. When reluctant Katharine finally opened her mouth, she sounded like a cross between Blossom Dearie, Betty Boop, and Billie Holiday. Jimbo started writing songs for the new outfit that owed nothing to what was currently popular. They chose the name Squirrel Nut Zippers after an old-fashioned chewy peanut candy. Its wax wrapper featured squirrels and lightning bolts.

One day at a What Peggy Wants practice in June, guitarist Tim Roven called a band meeting. "Fellas," he said, "I'm moving back to New York." Tim wanted to stay in town for the remainder of the year, so we planned on a December farewell. There was no question in my mind about continuing past that. I wasn't interested in playing rock and roll anymore.

My first instinct was to put a new band together in order to play the hot jazz and calypso songs I'd been writing. It was going to be called the Minor Drag. I never really got anything cooking except with Stacy Guess, the trumpet player in Sex Police. Stacy was a soft-spoken and learned soul. He phrased his trumpet lines like Chet Baker. We knocked some parts together. Even though I'd been writing and performing this material since the late eighties with Teasing the Korean and was going to incorporate horns, I had a lurking fear that the first thing people would ask is, "Why are you ripping off Squirrel Nut Zippers?"

Dish's *Mabel Sagittarius* EP was issued on June 10. It was produced by Mitch Easter. Claire Ashby, Sara Bell's friend and former Angels of Epistemology bandmate, released it on her Tenderizer Records label. Laura Ballance starred in the music video Claire made for "Leave Yourself Alone." Dish's sound might have been more aggressive than blackgirls, but they were no less melodic.

The Cat's Cradle suddenly closed. "We ran out of luck, I guess," Frank Heath told me. "That venue was a borrowed space. We didn't have any long-term commitment from the landlord beyond, 'We'll let you know when you need to move out six months beforehand.'" Frank was finally given notice. The Cradle stayed closed while its owners looked for a new home.

At the same time, Moist Records' Kelley Cox was asked to run another club, Smokin' Joes, on the east side of town. The Cradle's absence sent additional business to that club as well as Local 506. "Frank and I were talking even before the Cradle closed about what acts would make sense for me versus him," Kelley said. "So, even though we were running competing clubs, and I was a nobody, he still worked with me so that things made the most sense for everybody. Frank's not greedy. He shares the wealth."

Kelley describes Frank as "the best club owner for a thousand-seat venue in the United States of America. He's first and foremost a music lover and doesn't have an alcohol or nose-candy problem. He cared as much about the up-and-comers as he did Blues Traveler."

The Squirrel Nut Zippers' first show took place in the summer, around three months after Katharine Whalen started singing. The venue was Henry's Bistro, a tiny basement restaurant on Rosemary Street. Katharine had to be talked into performing at all, only consenting after being assured that the band was just an art project. The acoustic lineup featured Ken Mosher on drums, Chris Phillips on a variety of percussion instruments called a contraption kit, Don Raleigh on string bass, Jimbo Mathus on vocals and guitar, Katharine on vocals and banjo, and a violinist named John Kempannin.

Ken is convinced that the Squirrel Nut Zippers' rise was coincident with the Cat's Cradle being closed. Because of this, there were no high-visibility gigs to be had around town. Why not indulge in an oddball art project?

"We were the accidental band," Ken told me. "It was absolutely a product of Chapel Hill. The way we looked at it was, 'Here's what we did on summer vacation: We put together this band and wrote some songs.' I wasn't nervous at all because it was performance art. It was like we were *playing* this band. It was our impression of a band from a time that was much easier and breezy and fun. It was the audacity of not believing you're gonna fail."

The Hardback Cafe's Jamie McPhail was at the Henry's Bistro show. "That place was *packed*," she remembered. "People were standing on the stairs trying to get in. It was a different sound coming up that everybody was excited about." Jamie sees no contradiction in Chapel Hill's ability to bring forth bands as disparate as Archers of Loaf and Squirrel Nut Zippers.

"Originality and creativity kept everybody interested," Jamie said. "We didn't want one sound, because everybody was different. That was the beauty of it. We didn't go listen to bands that sounded the same as other bands. We went and listened to bands we enjoyed, and that diversity helped spark creativity. You needed to follow what you felt in your heart and not a trend that was happening around you. Everybody was doing their own thing and being supported by everybody else."

I was tending bar at Crook's Corner the night Squirrel Nut Zippers debuted. Lane Wurster had the night off and went to see the show. "Two songs into it, I thought, 'This is that crazy music that Tom Maxwell turned me on to!'" Lane remembered. "'It isn't punk rock, but it's punk rock. It's so disarming.' It was incredible. I remember calling Jay Faires and saying, 'This is really something.'"

Lane also called me at Crook's. "Tom! You gotta come down and see this! It's the greatest thing I've ever seen!" I was like, "Lane, I'm on the goddamned clock!" Then John Ensslin, who also had the night off, called. "Squirrel Nut Zippers—amazing!" he said. "Katharine Whalen—amazing! Billie Holiday, right there in the room. You gotta check it out."

"I'm not gonna see that band," I told John curtly. I was miffed that Jimbo hadn't asked me to join. At that time, I was insecure and therefore a brittle combination of petty jealousies and compensatory arrogance.

"Insecurity is why people might not want somebody else to do well," Archers of Loaf's Eric Bachmann told me. "I was one of the most insecure people. I still am in many ways. I think everybody is at some level. Whatever it is in the community that makes you feel like you can just be yourself and not be insecure is the magical part of it. You have to engage with human beings. The more you engage with human beings, the more you get to know them. The more you get to know them, the more you can lose your insecurity.

"That's how you develop a nurturing infrastructure," Eric continued. "Because there were so many places to go and hang out with people in Chapel Hill, Greensboro, Raleigh, and Durham, you got to know people on a personal level. When you do that, you root for them a little more."

Inevitably, Moist/Baited Breath imploded. "Everybody else said, 'We can't do this anymore,'" Andrew Peterson remembered. "It was clear that it was time for me to go," Kelley Cox said. "In lots of things in my life, when it's time for me to go I don't raise a big ruckus. I just walk. That was one of them. Like, 'Good luck to you!'" Shawn

Rogers, who had already hung out his shingle as a band manager, left too.

The last Baited Breath Productions record was the prophetically titled *Betty's Wake* by a band called Well-Nigh Forgotten. "We got those pressed, but I was like, 'I don't have the money to promote this,'" Andrew said. "'I gotta make a decision.' The band were buddies with D-Tox Records in Greensboro, so I ended up just giving them the CDs and saying, 'Look, these are your friends. If you can promote them, please do.' At that point I was operating out of a bedroom in my house and slowly shut things down. It was all over but the crying at that point." After his lease expired, Andrew moved down east to live with friends in Wilmington.

Chew Toy released *The Touch My Disney EP* that summer. "We recorded with my then-boyfriend, Greg Adams," singer Christina Pelech said. "He had never recorded anything before. That was something he wanted to do. He got some equipment and we were like, 'We can do this.'" The group took the single out to local record stores and sent them to college radio stations.

"I was teaching an English class at High Point University at the time," Karen Mann said, "and WQFS played my song. I almost had to pull over. If you told me at that moment that I'd won the lottery, it would be the same feeling."

The Chapel Hill used clothing store Time After Time wrote Chew Toy asking for a cassette. This is where the band bought old wedding dresses to perform in for one show. "Frank Heath told somebody that if we did that for every show, we'd be world famous," Karen said. "I know he didn't mean it as an insult, but at that point I thought, 'I'd rather be known for our music.'"

"I'm pretty sure the first song I ever wrote lyrics to was 'Fox,'" Christina said. "It was originally going to be called 'Al Gore, Fox, Fox' because both Karen and I had big crushes on Al Gore. But then I wrote the lyrics and it ended up being about being a woman and feeling like you were always being looked at by men. I was an art class model at the time. I wrote that song on one of my breaks. It's not

page

lost on me that I was modeling nude and writing a song that's partly about feeling like you're always being looked at."

It's not how I walk or dress or smile
It's nothing I do
There's nothing I'm changing
'Cause it's all you

Archers of Loaf's debut album, *Icky Mettle*, was released by Alias Records on September 7. It was produced by Caleb Southern at Kraptone. "You had to go in after the Cradle closed," Eric Bachmann said. "We would record from two until seven in the morning. Then I'd have to go back to work at the coffee shop. I'm not a druggie guy, but I would get a little bag of coke just to stay awake." The band worked a deal with Caleb to record the album for $3,000 of the $5,000 advance so they could pocket the rest.

"When I did the first Archers album, I was trying to make them something they weren't," Caleb said. "I tried to make it Nirvana or something like that, but I didn't know how to make the sounds. I was just twisting EQ knobs. The drummer Mark Price said, 'Caleb, your rough mixes always sound better than your final mixes!'"

Still, Caleb was evolving into something more than a capable engineer. "As a producer, I was starting to know what a single was," he said. "It's not about making money. It's about hitting the listener over the head with a great song. I thought there were several singles on that first Archers' album, not just 'Web in Front': 'Wrong,' obviously; 'Last Word'; 'Might'—here was a whole lot of them on that one."

Icky Mettle was enthusiastically received by the outside world. "I think it got to number two on the college music chart," Eric Bachmann said. "It did better than we ever thought it would have done." This was around the time that Eric's professional ambitions began to coalesce.

"I understand the disdain for corporate companies that want to exploit people and not pay them what's fair," Eric said. "I still have a

healthy disdain for it. But there's nothing wrong with finding something you love and trying to pull a living out of it, you know? That
was a battle, though, an internal battle. You would just not say anything and smile, then go like hell to get your stuff heard. I don't know
if all four of us were on the same page. I think people just wanted to
do it for fun. I was obviously more ambitious. It was a thing we hadn't
sat down and talked about because it was too uncool to talk about."

Caleb also produced *White Trees*, a Flat Duo Jets record that came
out in 1993. "It was a weird album," he remembered. "One time Dexter came in and said, 'Caleb, you're not doing it right! You don't know
how to mix this stuff.' He was right. I was making them sound like
Zen Frisbee.

"It was Dexter and Crow," Caleb said. "One time I asked Crow,
'How do you follow this stuff? Because Dexter's all over the map. He's
like a tiddlywink jumping around and he's not even on beat half the
time.' Crow said, 'It's real simple, Caleb. I just play a straight beat
along with him and when he goes off on some tangent, I start doing
fills until he locks back into another beat. Then I pick it up again.
That's my secret.'"

Crow got to sing one of his original songs on *White Trees*. "Where
Are You Now" sounds a little bit like Syd Barrett-era Pink Floyd by
way of Black Flag.

Alias Records released Small's debut *True Zero Hook* on September 27. The band is credited on the album as Small 23. The label
was going to press with the CD insert that spring when they received
a cease-and-desist letter from a lawyer up north. There was another
band already named Small that had a minor MTV presence. Alias
called the Chapel Hill Small as they were about to play a gig at Local
506. "We need a name," they said.

"We were all sitting there scratching our heads," Mike Kenlan
remembered, "and Chuck Garrison was like, 'What about Small 23?'
We said, 'Fine. Good. Go.'"

I asked Chuck how he came up with the "23" addendum. "Our
bassist Matt Walter wanted to call us Ultrasmall," Chuck said.

"Having just been through the Chunk-to-Superchunk business, I thought that was a little on the nose. We only had an hour to come up with another name.

"I'm not into numerology or anything," Chuck continued, "but twenty-three was obviously Michael Jordan's number at UNC. It's the angle of obliquity of the earth, one half of two sexy prime pairs, an Eisenstein prime, and has a bunch of other random number theory features. It's also allegedly the number of times Julius Caesar was stabbed.

"Right around the same time, Michael Monroe from Hanoi Rocks formed Demolition 23," he added, "so we were in decent company."

Unsurprisingly, *True Zero Hook* was also produced by Caleb Southern. Preproduction was done out in the country at Kudzu Ranch, Southern Culture on the Skids' place, where Small rehearsed. The band began recording the night of the last Cradle show at the Chapel Hill location. They had just enough time to track live on the Cradle stage before the venue closed. Consequently, *True Zero Hook* was mixed in Caleb's bedroom.

"Caleb was a genius," Mike said. "The sounds he could get! He did *Icky Mettle* there; he did so many great recordings. He always had a cup of coffee, a cigarette, and a Rolling Rock going at the same time. Just this manic energy. I would think I had a perfect take of something, and he'd be like, 'Aah . . .' and go out and fiddle with my amp a little bit. 'Do it one more time.' And then I'd do it and he'd be like, 'Yeah. That's it!'

"Caleb was always right," Mike remembered. "He had this ear for things. He always told me to clean up my guitar sound and I always fought him on that. Now I realize that he was right and my guitar would have sounded so much better if I'd just knocked down the distortion by about 50 percent."

Alias Records also bought a van for Small and even provided tour support. "At the time, it seemed like, 'Ooh, nice,'" Chuck said. "'They're paying me four hundred bucks to help cover my rent this month!' It seemed like a really big deal. Now it's like, 'Ah, whatever. They just have deep pockets.'"

"You're breaking something," Mike sings on the *True Zero Hook*'s title track, "but it's not my heart."

The Sex Police called it a day. "We decided we were going to stop pretty soon," singer John Plymale recalled. "We said, 'Let's go play every place that we play one more time, which is twenty or thirty gigs. Then we'll just stop.'

"Around that time, I was like, 'Man, I want to build a recording studio,'" John said. "I didn't know shit about recording, but I wanted to do it because when I was seventeen and went into Mitch Easter's studio with the Pressure Boys, I fell in love with it: the smell of the tape, the process." John produced The Popes' EP years before, which he described as Steve Gronback recording and him sitting around "acting like a producer." He did something similar with the *Dillon Fence* EP soon after.

John realized that he needed to learn how to engineer on his own but wasn't sure where to start. As it turned out, Wes Lachot had to relocate Overdub Lane, his ten-year-old studio in part of what was to become the Cat's Cradle's new location in Carrboro. John and Wes met by accident one day and chatted over a cup of coffee.

"He said, 'Dude, I'm moving out of the Cradle,'" John remembered. "'I'm building a place in Durham. Why don't you come work in my studio? I'm trying to stop engineering. I'll let you start working with a bunch of my clients. I'll pay you thirty bucks an hour,' which was a shitload of money." In the new year, Overdub Lane reopened in Durham and John Plymale had a new gig.

The Cat's Cradle's new location was several blocks west of the former one, at 300 East Main Street in Carrboro. Frank Heath was initially hesitant to move that far afield when the previous venue had practically been across Franklin Street from the UNC campus. The new space boasted the largest room yet, with a capacity of 750.

"That last couple weeks was me and Andy McMillan going on no sleep," Frank said. "He was my housemate and always very handy, very capable. He was willing to work his butt off to make sure every-thing that needed to be done could get done."

Jesus Lizard was set to perform opening night, but the club couldn't open without the fire marshal's final inspection. Every employee at Smokin' Joes, the club Kelley Cox managed, was on standby in case the show had to relocate over there. Back inside the new Cradle, Zen Frisbee's Laird Dixon was finishing painting a mural of Carrboro native and blues legend Elizabeth Cotten.

"Boy, people were scrambling," Laird said. "I remember seeing Frank running in the empty Cradle with a big bat of insulation, hur-riedly climbing up a ladder, cramming the insulation in there, and slapping the ceiling tile back on. He was literally footsteps ahead of the inspectors."

"It was down to the wire," Frank said. "The Jesus Lizard was help-ing us pound nails into the stage." The Cradle got the all-clear to open late in the afternoon. "I was prepared to throw myself at some-body's feet and beg," Frank said, "but luckily I didn't have to." When the venue passed inspection, Smokin' Joes closed so their employees could work the Cradle that night.

"When Frank got a chance to catch his breath," Laird said, "I went up to him and asked, 'How do you feel now that you're open and all these people are spilling in?'"

"Now it has a life of its own," Frank replied.

"It's like moving water," Laird mused. "You open the floodgates and, bam, it's out of your hands."

"That sounds like something I would've said to Laird," Frank told me. "I always felt like the club was this thing where all we had to do was provide an open room and the magic created itself."

I remember going out to Jim and Katharine's farmhouse to visit a Squirrel Nut Zippers rehearsal, which at the time largely consisted of smoking a lot, laughing a lot, drinking bourbon, and eating fried chicken. People also played music. I sort of remember sitting in on snare drum alongside Chris Phillips on the contraption kit.

"Of course, having a drummer with a kit would have been better," Ken Mosher said, "but I loved the disjointed, two-headed rhythm section. There were times it would get this gallop that I swear just couldn't be done by one human being. It was otherworldly. That was typical for that band: taking something that could be an extreme handicap and making it a defining element."

What I most remember from that day is sitting on the porch swing with my girlfriend listening to the band play through an open window before the whole thing crashed to the ground because the bolts had pulled out of the rotted porch ceiling.

Queen Sarah Saturday released their debut album, *Weave*, on October 12. It was issued by Thirsty Ear Recordings. I will be the first to say that every one of the guys in this band is an absolute sweetheart, so the following story that Zen Frisbee's Laird Dixon told me is no reflection on them.

"Queen Sarah Saturday had a big show at the Cradle—maybe a release or something like that—and then an after-party, as so many people did," Laird recalled. "The bong breaks out, people are smoking pot, and acoustic guitars come out as well. They're riding on their high, as they had every right to do. So, they start playing their songs acoustically in their living room with their girlfriends.

"It was just a scene that bugged me," Laird admitted. "I didn't want to hear it. I went into a back bedroom and called the police. Sure enough, ten or fifteen minutes later, everyone scrambles and hides the bong and the police shut 'em down. Then the party continued the way I wanted it to, without Queen Sarah Saturday showing off in their own house.

"On the one hand, Zen Frisbee didn't play the game because we were oblivious," Laird said reflectively. "On the other, we could be kind of vicious."

Dish's Dana Kletter was asked to record vocals on the sessions for Hole's *Live Through This* late in the year. "If I had known how much they were paying me I would have stretched that out forever," Dana laughed. "I spent three days in a fancy hotel filled with well-heeled businessmen and people who brought sushi to my room." According to Dana, Rosemary Carroll "coerced" Geffen into giving her an "additional vocals" credit. When I pointed out that "additional vocals" sounds more extensive than "background vocals," Dana agreed but refused to elaborate.

What Peggy Wants played their last show at the Cradle on Thursday, December 2. I remember seeing Jimbo and Katharine dancing in front of the stage. Afterward, Jack Campbell wrote a pseudonymous tribute to a local paper. "Standing in the darkness of the Cradle with 300 or so fellow fans," he wrote, "I thought to myself that what is precious about our little scene is that it produces unique bands like What Peggy Wants—bands that are willing to toil in relative obscurity with the simple goal of producing something cool."

"It was very hard to be wearing makeup when Nirvana exploded," John Ensslin said. "Nirvana would do drag, but they looked like Monty Python. It was very hard for me to continue in my Dark Prince persona with all that shit going on. Then we said, 'We're going to be like Cheap Trick. We'll just do these three-minute songs.' We got good and wrote the best songs while the crowds just dwindled away. But I think our integrity was completely secure. We were happy because we knew we were making a better product. Our success was not based on what people thought of us at all. Then we were able to exit gracefully. I'm very proud of that."

Chuck Garrison played two sets at the Hardback Cafe on New Year's Eve: the first one with Evil Wiener and the last one with Pipe. His former band Zen Frisbee played second, followed by Family Dollar Pharaohs, ex–Metal Flake Mother Randy Ward's new band, who also shared Zen Frisbee's bass player Andrew Maltbie.

By this time Chuck, formerly of Zen Frisbee and Superchunk, was drumming for Small, Pipe, and Evil Wiener. "I was always a little more awkward watching bands," he told me. "If I was going to be there, I'd just as soon be up onstage playing. That's how I developed this reputation of playing in every band in town—which wasn't true, but if you caught it on the wrong night it might seem like that."

1994

O N FRIDAY, JANUARY 14, I DROVE OVER TO SQUIRREL NUT ZIPPERS bassist Don Raleigh's cottage on Barclay Road for a jam session. Jimbo Mathus and Ken Mosher were there too. I forgot to bring drumsticks, so Don found a couple toothbrushes for me to play the snare drum. It reminded me of when I would use pencils to play air drums along to my favorite records as a kid.

As I was leaving, Jimbo beat me to the door and turned around. "What do you want to be in *my* band?" he asked with an anxious look. It was an odd question. All my previous band experiences were egalitarian, if not familial. This was a red flag. It was also true that the Zippers had the wind firmly at their back, at least locally. If I was ever going to do anything with music, this was my opportunity. "I want to bring Stacy Guess in on trumpet and play my songs," I said, after a moment thinking about it. And that was it. I was in Squirrel Nut Zippers—even though, as Quince Marcum said about rejoining Metal Flake Mother, it felt like I was violating some sort of principle.

The first thing I did was go out and buy a used tuxedo. The others did the same. We started gigging in black tie and tails. The de facto Chapel Hill uniform of cargo shorts and Converse high-tops was getting old. To me, the whole Squirrel Nut Zippers vibe seemed like a surefire way of sparing us from the corporate music industry feeding frenzy.

"I just loved that Squirrel Nut Zippers got dressed up for the show," Eric Bachmann said. "That was so against the aesthetic and I loved it. They got dressed up because it was a fuckin' event. That's a great thing to do."

Soon after, Ken and Jimbo came by my new house in Pittsboro to learn some of my songs. I pulled out two numbers cowritten with John Ensslin five years previously: "Plenty More" and "Club Limbo." It turned out that Ken, a dire drummer, was a stellar guitar player. My replacing him on drums made a lot of sense, but only in the way that each person was in the service of the collective.

The whole of Squirrel Nut Zippers was greater than the sum of its parts. We all existed on a spectrum of technical ability, from rank beginner to tolerably good. But that wasn't the organizing principle. The organizing principle was to build the most appealing, idiosyncratic musical landscape possible.

Small's Mike Kenlan and I used to work in the same bookstore together, the Avid Reader, up the street from the old shoebox Cradle location. The owners would play Django Reinhardt and Stéphane Grappelli's Hot Club of France. It made me feel like I was at a picnic. It was more than music; it was a destination.

It was so freeing to be in the Zippers, assembling musical elements taken from Harlem hot music, blues, calypso, country, and whatever else would work for a song. I was never interested in attaining virtuosity, which is just as well as that was never an option. Anyway, you don't need to be able to talk fast or have a big vocabulary to tell a good story.

Merge released Pipe's *Human Gutterball* single in January. It was their last record with Mike. "We had put out two seven inches on Merge and that EP," Ron Liberti said. "We were getting ready to make our first full length and we were primed. Mike ended up touring England and all over the country with Small. He couldn't do two bands and he chose Small."

Chuck Garrison was still in both bands. "I thought in some way that Small was the band that was gonna pave the way for Pipe," he said.

"I was working full time trying to put myself through school," Mike told me, "writing songs for two bands, and trying to keep a girlfriend happy at home. There wasn't enough time in the day. I remember Chuck giving me a ride home after a Small practice one day. He said, 'Yeah, I don't know if Pipe's gonna make it.'"

"What do you mean?"

"We've been auditioning guitar players. You knew about it, right?" Mike didn't, but it wasn't lost on him that this was basically the same way Eric Bachmann and Small parted company.

Pipe was about to enter a new phase. "I said to the guys, 'I don't wanna break up,'" Ron remembered. "'This is fun. We've got something going. Let's try to find a guitar player.'"

Mike's replacement was a veteran. Clifton Lee "Clif" Mann was the bass player in local swamp punk legends the Bad Checks. "I'd seen Pipe a couple of times at the Cat's Cradle," Clif said, "and I really liked their music. I liked their singer's onstage presence a lot. I was sittin' at the bar one night and Ron was there. I was older than those guys a little bit. I said, 'If you guys need a guitar player to sit in till you find somebody, I'll be glad to do it.' Because I'd seen Mike play and figured I could play pretty much the same stuff. So, I got together with those guys and started playing guitar for Pipe."

"Clif showed up," Ron said, "and he was a shredder. Some of the best songs I've ever been part of writing were with Clifton Mann."

The Veldt released a new album, *Afrodisiac*, on February 8. Half of it was recorded in Harlem, half in London. "We went with Ray Schulman as a producer," Daniel Chavis said, "because he had just done a song with Robin Guthrie and A. R. Kane called 'Sado-Masochism Is a Must.' I was crashing with a friend and saw this album cover of a girl with a knife behind her back. I put it on and said, 'What the fuck is this? Hell yeah! This is who we are.' It was loud. It was distorted. It had beats. It was ethereal."

Afrodisiac is quintessential Veldts. Cocteau Twins' Robin Guthrie contributed some guitar work. "It's not cluttered," Marvin Levy said about the album. "It has space, it breathes, it's fresh. For songs and production value, it's our definitive record." Marvin's drumming on "Soul in a Jar," the album's single, is explosive and rock solid. His kick drum trashes the place. The Jesus and Mary Chain made an industrial remix of "Soul in a Jar." Its quality made it an exception.

"We had been trying to get PolyGram to do remixes for I don't know how long," Danny Chavis said. "We gave 'em hip-hop people. We gave 'em everything. They still didn't get it. They hired this guy to do remixes for us but wouldn't let us come into the studio. He made it sound like the fuckin' Soup Dragons. We wanted the Bomb Squad.

"I was so frustrated," Danny said. "Then here comes Beck. He does 'Loser' and it has a beat to it. My Bloody Valentine did the same thing. Then the label got it. Had we gotten the Bomb Squad in there, we would have been way ahead of the curve. We begged them."

Back in Chapel Hill, a new group of iconoclasts had arrived on the scene: a three-piece consisting of drums, bass, and piano called Ben Folds Five. Ben used to play bass in a Greensboro band called Majosha but now wanted to play piano. Robert Sledge was another bass player from Greensboro whose old band was called Toxic Popsicle. The drummer, Darren Jessee, was originally from Houston, Texas. Ben met Darren when both were trying to make a go of it in Nashville. Ben initially tried getting something started in New York.

"Ben calls around Greensboro and says, 'I'm having a hard time putting a band together in New York that won't cost me a million dollars a day to rehearse,'" Robert said. Ben's brother Chuck recommended Robert.

"I was about to move out of town because a friend of mine had a gig in Nashville," Robert said. "When I came back from the trip, Ben had left me a message saying he wanted to start a band and heard I was good. I was like, 'Well, that's kind of cool.'

"The decision was, 'Where do we want to move?'" Robert remembered. "I immediately said, 'I want to move to Raleigh, because

I don't want to seem like I'm capitalizing on the Chapel Hill thing.' I felt like we would become stigmatized as foreigners and disowned.

"Ben was like, 'The heck with that! I've been playing Chapel Hill since I was sixteen,'" Robert said. "'Let's move to Chapel Hill. That's where it's happening.' I'd been coming to the Cat's Cradle every week for two years to see shows. Ben was ultimately right. It was a lot easier to develop a band in Chapel Hill than it was having all the distractions that a bigger town creates."

"I came back to North Carolina because everyone was having such a good time in the music business," Ben told me. "It was so not fun in Nashville at that time. You didn't play gigs, you played showcases. The whole time I lived in North Carolina, I would make my recordings on a four track and go play a gig to find out if the stuff worked. You could have thirty or forty people come out when you started who were listening to the notes and the words. That's huge, and not something I'd seen in other parts of the country."

"Ben's songs were so good," Robert said. "I wanted to get on top of that and internalize it. I wanted to do as good as I could all the time. It was such a weird opportunity, like getting a scholarship to the best music camp. Suddenly, everyone around you is just like you: 'Oh, I get to be myself now!'"

Soon Ben, Robert, and Darren were living in a house on Isley Street and gigging around town. Some Chapel Hill gatekeepers were slow to accept a newly arrived piano-based pop/punk band. "A lot of people were like, 'You just moved here just so you could say you were from Chapel Hill in the press,'" Robert said. "I was like, 'Dude. I'm from an hour away. I have that right. You moved here from Asheville two years ago and now you say you're from Chapel Hill when your band gets signed. I just didn't go to UNC.'"

"I was aware of the snobbery," Ben said, "but I always figured it came with the pride. In my experience, there's something great about going into a punk rock club and not being accepted. That's kind of cool. That feels right to me because you've reestablished the establishment: 'Well, the establishment is now punk rock.' 'Oh, great. I don't fit in. Who's punk now?' It works for me."

One night Bicycle Face and Ben Folds Five were booked to play a double bill at Local 506. "I knew Ben and Robert from Greensboro," Mitch McGirt said. "I always thought Ben was a brilliant songwriter. For some reason, they booked Ben first and us second. So, I called him and said, 'We need to talk about the gig.'"

"What?" Ben shot back. "You don't think we're punk enough?"

"'What? No! What I'm saying is you guys should go second,'" Mitch told him. "'Nobody really comes to see us play anymore. You guys are the hot new band.'

But, no, he insisted on playing first," Mitch said. "So, of course, Ben Folds Five sets up, the place is packed, they're rocking it. Then they pack up their stuff and everybody left before we even got onstage."

Ben Folds Five recorded a seven inch with Caleb Southern: "Jackson Cannery" b/w "Eddie Walker This Is Your Life." Kraptone was now a pop-up studio, occasionally located in Hillsborough at a place called Wavecastle Studios. Caleb would set his stuff up in front of the Wavecastle gear when he was producing a record. He knew about Ben from having run sound for Majosha.

"Ben Folds Five didn't fit into the Chapel Hill scene," Caleb remembered. "They weren't hanging out with the same people. They didn't sound like all the indie rock guys. I didn't care, because I was just happy to work with people who could play their instruments! It was really rewarding. I liked the stuff. Ben was like, 'This is punk rock for sissies.'"

"Jackson Cannery" starts off with some mechanical noodling before settling into a solid groove. Darren Jessee's effortless drumming was what I always worked so hard to achieve: impeccable timing, jazzy, and melodic, with occasional, unfashionable triplet fills. The band's three-part harmonies are completely on point. "Stop the bus, I wanna be lonely," Ben sings in a voice that would be at home on any 1970s Top 40 FM station.

When seconds pass slowly and years go flying by
You gotta stop the bus and get off here
Enough's enough
And I'm leaving this factory

Mammoth Records had entered a new phase in its joint venture deal with Atlantic Records. Danny Goldberg got kicked upstairs and became Atlantic's president. He moved to New York and took Jay Faires with him. "He wanted me as his guy," Jay said. "So, I had this crazy office and fifteen A&R people reporting to me, but they wouldn't let me put any structure on it. It was every A&R kid trying to get in my door every day, and I was still trying to run Mammoth."

"Atlantic loved us because we'd learned how to sell forty thousand units at a marketing cost of four bucks per unit," Jay said. "They would spend millions of dollars making thirteen records, and if they'd had a bad previous quarter, they'd put out thirteen albums with zero marketing budget. It was ass-backwards business practices. They started borrowing tools that we developed." This is what Jay considers the second phase of the Mammoth/Atlantic relationship. There would be one more.

Archers of Loaf and Small completed a tour of the UK toward the end of March. By this time, Small was just called Small again instead of Small 23. (The other Small had changed their name to the Ladybird Unition.) Chuck Garrison flew back to the States on March 21, his birthday. "You get a few extra hours flying west with the sun, so it was my longest birthday ever," he noted.

Chuck came home at 4:00 a.m., starving, to a house with no food. The tour had lasted several weeks, so the cupboard was bare. He decided to meet whoever was opening the Hardback Cafe and grab a bite to eat. Chuck rolled in around six and made himself some breakfast. An hour later, Hardback co-owner Grant Kornberg came in and told the staff not to open.

"We'd been hemorrhaging money in that last year," Grant said. "I had a bill with the IRS for about twenty or twenty-five grand that was due. We were gonna have to go borrow money again, which we were having to do a lot. We just decided this was it.

"The day after we closed, word got out that we were out of business," Grant remembered. "We had hundreds of notes plastered all over the walls outside, the glass windows, the side windows: 'Please come back.' 'You can't be gone forever.' It was heartbreaking for me, seriously. I guess I never really understood the full extent of that organism until it had gotten away from me." The last good deed the Hardback Cafe did for Chapel Hill was feed a hungry musician.

Chuck Johnson, guitarist for an experimental two-piece band called Spatula, used to hang out at the Hardback when he wasn't gigging there. "It was the heart of the community, from my perspective," he said. "It was the first time I felt like I'd transitioned from being someone who's moved there to go to college to being a local. Ron Liberti, Jamie McPhail, Alvis Dunn, and Groves Willer were extremely kind, friendly, and welcoming people who were also very supportive of other people's art. What a gift that place was."

"I do not remember any overt meanness or competition," Alvis said about the scene. "Now, there may have been underlying jealousies, but it was not cool to be that way. What was cool was to be supportive, or at least keep your mouth shut if you didn't have something good to say. Even when there were breakups—which could be very nasty—there seemed to be efforts to tamp it down: 'Let's be smart about this. Let's be human about this. Let's embrace the community that we have and don't fuck it up.'"

It turns out there was a term for what Alvis described: "Chapel-Hilling It." Polvo's Dave Brylawski thinks the phrase originated as a result of the finite local dating pool. "You're gonna have to coexist—and maybe even like—the next suitor for your ex-partner," Dave explained. "So, Chapel-Hilling It is just being cool, being kinda cruisy. 'All right, that's pretty fucked up. But here we are! Let's have a beer.'"

It also applied to the limited number of available local musicians. "We shared three drummers in the whole town," Ron Liberti said. "Like, bravo for Small. Go for it, dude. You needed to be able to hang with people at random house parties and not let other shit get in the way."

Superchunk released *Foolish* on April 19. It was their first full length on Merge Records. "Once Superchunk's deal was up with Matador," Mac McCaughan said, "they were in the process of entering into an arrangement with Atlantic Records. We had the choice to re-sign with Matador or just stay on Merge, because we had a way to be on Merge and put out full lengths. We loved the guys at Matador, but it was too appealing to just be on our own label. It felt like the right way to go. We had lunches and meetings with labels like Atlantic and Capitol when they were trying to find the next Nirvana. I think by this time they knew it probably wasn't gonna be us."

"Danny Goldberg wanted us to come to his office," Laura Ballance remembered. "I didn't go. I said, 'You guys go.' We were staunchly like, 'No, we're an indie band. We've seen what happens when a major label signs an indie band. They chew them up and spit them out.' Jon Wurster had been in a band that that had happened to. I was like, 'Why bother?' but Mac and the other guys said, 'What's the harm in having a meeting? If you don't know what they say, then you've never learned anything.'"

"We had this feeling, like, 'The Matador guys can be as cool as they want,'" Mac said, "'but if someone at Atlantic decides to do something fucked up, we don't know if they're going to be able to control that.'"

Foolish was, in its own way, a breakup album. Mac and Laura had ended their romantic relationship but decided to stay in the band and continue running Merge together. Superchunk hit the road.

Merge Records also released the first Squirrel Nut Zippers EP, *Roasted Right*, in May. Katharine Whalen created the cover, a color collage of a four-armed girl in a grass skirt in front of a black-and-white boat filled with disreputables. *Roasted Right* was recorded at the Yellow House with Mike "The Cheese Man" Beard and Bryon Settle on December 15, 1993, about a month before I joined. (It's testament to the ubiquity of Caleb Southern that Ken Mosher remembered doing the EP with him in Hillsborough. That never happened. Squirrel Nut Zippers were practically the only Chapel Hill band who *didn't* record with Caleb. He even did a session with Superchunk.)

Roasted Right is a good document of the early Zippers sound: acoustic, ramshackle, and charming, owing more to Tom Waits than Duke Ellington. Just as Bill McCormick observed with Chew Toy, all apparent Squirrel Nut Zippers liabilities were actual assets.

Roasted Right was a group effort. Don Raleigh contributed a song called "Anything but Love."

> *I sing a song about clouds and rainbows*
> *I hum a tune that sings like a dove*
> *Rhyme some words 'bout anything*
> *Anything but love*

The band was named after the Nut-Zipper, a chewy peanut candy that had been manufactured by the Squirrel Brand Company of Cambridge, Massachusetts, since the 1920s. Prior to the single's release, Don had the presence of mind to reach out to them. He enclosed a copy of the EP and asked their permission to use the name. The reply came on an engraved letterhead that looked positively Edwardian. The company told us how much they enjoyed our music and had no problem with us using the name. I still thought it was a dumb name.

Squirrel Nut Zippers shows in the area were rapturously received but few and far between. Over at Mammoth, Lane Wurster was pitching the band hard. "Jay Faires was really excited about the band at the time we did a ski retreat," Lane said. "He asked, 'What's the latest on the Zippers?' I said, 'I love the band, but Katharine is saying she has no interest in pursuing it as a career. I think we might be wasting our time. I'd hate to put all our efforts into something that we can't tour and promote.' I thought Katharine was a secret weapon."

Back in the Mammoth offices, Lane's job involved more than just creating posters and album art. "Jay was always driven by numbers," he said. "There was a weekly thing he would have the art department lay out called a 'hype sheet.' It was a form that talked about the status of whatever four or five records we were working at the time. It would be like, 'Number 67 on *SoundScan*! Number 5 Heatseekers track! *CMJ*'s Top 12! Top 5 phones at KROQ!' or whatever. He would fax it to all his industry peers and press people. It was the bane of the art department's existence putting that thing together each week. It wasn't the soulful part of the music that we were excited about."

One day, a hype sheet accidentally got printed and sent to the poster guys, who put them up all over the phone poles and kiosks around town. "It was all like, 'Number 25 on MTV's *120 Minutes*!'" Lane said. "We were so embarrassed. 'Oh, the business speak is suddenly in our indie rock town. Busted!'"

Band posters were everywhere. They were stapled on top of each other on kiosks that dotted the length of Franklin Street, creating layers sometimes inches deep. They appeared in the windows of clubs and restaurants. Making a poster was the primary way of promoting your show. Some bands were better at it than others.

Back in the day, John Ensslin was an expert poster designer. By this time, Ron Liberti was king of street art. "I was doing Pipe posters," Ron said, "and people seemed to be digging them." In 1992, Ron approached Frank Heath and asked if he could make posters for upcoming Cradle shows. A couple months later, Frank said yes. "That's when I started doing a poster or two a month," Ron said. "Frank let me pick the shows that I cared about, so I knew what the band sounded like. My most successful posters are ones that look like the band sounds in as few images or words as possible."

Ron combined his love of Saul Bass, punk rock cut-and-paste, and psychedelic posters of the sixties. Kevin Dixon told him to come into Kinko's after 10:00 p.m. to perfect his technique. "They had these killer two-color photocopy machines," Ron remembered. "Kevin let me go nuts and experiment. That's where I learned how to do color separation on a photocopier.

"I loved the immediacy of it," Ron said. "Doing something, puttin' it up on the pole, and there it is. Instead of working on a painting for three months and waiting for a gallery to put it up. I liked the spontaneity of it. I liked that it was doing a job. It warmed my heart when people would say, 'I came to the show because of your poster.'"

By this time, Kirsten Lambert was a DJ at WXYC and cohosting *Backyard Barbecue* as well as hosting her own Sunday night local music show called *Local Licks* on WZZU 93.9, a commercial FM station in Raleigh. "I was the first person to play Hootie & the Blowfish on commercial radio," Kirsten said. "Also, probably Ben Folds Five."

Through friends, Kirsten was introduced to an A&R person at RCA. "He asked me to bring him stuff from the Chapel Hill area," she remembered. "Whatever I liked, whatever I thought was worthwhile." She sent him the Squirrel Nut Zippers and Ben Folds Five seven inches and flew up to New York to find out if he saw the same commercial potential she did.

"These bands will never amount to anything," the A&R guy told her flatly. "We couldn't sell either one of 'em."

Former WXYC program director Glenn Boothe had been living in New York and working for record labels—first Island, then Sony, then Epic. While at Epic, Glenn submitted an early Ben Folds Five demo. It was rejected. Around that time, Glenn met the Caroline Records people out at the band's shows, worked up a rapport with the label's brass, and was offered a job. Almost immediately after, Caroline offered Ben Folds Five a deal. "I remember charging them at a show for a single," Ben chuckled. The band tried to get signed to a Chapel Hill label before committing.

"We went to the two obvious local labels and dropped off our single," Ben said. "Didn't even charge 'em for it. It meant a lot to us to try and do it that way. I was hoping we could get some kind of yes or no out of Mammoth and Merge quickly, so we could move on, or not, with our offer from Caroline. I don't think we heard back from either one."

"There was a Ben Folds Five show at the Cradle that all the Mammoth people went to," Lane Wurster said. "It was the first time we had seen a big piano up onstage at the Cradle. We were all jaw-dropped at his musicianship and voice. We had an A&R meeting shortly thereafter and I remember Jay Faires saying, 'It just seems like Elton John. There already is an Elton John. Why do we need another one of those?' Chris Sawin, who was kind of no bullshit, said, 'That's like saying someone plays guitar too much like Prince.'"

Ken Mosher was at that show. Ben Folds Five opened for Southern Culture on the Skids. "No one knew who they were," Ken said. "They walked out onstage and were my favorite band immediately. It was loud as bombs. Caleb was running sound, so that was helping. I thought, 'My God. Chapel Hill finally has a band from the sixties.'" Ben Folds Five signed with Caroline.

Having pressured Katharine Whalen into making a go of it, the Squirrel Nut Zippers also signed a record deal that summer. We had competing offers from Mammoth and Merge. "Steve Balcom was one of the last of us to get to see the band," Lane said, "because he had been traveling and kept not being around when there were shows. Maybe two songs into the set I remember him coming up to me and saying, 'We gotta sign this band. We gotta sign this fucking band.' I'm pretty sure he was in drag because it was Halloween."

Unusually, Merge was offering Squirrel Nut Zippers money up front, something like $1,000 ("A really sad advance," as Laura Ballance described it). Mammoth was offering more. "The Mammoth aesthetic, for lack of a better word, was trying to be like a small major label," Mac McCaughan said. "They were clearly going to spend more money promoting all that. I loved the single we put out. I remember a *CMJ* show Merge did with Magnetic Fields, Squirrel Nut Zippers, and Polvo. It was such an interesting lineup. But at the same time, we were never going to be like Mammoth. Our feeling was, 'We're not going to try to make an offer that's making it seem like we're going to be like Mammoth. This is what we do and if you want to be a part of that, great.'"

The Zippers held a meeting. "I just want our music to be heard by people who might like it," I offered. This seemed perfectly reasonable. Ken asked a related question. "I said, 'My aunt lives in Colorado,'" he remembered. "'When we put this record out, will she be able to get it?' The Mammoth people said yes. Merge might have been like, 'Well, if your aunt goes to a really cool record store, she'll be able to get it.' I meant your local Record Bar or whatever. I wanted us to have a chance. We weren't gonna have a chance if the albums weren't out there."

In that sense, the Mammoth deal was more appealing. They had a distribution relationship with Atlantic Records, who could put some promotional muscle behind our albums if need be. As it turned out, Atlantic had nothing to do with the band.

We also knew that the Merge people were straight up, and that going with Mammoth meant signing a deal with some kind of devil: they made their recording agreement contingent on us also signing a copublishing agreement. Its terms were functionally the same as what Dillon Fence's Greg Humphreys had signed a few years earlier.

We signed both agreements. At the time, Jimbo, Ken, Don Raleigh, and I were the band's songwriters. With the copublishing deal, I have a distinct memory of not fully understanding exactly what I was signing and figuring that if anyone was gonna write an actual hit song—whatever the fuck that meant—it would be Jimbo. His stuff in Metal Flake Mother was so good, as were his new songs. Given the fact that we were heading in the opposite direction of anything that was selling, I didn't waste much time thinking about such things.

In retrospect, my former self was signing away half of the intellectual ownership of everything I would ever write during the term of that agreement, while the entirety of the band benefited from the

Superchunk rocking Cat's Cradle, October 1990: (*left to right*) Laura Ballance, Mac McCaughan
Photo by Mary Robinson Crews

Bicycle Face, 1991: (*left to right*) Brian Huskey, Mitch McGirt, Chris Longworth
Photo by Michael Traister

Southern Culture on the Skids (and friends) performing at Cat's Cradle during a North Carolina Music Showcase, June 6, 1991: (*left to right*) Dave Hartman (*on drums*), Rick Miller (*on guitar*), Mary Huff (*on bass*)
Composite photo by Mary Robinson Crews

Metal Flake Mother at the Hardback Cafe, July 1991: (*left to right*) Ben Clarke, Quince Marcum
Photo by Mary Robinson Crews

Frank Heath manning the Cradle till, September 16, 1991
Photo by Mary Robinson Crews

Sex Police, 1992: (*left to right*) John Plymale, Robert "Robo" Jones, Je Widenhouse, Stacy Guess, Norwood Cheek, Jody Maxwell
Photo by John Kenan

What Peggy Wants lurking behind University Massage, 1992: (*left to right*) Tom Maxwell, Jeff Taylor, Tim Roven, John Ensslin
Photo by Maura Partrick

Flat Duo Jets' Dexter Romweber performing at Cat's Cradle, August 1992
Photo by Mary Robinson Crews

Polvo, 1993: *(left to right)* Steve Popson, Dave Brylawski, Eddie Watkins, Ash Bowie
Photo by Jason Axel Summers

Chew Toy, 1993: *(left to right)* Amy Wilkinson, Christina Pelech, Karen Mann, Stacie Smith
Photo by Brian Huskey

Dillon Fence outside the gas station practice space, 1993: (*left to right*) Greg Humphreys, Chris Goode, Kent Alphin, Scott Carle
Photo by Jason Axel Summers

Family Dollar Pharaohs, 1993: (*left to right*) Randy Ward, Groves Willer, Andrew Maltbie, Scott Goolsby
Photo by Jason Axel Summers

A cartoon included in *SONY FREE!*, April 1995
Illustration by Todd Morman

Ben Folds   Eric Bachmann   Caleb Southern

Barry Black

PH (818) 566-1034
FX (818) 566-6623
©1995 Alias Records, 2815 West Olive Ave., Burbank, CA 91505

Barry Black, 1995: (*left to right*) Ben Folds, Eric Bachmann, Caleb Southern
Photo by Jason Axel Summers

Spatula on tour in Minneapolis, June 1995: (*left to right*) Chuck Johnson, Matt Gocke
Photo by Bo Webb

Pipe backstage at Cat's Cradle, 1995: (*foreground, left to right*) Ron Liberti, Chuck Garrison; (*background, left to right*) Clif Mann and Dave "IT" Alworth have apparently found something of interest on the floor.
Photo by Jason Axel Summers

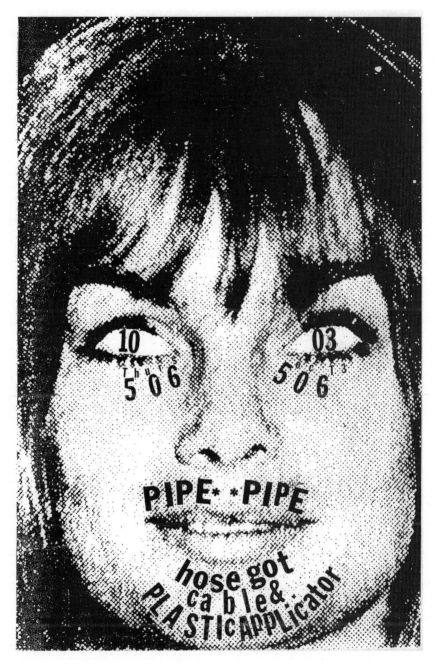

A poster for a Pipe show with Hose Got Cable and Plastic Applicator at Local 506, October 3, 1995
Illustration by Ron Liberti

Zen Frisbee sitting on the stoop of the Zen Frisbee house, 1995: (*clockwise from top left*) Andrew Maltbie, guest drummer Chris "Crow" Smith, Kevin Dixon, Laird Dixon, Brian Walker
Photo by Jason Axel Summers

A panel from the *Mickey Death* comic book, 1996
Illustration by Kevin Dixon and Eric Knisley

Archers of Loaf in front of their 1983 Ford van, The Dragon Wagon, 1996: (*left to right*) Matt Gentling, Mark Price, Eric Johnson, Eric Bachmann
Photo by Jason Axel Summers

Ken Mosher (*left*) plays while Mike Napolitano (*right*) works in Kensway Studios, November 1996.
Photo by Jason Axel Summers

Ben Folds Five performing in Charlotte, 1998: (*left to right*) Ben Folds, Robert Sledge, Darren Jesse
Photo by Daniel Coston

resulting advances, and he was likely baked when he did so. I mean roasted right.

"I remember meeting with Jay about signing the Zippers and saying, 'I don't know how we're gonna do it, but I think we can do a lot with this band,'" Steve said. "'I think this band can open doors. I think it'll get played on college radio.' What hooked him was when I said, 'Jay, they could be scoring stuff on Broadway!' I had all these wild-eyed ideas."

While everything looked solid on the outside, being *in* the Zippers was like standing on shifting sand. At some point, both John the violin player and a saxophonist named Spencer were ousted without the band discussing it. I now realize that that was a way of Jim and Katharine maintaining control. The familial, horizontal power structure I'd had with every other band I'd been in was never really the case with Squirrel Nut Zippers when it came to business. The fact that we were creative socialists was the only thing that made it work.

It took me years to figure out that the instability was the point. I remember Ken calling me about a meeting after somebody had been let go. "Is this bad news?" I asked, thinking I was about to get the boot. "Not for you!" he said with a sort of sad, phlegmy chuckle. Turned out I was being asked to be the third lead vocalist, a choice that I still don't fully understand. I couldn't really sing for shit back then.

Atlantic Records released Hootie & the Blowfish's debut *Cracked Rear View* on July 5. Tim Sommer, who had brought the MTV *News at Night* crews down to Chapel Hill years before, had become an A&R rep for Atlantic in 1993. He's the one who signed Hootie.

Tim teamed up with Hootie's manager Rusty Harmon as well as Atlantic's product manager Kim Kaiman. "We assumed that Atlantic would do nothing for Hootie & the Blowfish," Tim remembered, "that we would have to do something ourselves, that the band would have to build it, and that Atlantic would come. Most bands on a major label assumed the label was going to do the work. That's wrong. That's bullshit."

"Usually, the day a record came out," Tim said, "the label's A&R person, the product manager, and the publicist wanted to be able to go down to Tower Records in New York and Los Angeles, look at their record on the shelves, and go, 'Oh, look—this is my new record that just came out!' We told the Atlantic record sales staff, 'I don't give a shit if there are no copies of this record in Los Angeles, or Seattle, or Boston, or Chicago. We literally don't care if there's not one single copy in any store in New York City. However, in North and South Carolina—stock this thing like it's Pearl Jam.'" This was an easy pitch to the Atlantic sales team: Hootie's self-released EP *Kootchypop* had performed very well at retail in the Southeast, where the band primarily toured.

Cracked Rear View sold through the roof regionally. "It was the number one *Billboard* Heatseekers entry for that week based entirely on sales in the Mid-South," Tim said. "Because of that, the company noticed."

Zen Frisbee drove up to New York to play a one-off gig at CBGB on July 17. Randy Ward came along for the ride. "That was a hallmark scenario for Kevin," Laird Dixon told me, "because he'd always dreamed about playing CBGBs. This was an iconic thing for him."

"We had managers who booked that show," Kevin said. "The gig had to be moved for some reason, so we took whatever they had. We got to the club and there was dog shit all over the floor. You really felt like you'd made it."

The band loaded in, avoiding the landmines. Kevin watched TV with club owner Hilly Kristal in his office. Brazil beat Italy in the FIFA World Cup Finals with a penalty kick. "That's when one of the managers found out it was audition night and we weren't getting paid," Kevin recalled. The gig had been moved to a Tuesday night. Audition night.

"Instead of getting mad at us, like they usually did, the managers started laying into Hilly Kristal," Kevin said. "They were like, 'No, no, no. You need to pay us something because we had a paying gig. We didn't know we were moved to audition night. Nobody told us that. We need to at least recoup gas money.'"

"They pitched such a fit that Hilly Kristal gave us an ultimatum," Laird remembered. "He said, 'Okay, either they play for free, or I'll give you eighty bucks, you get the fuck out of here, and Zen Frisbee is banned from CBGBs for life.' We took the eighty dollars. As we were loading out with our tail between our legs, Randy was like, 'Chin up. Fuck that. You guys are standing up for yourselves and good for you.'"

Shocked, the band loitered on the sidewalk outside the club while their managers called other venues from a pay phone trying to book an emergency gig. "The club Brownies remembered us and said, 'Well, they can't get on the bill, but have the band come on over and hang out,'" Kevin said. "'They can see the Giant Sand show for free.' So, that was our consolation prize."

"Wow," Laird thought after hearing about Brownies' offer. "There's a red carpet."

Later that night, Kevin and Laird walked over to Brownies. "We tell them we're in Zen Frisbee," Laird remembered, "and the person at the door said, 'Hang on. How many fucking people are in this band?' They go get a manager. There's some confusion. The place is packed. They're agitated. It turns out there was a gang of bums that had been hanging out on the street in front of CBGBs. They overheard our conversation, beat us to the punch, and went to Brownies all claiming to be in Zen Frisbee."

Southern Culture on the Skids did more in 1994 than release their second Safe House album, *Ditch Diggin'*. In August, they founded an annual Chapel Hill music festival called Sleazefest. This beat being out on the road: SCOTS would usually take August off from their busy touring schedule because it was invariably too hot to play.

"I'd always tell my friends in bands like The Fleshtones or Ronnie Dawson to come to Chapel Hill, and there would never be that big a crowd for 'em," Rick Miller said. "I thought, 'We should have a really cool festival at Local 506—a small place—where we can put together all these bands that struggle to bring people in on their own.' We started off with a lot of bands from the Southeast like The Woggles, Hillbilly Frankenstein, Family Dollar Pharaohs, and Dexter."

Rick had the idea of putting three different generations of bands together to play each night of Sleazefest. The festival would feature legends like rockabilly wild man Hasil Adkins or New Orleans rhythm and blues singer Ernie K-Doe as legacy acts. Newer, established touring groups like SCOTS or Bodeco were considered the "middle" bands. Lastly, there would be younger groups just getting started who would benefit from the platform and association. "It was cataloging all these great bands," Rick said. "Each night would be a different genre. We'd do a garage night, a rockabilly night, and a surf night. We'd line 'em up, from young to old."

One hot inaugural Sleazefest night at Local 506, Family Dollar Pharaohs came on after Dexter Romweber finished his set with "Hurricane's A-Coming," a slow-burn blues. The Pharaohs' opener "Patina in 'Em" sounds like the television theme song from a 1960s Japanese spy show. Hasil Adkins closed the night with "Leaves in Autumn," an acoustic ballad from his new album *Achy Breaky Ha Ha Ha*. When he sang "I'll be looking out my window; I'll be looking for you to come home" it was so ragged and sincere you could be forgiven for thinking you were listening to Dexter's long-lost dad.

Future Sleazefests were predictably raucous and horny. Sometimes there would be go-go cages or a banana pudding fight. Once, Southern Culture wanted a piñata filled with condoms at their show. To cut costs, they sent bassist Mary Huff down to Planned Parenthood to secure some free samples.

"I need some condoms for this weekend," Mary told the attendant.

"How many do you need?" the lady asked.

"A couple hundred," Mary replied.

The lady looked at Mary for a moment. "Girl," she said finally, "you're gonna need this too," and handed her two hundred tubes of Astroglide.

On August 28, Bicycle Face played their farewell gig at Local 506. "Nobody was coming to our shows," Mitch McGirt said. "Not even our girlfriends would come to our shows. Our girlfriends didn't even like the band."

"I made a slideshow about the history of Bicycle Face and it was totally fake," Brian Huskey remembered. "It talked about our huge drug use and our car crash and how our drummer Chris Longworth died and came back to life. We played 'The Long and Winding Road' underneath it."

Dillon Fence's third Mammoth Records CD, *Living Room Scene*, was released in the fall. The band's previous record, *Outside In*, had gotten them some national attention. It was played on MTV's *120 Minutes*. At the same time, their southeastern touring base began to erode.

"For a two- or three-year period for Dillon Fence, everything was just so easy," Greg Humphreys said. "It just all unfolded in front of us. We would show up and had sold a thousand tickets. There was a vacuum for new music because there was no new music format on the radio. So, bands like Dillon Fence came in and cleaned up. But when the Commercial Alternative format hit, that was over. Because not only did we have competition, that competition was getting played on the radio every day. Organic, grassroots growth was no longer happening for us."

Greg remembers doing a radio performance for 99X, the Commercial Alternative FM station in Atlanta, which would host the band but not play their records. If a visiting group wasn't being backed by label promotional money, the 99X program director would usher everyone into a certain room to have his picture taken with them. This is where he took Dillon Fence. They all stood in front of a Sex Pistols poster that read NO FUTURE in big letters.

Greg thinks the recording budget for *Living Room Scene* was around $75,000. "We took three weeks to record it," he said. "We took two weeks to mix it. We went to Memphis, to Ardent Studios. It was a big swing for us as far as the amount of time and effort and money put into it."

The trouble was, Dillon Fence weren't selling enough records to recoup these kinds of advances. "I remember looking at our balance sheet and going, 'Wow. How are we this much in debt to the label?'"

Greg said. "I think part of it was that our budgets went up as our contract went along, but our sales did not increase commensurately. Each one of our records sold around twenty thousand copies. But on paper, we were in the red to Mammoth for six figures because of the nature of our deal. We made such a small percentage of each sale, and all the Mammoth investments in our records were taken out of our end before we made a cent." Greg was starting to feel trapped.

Up in New York, David Letterman heard Hootie & the Blowfish's song "Hold My Hand" the only time it was played on a local station. That was on a Tuesday. Letterman pulled his car over and directed his booking agent to book the band for Friday. Hootie played *Letterman* on September 2. You wouldn't have known it at the time, but grunge had just been bumped off.

Small's second full length, *Chin Music*, was released by Alias Records on September 12. It was recorded back in May at Wendell Recording Studio in Massachusetts. Mike Kenlan painted the cover.

"The records I did with Caleb were like, plug in and the band plays," Mike said. "I might come back and throw one more guitar track on top to fatten it a little bit. Then you do what you do to make it sound professional. Small had a bigger budget for our second record and we used all this fancy gear. I played one little solo on a '52 Fender Broadcaster through a vintage amp. It was like, 'Oh, this is great!' but it didn't make the record better. It was fun to dick around with that stuff, but on some level, it didn't feel like it was correct for us."

Some of the national attention Small was getting also didn't seem to make much of a difference. "I remember one of my brothers getting really excited when we got a positive record review in the *New York Times*," Mike said. "He was like, 'Oh my God, you've made it!' I said, 'Yeah, that doesn't really matter. The people that I care about aren't reading the *New York Times* to be informed about indie rock.' It was cool, but it didn't necessarily put butts in the seats."

On October 4, Mike's former band Pipe mastered their debut album, *6 Days till BELLUS*, with Brent Lambert in his house in

Chapel Hill. Brent got into mastering records indirectly. In the early nineties he had a gig doing voice-overs and recording jingles for WZZU. "The cool thing was that I would give a quarter-inch tape to my wife Kirsten, who worked at the station," Brent said, "and I could hear it on the radio that night. I would go, 'Oh my God. That sounds freaking horrible!' Too much low end or whatever. I would keep changing it until it got better. I finally figured out how to make those recordings sound good on the radio.

"There were great studios in the area," Brent said, "but no mastering places except for one and he specialized in bluegrass. So, everybody went to New York or LA or Nashville. It was expensive." Brent bought a digital workstation made by a British company named Sadie. "Once I got that, then bands could come to me before they went to the mastering place and sequence a record, do the fades, all that stuff," Brent said. "It would save them thousands of dollars at Masterdisc or Sterling. Then I made that transition from commercials to mastering because I hated doing commercials. With mastering, I felt like I was helping a lot of people." By the time Brent mastered the new Pipe record, he had almost completely phased out of commercial work. He called his mastering lab The Kitchen because that's basically where it was located in his and Kirsten's house.

Even to someone like me who spent years as a professional musician, mastering is an almost occult art that cannot be told from magic. Brent explained the process. "Mastering is the parallel to what a colorist does to the final print of a film," he said. "You look at a scene and go 'Man, that green has too much yellow in it,' and you make it a little greener. Or you're trying to interpret the mood of the scene: 'Hey, if we made the light a little bluer here, it would be colder and scarier.' It's that kind of approach, except with what I call forensic audio tools like equalization. It's the marriage of technical requirements with aesthetic interpretation."

From his vantage point as a mastering engineer, Brent was able to survey a broader landscape of local music beyond Chapel Hill's little indie bubble. "The one thing that people don't ever talk about is what was also going on around the fringes that wasn't part of the Caucasian, educated music scene," Brent said. "All the gospel, all the bluegrass. Some major stuff that people don't even think about: Shirley Caesar, Charles Johnson & The Revivers, and all these other amazing gospel artists in the counties outside of Chapel Hill. I would hear music that would just blow my mind. It was funny, from my perspective, to see these disparate music scenes coexisting. I thought it was cool that it was all going on and a lot of them weren't even aware of each other."

Dana Kletter's close relationship with entertainment attorney Rosemary Carroll was opening doors. Both Epic and Interscope Records showed an interest in signing Dish as well as guitarist Bo Taylor's other band, Motocaster. Bo insisted that the two bands were a package deal.

The major label A&R people Dana interacted with were generally awful. They had no problem telling her how much they were interested in Motocaster without appearing to understand how rude it was. "We don't really want to sign *your* band," they'd say breezily.

"There were catchphrases they'd use," Dana said. "That year's buzzwords were 'organic' and 'violent.' Pushing Up Daisies had just been signed to Island Records. One label rep said, 'Their organic violence is so beautiful.' We laughed about it, but it was also distressing. These were the people who would own us, in a way."

Interscope won the day. "They signed Dish because they wanted Bo Taylor and Motocaster," Dana said. "Jimmy Iovine was convinced that Bo was going to be the next Kurt Cobain.

"Sara Bell and I both have these punk and hardcore morals," Dana said. "I knew it was an immoral decision to sign to a major label and I think Sara believed that as well. She was very hesitant about working with them. At one point I yelled at her, 'Look: when Anne Frank has her own record label, we'll sign with her! But in the meantime, these are the offers.' Of course, Sara was right."

"Interscope was not really super excited about Dish," Sara told me with typically gentle understatement, "except our A&R person Anna Statman. She had signed Rocket from the Crypt. She loved Dish."

"Interscope was like, 'We need a story for you,'" Dana remembered. "One of the things that they wanted me to do was possibly be a junkie. It's easier to manipulate musicians when they're on drugs." Label reps took Dana and Bo to a sketchy part of LA and scored heroin, presumably for them to use.

Dana was stunned. "'You know what? Heroin hurts my stomach,' she told the label people. 'I'm not going to do it.'" Rosemary had to send a car to fetch her.

On November 7, WXYC became the first radio station in the world to offer a live Internet simulcast. "Already famous within its limited on-air signal range, WXYC now takes advantage of the Internet to send its broadcast world-wide," read the station's press release. "Listeners in Hong Kong, Johannesburg, Moscow and Guadalajara can now listen to the Chapel Hill station using public domain software that is readily available on the Internet."

Paul Jones headed the project. At the time, Paul was employed by UNC Campus Computing to run an archive called SunSITE. He and his students were working with emergent technology to archive the World Wide Web.

Work on simulcasting WXYC began in August, when one of Paul's students, a DJ, asked, "Why can't we broadcast the radio everywhere?" Paul brought grad students Mike Shoffner and David McConville on board to see if they could, in fact, accomplish this task.

Cornell had a client-based computer program called CU-SeeMe. It worked badly for video conferencing, but its audio file was easy to compress. The team decided to use this. Their simulcast setup was as DIY as the local music scene. "I borrowed my younger sister's little junker boombox," Mike told a journalist years later. "We set that up down at SunSITE. I bought an adapter to put into David's Mac. He plugged that adapter in there and then the boombox went to the adapter and that was where the signal came from."

"We had been streaming twenty-four hours a day before November 7," Paul said. "We could have announced it in September, but the board of WXYC was concerned that they could lose their broadcast license because we might be violating the copyright agreement. A couple of the board members were in law school. Nothing is worse than a law student because they think they know things they don't. There was no law about the Internet at that point. Nobody knew it was even viable for this kind of application." A workaround was instituted using a carrier current to take the station worldwide. Nothing was actually going out on the air; therefore, no FCC regulations were being violated.

Once people got wind of WXYCs simulcast, Paul's team received immediate feedback, much of it negative. "I heard all these things like, 'Once you start doing radio, it's gonna be the end of the Internet,'" Paul said. "'It'll be too congested.' 'Nobody's gonna be listening to it.' 'Nobody will be able to use email because people will be too busy listening to radio.'" A month later, two DJs in Basel, Switzerland, streamed WXYC and discussed whether it signaled the end of the Internet.

"I certainly hope this is NOT the start of a trend," one critical email read. "I hope that things like WXYC are stopped as soon as possible, particularly if they get small numbers of listeners, but in fact, after the trial stage, even if they get lots of listeners."

The hand-wringing was all for naught. "Nobody went to jail, WXYC kept their license, and other people started doing it," Paul said, "and it all got better."

Pipe's 6 Days till BELLUS came out at year's end on Jesus Christ Records, a new local label. Kirk Ross, the Copytron employee who used to drink coffee with Jamie McPhail at the Hardback Cafe every morning, had saved up enough money to release records by a few of his favorite unsigned local bands.

Clif Mann slotted right in with Pipe as a guitarist and songwriter on 6 Days till BELLUS. Monumental riffs, tectonic chord changes— it's all there, now colored with a slight seventies stadium rock sensibility.

Kirk was in a band of his own, Lud, with the Yellow House's Bryon Settle. "Bryon had just bought a half-inch tape machine," Kirk said.

"I got hooked up with WXYC program director Randy Bullock, who wanted me to put out the Pipe record. I had worked in studios in Indiana, just like I had worked in restaurants in Indiana. When I came to Chapel Hill, I decided I wasn't going to work in restaurants and I wasn't going to turn knobs. So, I just sat and listened for some of these sessions."

The other Jesus Christ Records release, issued on the same day as Pipe's CD and also mastered in The Kitchen, was Spatula's *Even the Thorny Acacia*. The band had formed several years previously. "I was living with the guys in 81 Mulberry," guitarist Chuck Johnson said. "We would also hang out with a couple other households of people who had not yet committed to band formations. Everyone had instruments and were always experimenting in basements and things like that. So, there was a lot of cross-fertilization.

"Matt Gocke and I were living in a duplex next to each other," Chuck remembered. "There was a drum kit set up in his kitchen. I just walked in one day with my guitar, plugged it into somebody's amp, and was like, 'Let's play,' because that's what we did all the time. Matt didn't even have drumsticks, so he picked up a pair of spatulas from the kitchen and started playing the drums. He had never tried to play drums before but was a naturally gifted musician."

Chuck was highly influenced by what Ash Bowie and Dave Brylawski were doing in Polvo. "They were experimenting with different kinds of open and alternate tunings on the guitar," he said. "That really does open up what's possible on the instrument, because you no longer have these rote chord fingerings and positions. You no longer even think about what notes you're playing—that's impossible if you completely retune the guitar. Then you're exploring by ear and tonality and texture.

"There were so many good bands in that moment," Chuck said. "But Polvo would do something very different from what other local bands were doing. It contributed to this feeling of, 'There's no rules.' They had more of a standard rock band format, but what they were doing within that, to me, was like, 'Okay, this really opens the possibilities. You can make sounds that really had not been heard before and still make it catchy.'"

Former Pressure Boy Bryon Settle and Mike "The Cheese Man" Beard coproduced *Even the Thorny Acacia* at the Yellow House. "Spatula had really good songs," Bryon said. "They were kinda hard rock, they were kinda weird, but they were also beautiful. For me to say that, it means they probably really were beautiful. I don't say that about a lot of things."

"The Yellow House would have been only our second time going into an actual studio," Chuck said. "We attempted to record some stuff with Caleb the year before, but we didn't get good performances and I wasn't happy with the sound. I'm glad we waited. I'm sure I knew Bryon from around town and being in the Pressure Boys. I didn't know Mike Beard until we worked in the studio with him.

"It was a great fit for us at that time, being really green and not terribly confident in what we were doing," Chuck said. "Having those two guys cheerleading us and getting sounds we liked in a comfortable environment—it was ideal. It was the Hardback Cafe of recording studios."

Zen Frisbee's debut album, *I'm as Mad as Faust*, was released late in the year on Flavor-Contra Records, a new label run by Dave Jimenez from *Trash* magazine and Dave's Videodrome. Todd Goss's Jettison Records had been responsible for issuing every other Zen Frisbee recording in the form of seven-inch singles, but Todd balked at doing a full length with the band. "Their records sold great in Chapel Hill," he said, "but I couldn't give 'em away anywhere else. I'd get 'em all back in returns."

I'm as Mad as Faust was produced by Caleb Southern and "recorded the Kraptone way" at Wavecastle Studios in Hillsborough. "Zen Frisbee was the quintessential Chapel Hill band," Caleb told me. "They embodied the spirit and ethos of the town. They were the Big Star of Chapel Hill.

"They cared about this record," Caleb said. "They took it seriously. That's one of the most produced records I've done, in a funny way.

We did a lot of preproduction. We rearranged songs. I used click tracks. They were all into it as far as I could tell."

Caleb thought the song "Fraidy Cat" was a single and carefully directed its production. Using a click track, he recorded Laird Dixon's delicate fingerpicked guitar part first, then Brian Walker's vocal, then Kevin Dixon's distorted lead guitar. Unusually, the drums were recorded last. Former drummer Matt Murphy had gone back to school and was replaced by Clint Curtis. "I slowed the tempo down at the end and had Brian sing the entire verse on top of the chorus," Caleb said. "I always liked that kind of arrangement trick."

The band told Caleb that they wanted a piano on "Fraidy Cat." He assured them he'd have one in the studio the next day and made a call. "This U-Haul showed up with a guy I'd never seen before," Laird remembered. "A nondescript, college-looking dude. It turned out to be Ben Folds, who I didn't really know. He and Caleb opened the back of this truck and there's a giant fucking grand piano. They turned it upright and squeezed it into the studio. I guess Ben was a fan of Zen Frisbee. The comical thing about it was that none of us are piano players. We just needed the sound. It was me and Brian pecking the part out with one finger."

"Chapel Hill bands from that time were almost British-style bands," Ben told me. "They were like, 'We're making hits!' Someone might not think that Polvo was trying to make it, but some of their songs have hit-record appeal. Zen Frisbee was the same way. You and I don't care whether they're playing it on whatever radio station, because once you've been through the process you realize how much chance there is in that."

News & Observer music critic David Menconi fell hard for *I'm as Mad as Faust*. "There is nothing that sounds more like what Chapel Hill was like back then than that record," he said. "It's almost wizardry how perfect it is. It puts you in a trance. Once I put it on, I cannot take it off until the whole thing has played."

1995

"I REMEMBER BEING IN ANDREA GANIS'S OFFICE," JAY FAIRES SAID. "She ran promotions at Atlantic. She was the gatekeeper. Jason Flom and Doug Morris were there. Hootie was at five hundred thousand and they were like, 'Are we gonna go after this or are we done?' Doug said, 'I wanna push the button and go balls to the wall.' Then there was a machine behind it."

"When a major label signs you," M-80 Management's Dick Hodgin said, "it's like starting a fire. They put a little kindling out there and light it. I'm talking about money. They see what kind of heat they get back from that money. If it goes out, there's no more money. If it gets hot, they push a little bit more money and then a little bit more. Atlantic was *bulldozing* money into Hootie & the Blowfish."

Around this time, Dick and Hootie's manager Rusty Harmon were at a wedding down in South Carolina, where, as Dick described it, they were "sitting out in the car getting high as a lab rat."

"Dude," Rusty confided. "I probably shouldn't say this, but they're telling me that *Cracked Rear View* could sell ten million copies."

"Easy, dude!" Dick responded. "Y'all are really tearing it up. But *ten million* copies?"

"Yeah," Rusty said. "Maybe fifteen."

Meanwhile, Hootie's buddy band Dillon Fence was coming apart at the seams. "Kent Alphin and Chris Goode quit and I replaced them," Greg Humphreys said. "Then we got a call: 'Hootie's record is taking off. Will you guys come support?' So, we went and started playing these big venues. They were on Atlantic. We were on Atlantic. But because we were on two different sublabels of Atlantic, which were fighting for attention and resources—even though we were on Hootie's tour and playing in front of thirty thousand people a night—we got no radio. Mammoth did step up and give us tour support."

Zen Frisbee's *I'm as Mad as Faust*'s matrix number was Flavor-Contra 0000. Flavor-Contra 0001, released around the same time, was *Haunted* by the instrumental band Family Dollar Pharaohs. In addition to ex–Metal Flake Mother guitarist Randy Ward, the lineup included Zen Frisbee bassist Andrew Maltbie, Scott Goolsby on second guitar, and Evil Wiener's Groves Willer on drums. Groves had been a Metal Flake Mother superfan. "I would religiously go see any show I could," he said.

Haunted was recorded at both the Yellow House and Wavecastle, but not with Caleb Southern. Another former Cradle soundman, Dave Schmidt, produced the record. Only three songs on *Haunted* last more than two minutes. It's a cobwebby surf record, owing much to tube amp reverb and whammy bar guitars. The best way I can describe it is "Marc Ribot meets The Ventures in the Munsters' house."

By now several albums into their career, Polvo was getting tired of the indie grind. "We had released three records on Merge," Dave Brylawski said. "We were happy with Merge, but other bands were getting signed. We wanted to test the waters and see if we could quit our day jobs. So, we left Merge and got a lawyer." Leaving Merge was not a legal issue since there were no signed contracts. Any Merge band could technically come and go as they wished.

Glenn Boothe was working for Caroline Records up in New York, which hired him and signed Ben Folds Five at almost the same time. "My favorite local band was Polvo," he said. "When I started doing A&R, I wanted to sign them. I reached out to Mac McCaughan and said, 'Hey, man, I want to sign this band.' He wasn't happy about it, but gave his blessing."

"Caroline offered us enough money to upgrade our equipment and maybe pay off some debt, which was great," Dave said. "That was more money than we'd ever been offered up front, but there was no quitting our jobs."

"We moved forward and started the contract negotiation," Glenn said. "The whole thing was stupid, because I became the conduit between their lawyer and our in-house lawyer." Negotiations would drag on for months.

Back in Raleigh, Kirsten Lambert became program director at WZZU. "Payola was still a thing, but it was indirect," her husband Brent recalled. "A Sony rep would come and say, 'Man, I was driving in and you know that billboard that's downtown, right where the interchange is? Your station would look great on that billboard. By the way, we could give you a bunch of TVs to give away. How about two hundred seats to this concert?' It was all this backdoor shit."

Sony was looking to increase their influence in The Triangle beyond radio. Chew Toy guitarist Karen Mann moved to Raleigh in 1994 and got a job at the *Independent Weekly*, an alternative Triangle culture magazine. "I was the calendar editor," she said, "the lowest rung on their ladder. I was also writing some music reviews.

"The *Independent* struggled in the early years," Karen told me. "They were not profitable. They had rich friends who would prop them up. There was a flimsy wall between the ad staff and the editorial staff. I was constantly fighting off ad reps who would say, 'This label or club bought an ad, so you need to make their show this weekend a Best Bet.' The only person who never tried that with me was Frank Heath."

Sometime in the new year, Karen was called into a meeting with the *Independent*'s publisher and the arts editor. "We're going to have this music festival and you know all the bands. We need your help," she remembers being told. "I thought, 'This is amazing! Yes, I'd love to do this.' They said, 'We've talked to Frank Heath. It's gonna be at the Cradle and we've already got a sponsor. It's Sony.'"

"Well, that's okay," Karen told her bosses. "We're gonna have other sponsors, right?"

"Absolutely!" the two men assured her. "But Sony is really hot to promote their new MiniDisc." MiniDiscs were erasable magneto-optical compact discs that could hold up to eighty minutes of digitized audio. Sony introduced the product in 1992. It was popular in Japan.

Karen's bosses at the *Independent* seemed genuinely excited. "What bands *wouldn't* want to play this thing?" they asked. There was talk that some lucky hopeful might even get a Sony record contract.

"As part of the festival, Sony wanted to have this panel to help people learn about making it big in the music business," Karen said. "They were determined to have Jeff Buckley be the headliner." Collectively, the music showcase and related symposia would be called the Sony MiniDisc Festival.

"Imagine a room filled with many of the area and nation's top movers and shakers of the record industry," read one *Independent* ad, ". . . right in your own backyard." This pitch would not land the way it was intended.

Archers of Loaf released *Vee Vee* on March 6, their second album on Alias Records. Bob Weston, who'd already worked with Polvo, produced. "I felt good about the record," Eric Bachmann said. "I like the way it starts." *Vee Vee*'s single, "Harnessed in Slums," became a college radio staple. "Thugs and scum and punks and freaks," Eric sings in a shredding tone, "are harnessed in slums but they want to be free."

Small's drummer and fellow labelmate Chuck Garrison wasn't convinced Alias Records knew what they were doing. "We were lucky that they showed up and signed the bands," he told me, "but at the end of the day it wasn't a well-run operation. They were all in over their heads. The Archers alone were a phenomenon that Alias could have managed a lot better. They should have been a much bigger band."

Alias was unusual because its wealthy owner, Delight Hanover-Jenkins, seemed to regard the label as a credibility factory. "The problem with Alias was that they didn't need the money," Eric Johnson said. "For the most part, they enjoyed having us on the label. That's all I can think, because they were made offers that would have made them rich. Then they would have been rid of us and have a lot of money.

"They didn't get us, to put it bluntly," Eric continued. "When *Vee Vee* came out, they were going to give away Gibson Flying V guitars as promotional items. Eric Bachmann and I were like, 'What the fuck? We can't afford a Flying V guitar and you're gonna give one away to one of our fans? Are you fucking out of your mind? Give them to us, we'll play 'em!' The disconnect was unbelievable."

Whether Alias had a hand in it or not, Small was big in Scandinavia. "I remember going to Sweden, first night in Gothenburg," Mike Kenlan said. "We show up and are whisked away to be interviewed by Swedish national radio. Every show we played there was packed 'cause we were popular. It was like, 'Holy crap.' Starting the first song and everybody's singing along with me.

"People only do that for famous bands," Mike thought. "What's wrong with them?"

On April 3, former WXYC station manager Todd Morman posted to the new alt.music.chapel-hill newsgroup. "FYI, Sony, your friendly neighborhood multinational corporation, is trying to interest some local folks in a three-day Sony Minidisc (tm) Music Fest to be held in April," Todd wrote. "It seems they want to do something to promote the (lame?) sales of minidiscs (I'll leave it to the audiophiles to explain) and they thought coming to Chapel Hill would be a great way to do it. I'm led to believe that this will be the first in a series of these events to be held around the country."

"In the wake of Kurt Cobain's suicide, there was some talk that *Spin* and *Alternative Press* and the rest of that ecosystem were lurking on alt.music.chapel-hill looking for the next Kurt Cobain," the *News & Observer*'s David Menconi said. "You know, checking out who from here is posting poetic things that will be worth printing somewhere if they blow up. Instead, the site was mostly a bunch of XYC DJs."

"There were some DJs from the Duke station WXDU," Skip Elsheimer added, "and some Raleigh people too." Skip lived in Raleigh and was a member of an artistic collective called Wifflefist. He also had a job with an Internet connection. "Instead of doing work," he said, "I'd read alt.music.chapel-hill. It had a kind of frenzy because people were bored. They were constantly chiming in. There was a camaraderie that came out of it, even with all the different personalities. There was also trolling behavior. People would come in and talk shit just to get people riled." In other words, the Internet. *Sic semper erat, et sic semper erit.*

Wifflefist was taking advantage of the *Independent*'s willingness to trade legitimacy for ad revenue by participating in a campaign the magazine was running with Zima Clearmalt, a lightly carbonated, citrus-flavored alcoholic drink. "The *Independent* ad rep called me and said, 'We want to feature Wifflefist bands,'" Skip remembered. "They would run a quarter-page ad with a picture of the band and a one-paragraph bio. On the other side would be a quarter-page ad for Zima."

Jumping at the chance for a complete own, Wifflefist chose to submit their most absurd project for the *Independent* Zima ad: a band called Krapper Keeper, responsible for songs like "Chewbacca Is Gay" and "I Fucked Your Grandmother." They sent the magazine a band photo that is pure Dada: two men in outrageous outfits assault a masked, wheelchair-bound person with a guitar. Their band bio was an impressive predictor of AI-generated text.

"Krapper Keeper is a carefully engineered spectacle of sound and music illuminating the fears, thoughts, and obsessions of the very young and the very old," it read. "They crank out an infectious pop-driven groove that doesn't comprimise [*sic*] their indie sensibilities."

"We just looked at previous issues and used the same words that were in the other band descriptions," Skip said. The *Independent* dutifully ran Krapper Keeper's ludicrous picture and bio under the heading "not the same old music." The Zima ad appeared on the facing page: "Not the same old drink."

"Once the details of this MiniDisc Festival started coming out," the *Independent's* Karen Mann remembered, "I thought, 'This is the evil twin of the Big Record Stardom Convention.' They genuinely believed people would be jumping up and down to play the Sony MiniDisc Festival in Chapel Hill. A group of people on alt.music .chapel-hill became incensed about it. They seemed personally insulted."

"It was just gross," Skip said. "They're coming in and putting their name on something that should be just The Triangle music scene, which is a bunch of friends who hang out and do this stuff."

While I don't disagree with this perspective at all, some on the alt .music.chapel-hill newsgroup undermined their credibility by working themselves into a conspiratorial lather.

"Here's what I learned," began one breathless email dated March 25. "Friday night is already rigged. The lineup is Jeff Buckley, Chris Stamey, Backsliders, Ben Folds Five. Apparently, Mama Sony has decided this is too good a chance to pass up and has ordered Mr. Buckley onto the bill, so Frank & Co. are trying to cover up the intrusion by putting some local artists on with him who would fit with his music."

In an apparent response to an angry Internet newsgroup, Sony scrapped the idea of Jeff Buckley headlining the MiniDisc Festival and appeared to take a big step back. Instead, the *Independent* took over the process of selecting who would perform.

"I was given a list at work," Karen said, "and asked, 'Are these good local bands?'"

"Yeah, I guess," she replied.

"Well, add anyone you want," her bosses told her. "We're gonna run it tomorrow."

Karen scribbled in a few other bands she thought were missing. Readers were supposed to cut the list out of the magazine, cast their vote, and drop it off in a ballot box at Schoolkids Records. The list omitted a couple big local bands like Queen Sarah Saturday, which caused more outrage.

"I kept telling my bosses, 'This isn't having the kind of effect you want it to have,'" Karen said. "'It's making us look bad.' They kept telling me, 'No. You need to get out there and promote it. You need to convince them that this is great.'"

The winner of one of the Sony MiniDisc Festival's headlining slots was a relatively unknown singer/songwriter named Debbie Likse, who had a small but devoted following. She also happened to be Karen's cousin. (Because of this, Karen had earlier declined to review Debbie's record.)

The *Independent*'s sales rep told Karen that he had heard concerns over ballot stuffing, even though Debbie had simply taken copies of the magazine to a show and asked her fans to vote for her. Minutes later, Todd Morman showed up in the *Independent*'s office and confronted Karen about ballot stuffing, among other things.

"I screamed at him so hard that he ran out of the building," Karen said. Consequently, she was sent home.

Todd has no memory of this exchange, but characterized his general feelings about what Sony was doing. "My main question was, 'What are they offering?'" he said. "At one point, there was a rumor that Sony was going to offer one band a contract. Then it was like, 'How good is that going to be for a band? How much muscle is Sony going to put behind this release? Or is it just gonna be a sop and then they just bury it?'"

Rattled, Karen went to a friend's house and saw Skip Elsheimer and others printing issues of SONY FREE!, a one-off zine that eviscerated the *Independent*, wallpapered itself with ads for local indie labels, and featured a number of essays ranging from reasonable to irrational. Skip and Todd worked at the AIDS Hotline together, and Skip had the equipment to do desktop publishing. He was also interested in making zines. The two were billed as SONY FREE! editors.

Carrie McLaren, who used to publish *Stay Free!* and who started out as a college rep for Sony making a zine called SONY LAND, wasn't directly involved with SONY FREE! but gave it her blessing. "It was right in the middle of my move to New York," Carrie told me. "I was completely bonkers out of my head with stress. I remember talking to someone about it." Actually, she wrote the zine's prologue.

The *Independent*'s Krapper Keeper Zima ad ran on April 19. The Sony MiniDisc Festival was held April 20–22. "It's not like this was done out of any affection for the music community here," David Menconi remembered. "It was just, 'Hey, here's this cool indie rock town. We've got a new music format. Let's launch it there.' It seemed about as poorly thought through as that.

"I got roped into being a moderator of an afternoon panel discussion called 'The Music Industry,'" David said. "They brought in some people like Melinda Newman, an editor at *Billboard* magazine, to be on it. She seemed even more mystified than I was about the point of the whole thing.

"I remember being embarrassed for them," David told me. "I tried to make the panel as nonembarrassing as I could, but the crowd was full of people who thought I was part of the problem."

Several pissed-off denizens of alt.music.chapel-hill, some wearing wigs, showed up to the panel discussions. Karen was warned that they might throw rotten tomatoes at the panelists. None did. Skip did not attend, but Todd did. "Todd was asking pointed questions," David remembered, describing them as "What do you think you're doing here? What is it you're hoping to accomplish? We don't need you here.

We had a perfectly healthy scene before you came in. When you leave with your tail between your legs, that will continue and you will have no impact. If you think you're helping us, you're not. You don't even know what that would look like."

"It was not a pleasant time," David added.

"There was a discussion about whether people should participate in the panels or not," Todd told me. "Ultimately, it came down to, 'Well, it might as well be people from the scene instead of people chosen by Sony.' Ultimately, they *were* chosen by Sony. My impression was that not a whole lot came of the panels, but we took advantage of them to have good conversations. There were people who raised a lot of good questions about corporate control in music. I don't have any memory of any of the panel discussions."

Todd considered himself a part of the scene—which was true—but it should be noted that he was never a musician. Because of this lack of lived experience, Todd appears to have been more willing to assume that most local musicians were happy to stay indie and remain destitute, which was not always the case. John Ensslin remembers a prevalent attitude among certain local culture mavens as described by an *Independent* freelance music writer: "What I took from it was that if there's no money in what musicians do, but they do it anyway, then they're going to produce more authentic art," John said. "Penury is a factor that contributes to legitimacy in critical circles."

"The people from Sony were mystified to encounter this indier-than-thou attitude here," David said. "They couldn't understand why any band would turn down a major label deal. It was completely foreign to their way of thinking—that any band would just be out there playing to play, putting their records out themselves, be satisfied with that, and not want to grab the brass ring."

Jesus Christ Records' Kirk Ross was also a MiniDisc Festival panelist. He had just released an improvisational album in collaboration with former dB Chris Stamey called *The Robust Beauty of Improper Linear Models in Decision Making, Vol. I.* "The way it was pitched to us was, 'If you agree to be on this panel, you'll get a MiniDisc,'" Kirk recalled. "David Menconi ran another panel, but he was also on this panel with me, Chris Stamey, Mitch Easter, and a couple other people. The panel was basically 'Is Chapel Hill the Next Seattle?'"

Kirk got the first question. "How would you describe the Chapel Hill scene?" someone asked.

"I like to think of it not as a scene but as a community," Kirk replied. "We're people, we have lives. Not everybody can tour. We try to support each other."

"I got a whole bunch of sentences out real quick and then just shut up," Kirk remembered. "I probably didn't get another question."

Karen Mann tried to back out of being a panelist. "I can't be involved in this," she told her bosses.

"You have to," they told her plainly, "because we can't get any other women to be on this panel." ("If Chapel Hill were a movie," Carrie McLaren told me, "it wouldn't have passed the Bechdel test.")

"I talked to one Sony rep at the conference. He looked like he was about twenty years old," Karen said. "You could tell he bought into this whole idea: 'We're Sony! We're great! Everyone's gonna want to be signed by us.' I told him I'd gotten a parking ticket going to the panel. He said, 'Don't worry. Sony's gonna take care of that.'"

During this entire process, which Karen described as traumatic, Frank Heath was the only person to offer any sympathy. "I'm sorry you found yourself in the middle of this," he told her. "It's gonna be okay."

Meanwhile, Archers of Loaf and Family Dollar Pharaohs had a gig at Tramps in New York City on April 20. Madonna's Maverick Records was actively courting the Archers. "Capitol, DGC, MCA, Epic, Maverick, and Elektra were all in the mix and interested in buying out the Alias contract," manager Shawn Rogers said. "Honestly, the only one the band would have truly considered was DGC. They had Sonic Youth, Nirvana, and Teenage Fan Club."

The Archers were afraid that whoever bought their contract would never recoup, confining the band to debt. "I remember Jimmy Iovine from Interscope saying, 'I feel bad for you guys,'" Eric Bachmann said. "'If you want to get out of your deal, we can do it. You gotta do something. All this rock music is big right now, but in two years it's gonna be bubblegum pop again.' Sure enough, Britney Spears came after two or three years. He knew what he was talking about."

"Maverick had an A&R woman named Mary who was very good," Eric Johnson said. "She was very sweet, very kind, and would take us out to dinner. But Maverick had Alanis Morrisette and Candlebox. We didn't want to be associated with those artists."

"A member of Candlebox somehow managed to get backstage at one of our shows," Eric recalled. "He said, 'Hey, I'm in Candlebox.' We said, 'How did you get in here?' I actively disliked their music."

"The night we played Tramps, Mary took us out to dinner in Hoboken," Eric said. "She's like, 'Yeah, Madonna's gonna come to the show tonight.' We were like, 'Are you serious?' We got back from dinner. I went downstairs, made a drink, and watched the Family Dollar Pharaohs. I noticed to my right there's this lit-up little corner with a bunch of big fucking dudes at a table. I could see a woman in between them. It didn't take me long to figure it out. I was like, 'Goddamnit, that's Madonna.' So, I pretended I didn't see what was going on."

Shawn Rogers saved Madonna the VIP table. "Mary came over to the side of the stage and said, 'Hey, I want to introduce you to Madonna,'" Shawn said. "It was really dark. I'm trying to get over to where they've saved me a seat, but I'm having to climb through people to get around. I tripped on a friggin' table leg and grabbed Madonna's arm to break my fall. I was like, 'Oh, I'm so sorry!' She goes, 'That's okay. Who are you?' 'I'm Shawn. I'm the manager.' I could tell she was not impressed."

The Archers played their set and then received Madonna backstage in the greenroom. "She sat down next to me and we started being silly," Eric Bachmann remembered. "I told her, 'I like your old records,' and she said, 'Well, I like all *your* old records.' I looked at her and said, 'Madonna, all our records are old records. We've got two records out. We don't have any new records.' There was this laugh and then awkward silence."

After a brief back-and-forth about Eric's Converse endorsement tennis shoes ("They're kinda dorky," Madonna deadpanned), the meeting ended. "Thank you so much for coming," Eric told her. "I'm not sure we're gonna sign with Maverick, but it was really sweet of you to come and watch the show.

"At that point, Randy Ward comes to the door," Eric said. "Randy was a phenomenally charismatic presence. He walks in carrying a Ziploc bag with toothpaste in it. I said, 'Randy, this is Madonna. Madonna, this is Randy.'"

"Oh, hey, Madonna," Randy said nonchalantly. "Say, has anybody seen my toothbrush?"

Chuck Garrison saw the whole thing. "Randy was not gonna let anyone else be the coolest guy in the room," he told me. "It just wasn't gonna happen. He was gonna do it one way or the other. That's the kind of thing you would say about someone you didn't like, but I honestly love it with Randy because he *was* a cool guy. He was cooler than you. He was cooler than any of us."

"It was the most surreal, perfect moment," Shawn said. "I was like, 'Oh my God, this is amazing.' They chitchatted for a little while longer. I was standing next to Mary, taking it all in.

"A couple minutes later, Madonna comes back up, leans over to Mary, and whispers, '*I feel like an alien. Can we leave?*'" Shawn remembered. "They went up this little side escape hatch to where the limo was waiting and that was it."

Shawn had interviewed Randy Ward three and a half years earlier for the Madonnathon, when Shawn was interning for Moist/Baited Breath Records and Randy was in Metal Flake Mother. The guitarist admitted that he hadn't thought about Madonna much lately before adding, "I've fantasized about her, but then that's just sex and how meaningful is that?"

Back in Chapel Hill, the Sony MiniDisc Festival staggered on. "The decision was made that the first night's lineup would be the winners, the people who got the most votes," Karen Mann explained. "The second night may have been Frank Heath curating the bill. The third night would be the *Independent* curating, which was basically me. It was all Raleigh bands because I was like, 'Fuck Chapel Hill! I'm just gonna call people I know in Raleigh and ask them to play' and none of them batted an eye."

By this time, *SONY FREE!* had become a bit of a cottage industry. Spatula's Chuck Johnson was working at the Cradle. "They sold *SONY FREE!* hats that had a little MiniDisc symbol," he said. "I fell on the side of the argument that this corporate attempt to appropriate the local music scene was not good. In hindsight, I don't know if it would have mattered that much, but I was like, 'Yeah, fuck Sony!'

"I was wearing the hat while I worked a shift at the Cat's Cradle during the festival," Chuck said. "Frank Heath was like, 'You gotta take that off.' He said, 'I understand where they're coming from, but Sony is keeping my lights on tonight.'"

Pipe's Ron Liberti was also working the Cradle that night. "That might have been the only time ever that Frank raised his voice at me," Ron said. "I had a *SONY FREE!* pin on when I went into work. Frank was like, 'Come here. Take that fucking thing off. I pay you to work here.' He got irked because everybody was coming down on him. I said, 'I'm sorry, Frank,' and took it off. I wasn't gonna argue with him. He's Frank Heath and he's never raised his voice. But he was pissed that everybody who was working at the Cradle was down with what was going on."

"Have you ever seen Frank Heath scream at somebody?" Kirk Ross asked me. "I have. After the end of the festival, I was standing in the back of the Cradle with Todd Morman talking to him about the controversy. Frank comes up with this copy of *SONY FREE!*, slams it down, and screams at Todd. 'It's fucking uncalled for! What the fuck are you doing? I have a right to run my business!'"

"I would say stuff like that to people," Frank told me, chuckling. "I had to. It was a very tense time. It was an opportunity for us to make a little money because they were paying to rent the space. So, I was torn between the Sony money and defending my scene. I didn't really buy into a lot of the conspiracy theories on alt.music.chapel-hill." It couldn't have helped that the Cradle had been struggling since it opened in the new Carrboro location.

Kirk Ross later found himself talking to one of the main Sony reps as the Cradle emptied out. "Why did it happen this way?" the dismayed Sony rep asked him. "Why did you guys get so pissed off?"

"It's like you threw a party at our house," Kirk replied.

I asked Kirk if Sony had followed through on their promise of a MiniDisc. "Hell no!" he said. "We got T-shirts." Not only did Karen Mann not get a MiniDisc, she also had to pay her own parking ticket.

Maura Patrick was both an XYC DJ and longtime Cradle employee. She has no memory of the MiniDisc Festival. "What I do remember is that XYC had a MiniDisc player installed to replace the cart machines," she said. "They were all converted into a MiniDisc. They lasted about twenty-five years."

Flat Duo Jets put out a new record on April 25. *Introducing Flat Duo Jets* was produced by Billy Miller, who released it on his own Norton Records label. Billy was in bands himself like The A-Bones, a rockabilly outfit. He founded the music archive *Kicks* magazine together with his wife. Before Flat Duo Jets, Billy produced Hasil Adkins and Link Wray. *Introducing Flat Duo Jets* is a great document of a great band. "Is life real tomorrow?" an echoey Dexter sings. "Is life real today?" Norton would also release 1996's *Red Tango*.

Apart from managing Archers of Loaf, Picasso Trigger, and Pipe, Shawn Nolan was offered another label gig. "Jay Faires came to me and was like, 'Hey, Mammoth is getting to the point where we can't really take chances on smaller bands,'" Shawn remembered. "'I'll fund the production, pay you, and cover your office rent.'" Consequently, Shawn formed Hep-Cat Records, an indie label with benefits.

"At that time, I had never had an office outside of my house," Shawn said. His new business was in Carrboro, next door to both Merge Records and Mammoth's art department. Most of the Hep-Cat money went to pay Shawn's assistant. "To be frank, I think it was off the books," Shawn added. "Some of it might have been Atlantic money. Mammoth used to fly fast and loose."

Five years after he quit, Chuck Garrison rejoined Zen Frisbee just as the band's fortunes were about to change. "It was extremely frustrating at the time," Kevin Dixon said. "Because as the scene got bigger, we were consistently ignored. Other than Jettison, we couldn't get a record label in Chapel Hill interested in us, let alone a real label. Bands that would play their first gig with us turned out to be Polvo and Archers of Loaf. Every band that would start after us and be like, 'We love you guys!' would go on to some kind of fame and notoriety and get to put out records."

Then Zen Frisbee played a showcase in front of some people from Ardent Records. Ardent was formed by legendary Memphis producer John Fry in 1959. For a while in the 1970s, the label released albums by Big Star and was distributed by Stax Records. By 1995, Ardent consisted of two divisions: Alternative Mainstream and Contemporary Christian.

Dave Burris claims responsibility for turning Ardent on to Zen Frisbee. Dave had been in North Carolina bands for years, starting in the mid-eighties with Light in August. He played bass in The Veldt for a while. Now he was in a band called Jolene, who were signed to Ardent and about to make a new record.

"Paul Ebersold, one of the producers at Ardent Studios, talked to me and said, 'Okay, who's the Chapel Hill band that's not been signed that should be signed?'" Dave remembered. "I said, 'Zen Frisbee, and here's their number. This is the band you want.'

"I will evangelize about Zen Frisbee until I keel over," Dave said. "I just think they're a *fucking* brilliant band. Paul Ebersold is a great producer. He had some hits. He has a warm, analog vibe that I thought fit Zen Frisbee perfectly, that would pull out some of the elements of the band that could appeal to a wider audience."

While a label contract was being drawn up, Zen Frisbee got to record at Ardent with Ebersold producing. "It was like going to Valhalla," Kevin said. "We saw the organ that was used on Booker T. & the M.G.'s

'Green Onions' in a broom closet. There were Big Star vibes every-where. Their drummer Jody Stephens was managing the place."

"It was so fun seeing those guys record in Studio A while we were recording in Studio B," Dave said. "Studio A! I mean, Big Star recorded there. Led Zeppelin recorded there. R.E.M. recorded there."

"This was the big time," Laird Dixon remembered. "This was the real stuff. We got our shit together for that. I remember one afternoon after a recording session, we spilled out into the parking lot, all going our separate ways. Big Star's Alex Chilton walked out of the building. Paul Ebersold had played him some of the tapes and he liked it. He was singing Brian Walker's lyrics as he was walking to his car."

Squirrel Nut Zippers' debut album *The Inevitable* was released by Mammoth Records on May 23. "I think we gave them $3,000 to make that record," Steve Balcom said. "The advance was so minimal. They recorded in that weird studio in Hillsborough." That studio was Wavecastle. To be fair, it was a little weird.

Instead of Caleb Southern, our record was produced by Brian Paulson, who had done Uncle Tupelo's *Anodyne*. The sessions took place over a few days in October 1994. By this time, Ken Mosher was playing alto saxophone because he'd done so in middle school and figured it was fair game.

I remember seeing Chris Phillips's brother bringing his old-school horn, a baritone saxophone, into the studio for Ken to play on the record. I thought, "Fuck it, I can do that too." I also played alto sax for years, through middle school and high school. I even marched in the UNC band one year to get out of a math class. I loved the punchy bari sax solo on Cab Calloway's 1930 version of "St. James Infirmary" and thought I could put the horn to good use.

"Club Limbo" and "Plenty More" made it onto *The Inevitable*. John Ensslin wrote the lyrics for both.

They say all the girls are monsters and all the boys are whores
So if you lose the one you love there's always plenty more

John was happy I'd found the Zippers. "I thought, 'This is such a great gig for Tom,'" he remembered. "'This is such a sweet deal, because there's no reason this band can't go on forever. It hasn't got a sell-by date. They can bring in audiences aged four to four hundred.' It was outside of the tweeness of music at that time. It's like what the poet Paul Valery said: 'Nothing ages faster than the modern.'"

"I listened to *The Inevitable* recently," Ken told me. "And I'm like, 'Wow. There is nothing in tune on the entire record,' which is fantastic. I swear, if the band that did *The Inevitable* had been on a bill with the Velvet Underground, it would have been the most unbelievable show you've ever seen."

Dish's debut, *Boneyard Beach*, was released on Interscope Records in June. It was also recorded in Ardent Studios. "One of our main criteria was that the studio had to have a great piano," Sara Bell said. "We talked about Bearsville in upstate New York. Anna Statman, our A&R person, flew to North Carolina. We rented a car and drove across Tennessee. We looked at a couple studios in Nashville. We looked at Easley in Memphis. Then we looked at Ardent.

"They were trying to push the big, beautiful Studio A—the fancy studio—on us," Sara remembered. "Then they took us into Studio C, which was a little back corner. We were like, 'Oh, yeah, we could do our record here.' It was a little cubbyhole. We met Jody Stephens, who is a delightful human being. We said, 'Let's do it in Memphis.'"

"We were totally happy with *Boneyard Beach*," Jerry Kee said. "It was pretty much what we wanted to do. Of course, it went nowhere and the record company's interest dropped accordingly."

"What I hoped was that I would live the life that I'd always wanted to live as a musician," Dana Kletter said about Dish's Interscope debut. "I'd been training for many years as a classical pianist. I went to music school. I played the pageant circuit. I thought, 'This will be great.' But as it turned out, Interscope really fucked us. Once Motocaster didn't make it the way that they wanted them to, they were not going to promote Dish. They printed three thousand copies of *Bone-yard Beach*."

Zen Frisbee's luck had also run out. "Almost immediately after we recorded, Ardent got bought out by Interscope," Kevin Dixon said. "Contracts were drawn up but never signed. It got sold and then it was like, 'Nope. Never heard of you. Who the fuck are you?'"

Ardent's mainstream division closed. The label chose to focus on Christian music instead. The Zen Frisbee recordings were shelved. Defeated, the band withdrew.

Meanwhile, there were tectonic rumblings in the music industry that few insiders felt. Joe Fleischer left A&M Records in 1993 to become a senior editor of the highly influential trade magazine *HITS*. "A friend of mine who was an electronica dance music dork said, 'Listen, this is a really cool thing,'" Joe remembered. "'Have you ever downloaded any MP3s?' I said, 'I don't know what you're talking about.'"

The two made a crude peer-to-peer connection on their computers. Joe's friend sent him a file. "I remember clicking it and then leaving to go to breakfast with my girlfriend because downloading it was going to take two hours," he said. "I came back, clicked on the file, and it played music through the speakers on my computer. It was obvious that it was something big.

"I went into the living room and was standing there, speechless," Joe recalled. "My girlfriend looked at me and said, 'What?'

"The music industry is over," Joe told her. "That's it. I need to figure out what I'm gonna do."

Just like that, Joe became a Cassandra. "The era of the top-down, undisciplined forcing of music into what the major labels wanted had ended," he told me. "It was irreversible. I was convinced it would be over in a day. It ended up taking a lot longer than that."

Ben Folds Five was released by Caroline Records on August 8. Technically, the album came out on Passenger Records, which was owned by Caroline and an "independent" subsidiary of Virgin/EMI.

Instead of Caleb Southern, the band tried using a new producer. "We started with Dave 'Stiff' Johnson," Robert Sledge said. "He'd produced G. Love & Special Sauce. I didn't really get along with the guy. It started sounding slick."

"It was a disaster," Ben told me. "We spent the entire budget on this producer and there was no soul in the record. One of my best friends came and listened to it and disappeared. I found her in a back room, crying. 'Who is that?' she said. 'I don't even know who this band is.'"

"She was like, 'Please go home and make a record with Caleb,'" Robert remembered. "'I'll put it on my credit card.'"

Ben played the Stiff Johnson tapes for Caleb. "You sound like a bunch of tired thirty-five-year-old men," Caleb told him.

"You're right," Ben said.

Ben Folds Five was rerecorded the Kraptone way at Wavecastle in three days for $3,000. "I just stacked up a bunch of blank reels ready to go," Caleb said. "I wrote up setlists for the band and told them, 'Start playing one song after another,' so they would get into it. I was trying to get a live thing going on. I'd flip the tape real quick in between songs."

"Caleb is younger but I consider him a mentor," Ben said. "He's not a particularly good musician, but he's a *proper* producer. He invented himself that way. He doesn't come from any school or anything. He's the real thing and a serious artist."

The producer was losing his perfectionist streak. "Caleb had this beautiful perspective on people as artists," Robert said. "He saw everybody as valid on their own terms. That was really refreshing. Here's the big thing: Ben can sing perfectly in tune, but Caleb would like the out-of-tune takes more than the in-tune takes. He would like the warm-up takes. He would say, 'I don't know if I believe those pretty, polished takes. I like the ones where you sound like you're in pain.' That changed the sound of the band."

Before he could finish mixing *Ben Folds Five*, Caleb had to fly out to LA to run sound for Archers of Loaf, who were going out on tour opening for Weezer. Caleb had the Wavecastle guys mix the two remaining songs he couldn't get to and FedEx the tapes out to the West Coast.

"We were out at Delight Jenkins's house in Burbank," Caleb remembered. "She lived in some mansion with a guesthouse. I got the tape and put it on the stereo. I remember looking at the Archers and going, 'I know this isn't really your thing, but this is important to me. I gotta see how this album ended up.' They didn't know what to think. I think they were impressed, but it wasn't their deal."

Immediately after, Caleb got a call from Ben Folds Five's manager. "You did it, Caleb!" he said. "It's perfect. This is the punk rock version of Ben."

The guys in Archers didn't know what to think about the tour they were on either. "Weezer's fans were kids," Eric Johnson said. "I don't mean kids like eighteen- to twenty-year-olds, I mean kids like fifteen- and sixteen-year-olds. That was their main audience. Some of them thought *we* were Weezer. It was probably their first concert and they didn't realize there were opening bands.

"They would start shouting for us to play Weezer songs," Eric said. "We had to tell them we weren't Weezer. Even when Weezer hit the stage and people knew it was them, the room would be half empty until they played a hit. Then everybody would run in and start jumping up and down. When they played something a little more obscure, the audience would go into the lobby and hang out."

Grant Alden was still writing the singles column for *The Rocket* in Seattle. "Peter Blackstock and I and a couple of other people were talking about starting a magazine called *No Depression*," Grant said. "I had moved into a converted garage behind the house where Peter lived. So, I'm sitting there in the middle of summer, writing my column for seventy-five bucks, which was a quarter of my rent. And I heard this Whiskeytown EP, *Angels*, which had probably been in the stack for a couple of months by the time I got to it." *Angels* was a four-song EP that the band recorded in one day shortly after they formed. It was released in May on Moodfood Records.

"The first recordings were at this crazy farm place," Whiskeytown member Caitlin Cary said. "The guy had an airplane. I didn't go up in the airplane because I was like, 'You're fucking high on drugs! No way!' but everyone else in the band went up in the airplane and threw biscuits at each other."

"I played *Angels* twice," Grant remembered, "and walked around to the front of the house. Peter was sitting in the front room on his computer with the window open. I handed him the single through the window and said, 'You need to listen to this. This needs to be our first issue.'"

Peter called David Menconi about writing a review. "Oh yeah, I could do that," David told him.

David was one of Peter Blackstock's closest friends. Peter had visited David in North Carolina in November 1993. "I really had no inkling of any sort of Americana roots thing going on there," Peter said. "It wasn't until a couple years later when Grant and I started talking about doing this magazine about alternative country music that David clued me in to it. He said, 'Oh, I probably have some stuff to write about for you.' He told us about Whiskeytown and we had them in our first issue. He also told us about Jolene, who had just formed."

"Whiskeytown happened to me by accident," Caitlin said. In 1993, she moved to Raleigh from Houston to attend grad school. She wasn't in bands and doesn't remember even telling people she played violin. "But Ryan Adams called me and asked if I wanted to be in this band," Caitlin said. "I said yes and can't even say why I did."

Caitlin immediately formed a close creative relationship with Ryan. "I was in grad school studying creative writing," she said. "I transferred all that discipline to writing songs with Ryan. I knew immediately that he was a good writer and a total mess that I could try to fix—workshop, make him slow down and actually write something good. I took a pedagogical approach. It's also an amazing, fun thing when you realize that you sing well with somebody. We could immediately harmonize great. That was a nonromantic romance, for sure."

Whiskeytown's lineup also included guitarist Phil Wandscher and bassist Steve Grothmann. The band's drummer, Eric "Skillet" Gilmore, owned Sadlack's Heroes, Raleigh's answer to the Hardback Cafe.

"The community of Sadlack's wasn't any one type of person," 6 String Drag's Kenny Roby said. "A philosophy teacher would be sitting there talking to a member of COC, who would be sitting next to a town drunk, who would be sitting next to a Deadhead, who would be sitting next to a punk. It was this weird melting pot of people."

The place had an indelible influence on a young Sara Bell. "Sadlack's was a sandwich shop right across the street from the bell tower of NC State," Sara said. "It was this incredible nexus of all the creative people in town. There really wasn't anywhere else to go. It was the meeting center for musicians, artists, and a lot of people from the design school. Many people in Sadlack's had dropped out of their PhD program because they were more interested in just hanging out and drinking beer, but they were brilliant. You'd sit around the table and learn extraordinary ideas and concepts."

"Whiskeytown had just gotten started," Lane Wurster remembered. "We used to see them play a lot because Whiskeytown and The Backsliders ran around together. They would open for each other." Mammoth had just signed The Backsliders.

"Mammoth never made a play for Whiskeytown," Lane said. "There was a feeling at that point that their early stuff sounded too much like Uncle Tupelo. We decided to focus on The Backsliders instead."

Between Jolene, The Backsliders, and Whiskeytown, it was clear that something very rootsy and American was coming out of Raleigh. 6 String Drag also gigged with Whiskeytown. "It appeared that Raleigh was based more in a Southern rock thing," Kenny Roby observed, "and Chapel Hill was more on the art rock side of things. It was a bit like the difference between the hardcore and the LA punk scenes of the late seventies: X and The Bags versus Blast. Raleigh was a little more working class.

"There were plenty of visual artists in Raleigh," Kenny said, "but many of the ones I knew were design students. There's this form-and-function thing working within their art, so it makes sense that these traditional forms would be there as a basis in the music." Most of these new Raleigh bands would soon be labeled alt-country, whether they liked it or not.

Southern Culture on the Skids released their major label debut that summer. *Dirt Track Date* came out on Geffen subsidiary DGC Records, the same label that Archers of Loaf considered doing a buy-out with. "We were touring the whole time," Rick Miller said. "That got us noticed by some people at major labels."

During the January recording sessions at Reflection Sound Studios in Charlotte, SCOTS realized they were out of material. "Hey," their producer said, "I really like that song 'Camel Walk' we did as a single a few years ago. Why don't we rerecord it and throw it on here?"

"We did," Rick said, "and buried it on the record as total filler."

"It's not clear what Geffen was thinking when it signed this Southern underground club-scene fixture," Lorraine Ali wrote in her *Los Angeles Times* review, "because it's unlikely that *Dirt Track* will rake in the big bucks." SCOTS hit the road again—buoyed by the Adult Album Alternative radio format and Geffen's support—to tour Europe, Australia, and the United States from coast to coast.

Conversely, after extensive touring with Hootie & the Blowfish and the Black Crowes, Dillon Fence called it quits. "I was really frustrated with how things happened," Greg Humphreys remembered. "I went to Jay Faires and said, 'I want to try a new project. I'm willing to do it with you if you'll renegotiate my contract. I'm in a publishing deal with my old bandmates who are no longer in the band. I'm only getting 9 percent of the profits from the albums and have to pay back everything from that. I'd like to get a fairer renegotiation in the spirit of good faith and continue working.'"

"No," Jay said, according to Greg. "I've got you under contract. If you wanna fulfill this contract, we can continue working together. Otherwise, you're stuck on the sideline."

Greg's response was to hire Hootie's Raleigh-based lawyer. "He went to Atlantic Records and said, 'My client would like to get out of his deal,'" Greg said. "'Can you help us facilitate an exit?' So, Atlantic went to Jay and said, 'Hootie's attorney wants one of his clients to get out of his deal. Can you help us out?' That's when Jay finally came to the table."

"We never officially broke up," Dillon Fence's drummer Scott Carle told me. "Greg said, 'I want to take a break. I want to do a side thing.' I understood completely. We wanted to keep building this thing and climbing the mountain, but understood that you don't have to knock yourself over the head doing it all the time. You can take breaks from it. When you're in the thick of it you don't see it that way."

A new project rose from the ashes of Zen Frisbee's Ardent Records heartbreak and Dish's Interscope disaster: Laird Dixon started writing songs with Sara Bell. "I became disenchanted with Zen Frisbee," Laird said, "and didn't feel they had the tools to fully realize what I was trying to do musically." Sara made sure her Interscope contract allowed her to potentially record with Laird. The two hashed out songs on a cassette deck. "We didn't own a microphone," Laird said, "so we used a shitty pair of plastic earphones plugged into the wrong jack."

The new instrumental group was initially called Mordecai. Former Ugly Americans bassist Chris Eubank, who had also just joined Spatula, showed up to a practice with his cello. "As soon as I heard that cello accompany my guitar, I thought, 'This is it,'" Laird remembered. "I loved it."

The drummer they'd been playing with tried to force Sara out and, since that wasn't gonna fly, Mordecai broke up. Laird immediately called Groves Willer from Evil Wiener and Family Dollar Pharaohs.

"Zen Frisbee used to do this thing called Zen Frisbee Brava," Groves said, "where they would do a more acoustic-leaning set. It was like diet Zen Frisbee. Laird also had a thing on Tuesday nights where a bunch of people would come over and play music. He called it 'Plop 'Em Doos.'" Groves was happy to team up with Laird, Sara, and Chris.

Scott Goolsby from Family Dollar Pharaohs rounded out the lineup. The new band was named Shark Quest, something Laird calls "the second dumbest name on the planet besides Zen Frisbee."

"I was walking down the street with a friend," Laird remembered. "We were booked to play Dave Jimenez's movie night at Local 506. I said, 'We don't have a name. Let's come up with something so we can draw it on T-shirts with a Magic Marker.' My friend said, 'Call it Power Quest.' I misheard her. Then Dave printed flyers with the name Shark Quest, so there was no going back."

"Laird didn't really have much capability or interest in doing any of the booking," Sara said. "Being in Dish gave me a model for how to do this. Dana, Bo, and Jerry are all amazing musicians who really did have their sights on having some kind of success in the music business. Since I came out of this weird little hardcore scene that was very much all about *not* having success, it wasn't an ambition of mine. I'm such a socialist, I can't understand commerce. But once Dish happened, I was like, 'Well, I have a better idea now for how to do this. I don't want to be on a major label necessarily, but I do want to keep playing and book shows.' So, I felt more empowered in that way."

Superchunk released *Here's Where the Strings Come In* on September 19. It was the band's fifth studio album, recorded at Fort Apache in Boston. Although never their priority, it was around this time that Mac McCaughan and Laura Ballance quit their day jobs. "By '95 we were touring enough that it was pretty hard to keep a job back home," Laura said. "We'd come home with money, pay ourselves from that, and go back and work at Kinko's. It dawned on me slowly that, 'Oh. Merge is my baby and I'm making a living in this band.'"

Small released *Silver Gleaming Death Machine* in the fall. "We did *Chin Music* up north with our manager producing," Mike

Kenlan said, "and it didn't really sound like us. We thought, 'For the next one, let's get back to Chapel Hill.' We did it at the Yellow House. We took a whole month to record and mix it. That was the most fun I ever had making a record. I loved Bryon Settle and Mike Beard.

"We'd show up, work for a few hours, then go get food from Mama Dip's," Mike said. "It felt like a very Chapel Hill kind of record. There was one point I was trying to get a high harmony note. Mike's like, 'Oh, hold on a second,' and goes into the control room and comes out with a bottle of whiskey. He's like, 'Let's do a shot of this.' We threw back the whiskey and I tried it again. And that was it. It loosened me up."

Alias Records proposed a very strange marketing strategy for *Silver Gleaming Death Machine*. "They loved the record," Mike said. "They thought it was gonna be big. But they were like, 'Let's put the record out, not advertise it for six months, and let it build word of mouth. Then we'll give it a real big push in the spring.' We said, 'What the fuck? That doesn't make a lot of sense,' but they were like, 'No, no. It's gonna be great!'

"So, we went out and had this amazing tour of the US—big audiences, selling merch—amazing," Mike remembered. "We wrapped up in Chapel Hill and packed the Cradle, then toured Europe and Sweden. But there were no posters up. The kids knew about it somehow. They were like, 'The club didn't have any flyers or posters up.' A guy came up and said, 'I own a record store. They sent the records, but no promotional material.' We said, 'Yeah, they're trying this thing,' and he said, 'Oh. Wow. Very stupid.'"

After months of contract negotiations, Polvo was still betwixt and between. The band might have moved on from Merge, but they still weren't officially part of Caroline's roster. "Maybe we were late in the game, but we hadn't signed anything," Dave Brylawski said. "We were like, 'Okay, can you give us health insurance?' We'd already booked a recording session in Boston, where Ash Bowie was living, at a studio called Squid Hell." The band commenced recording in October, confident that they were about to sign an agreement.

"The Polvo contract was done," Caroline label rep Glenn Boothe said. "It had the 'sign here' stickers on it. The negotiations had taken a long time because things would come up. They'd come to me and say, 'Thurston Moore is trying to sign us to Geffen and he's offering this. Can you guys do that?' Every time we'd have to go back to the drawing board and reconfigure the deal."

"We had a deadline," Glenn said. "They'd booked studio time and they needed the money to pay the studio. Ash Bowie was also in the band Helium and was about to go out on tour with Sonic Youth. I'm walking across the office to get the FedEx envelope to overnight the contract to the studio for them to sign. I walk by our attorney's office. He's in there with our COO. They're like, 'Hey, let's talk for a second about that insurance clause in the Polvo deal.'"

"We had agreed to give them health insurance, which was pretty uncommon," Glenn said. "Our COO thought that the $3,000 was a one-time payment." In fact, the health insurance clause was negotiated out to be a recurring annual expense. This was not acceptable to the label.

"I could have put those contracts in the mail and had the band sign them," Glenn reflected. "But, no, I reached out to a lawyer. The Polvo deal completely fell apart at that point."

"We had started to track when Caroline said, 'No, we're not gonna give you insurance,'" Dave remembered. "We had this come-to-Jesus moment: 'This is not going to be worth it. We're not quitting our jobs, we're going back to our jobs. It's not enough money.' The insurance thing was the final straw."

Polvo was recording with Bob Weston again, who'd produced *Today's Active Lifestyles*. Bob called Corey Rusk from Touch and Go, which already had a distribution deal with Merge. In Europe, Polvo records were released on the Touch and Go label. "This band's in a jam," Bob told Corey. "You know these guys. Can you pay for the session and sign 'em?" Corey said he would.

"Which was unbelievable," Dave said. "Then we were on Touch and Go."

"It's all water under the bridge," Laura Ballance told me, "but at the time we were mad at both Polvo and Corey. It just seemed weird. But the stupid thing about not having contracts is that you have people making assumptions, and that's a bad thing. Ultimately, it's good to have contracts. Because we didn't have that clarity with Polvo, it felt shocking."

"That was a weird one," Mac McCaughan said. "That was one of the first times I felt a little conflict with Touch and Go. Corey basically went to Polvo and said, 'Look, if you just sign with us directly, there won't be another label that you're sharing the money with, and we'll give you this bigger advance.' I was like, 'What the fuck?'

"I hope it worked out for Polvo," Mac continued. "I mean, the math makes sense. We were bummed out. It was a whiff of the major label thing of, 'Oh, you little labels are the farm teams, but we're the big leagues.'"

Merge would go on to offer Todd Morman, of SONY FREE! notoriety, a job. At the time, Todd was working for a small graphics software company in Raleigh. "I had health insurance," he said. "I was so tempted. But what stopped me was that Merge was too small at that point to offer health insurance. I would have jumped at the chance, but had some illness. I couldn't imagine not having my health insurance."

On October 10, Alias Records released *Barry Black*, an Eric Bachmann solo album. "It was recorded with Caleb Southern," Eric said. "I worked with local musicians in Chapel Hill. I brought friends in and we made this front porch, ambient jazz record. I play a lot of saxophone on it. I missed playing saxophone." Eric had been a saxophone performance major back at Appalachian State University in Boone.

"I had a saxophone teacher who was very honest," Eric remembered. "He asked me if I wanted to be a teacher. I said, 'I want to write. I want to be in a band. I want to perform.' He said, 'Well, you're getting a performance degree from a place that doesn't really nurture performance. We're a teaching college. If you want to perform, you need to move to New York or LA or somewhere where there's more action.' I didn't have the financial ability to do that. I knew stuff was going on in Chapel Hill, so I moved there and immediately started looking to play in bands."

Ben Folds played drums on *Barry Black*. "Percussion is his best instrument," Caleb said about Ben. "Drums are second best, bass is the third best, and piano is somewhere down the list. Ben is one of the most amazing drummers I've ever seen. It was my idea to have him on Eric's record. I don't think they knew each other before then."

"Ben and I got along really well," Eric said. "He's a consummate musician and a cool guy. He worked hard in his writing. He wasn't afraid to tell you, 'I'm trying to do this. I'm gonna do this.' Which, I think, speaks to his success."

One day during the *Barry Black* sessions, Eric stopped what he was doing and looked up. "Caleb," he said, "I think the reason I smoke is because a cigarette is the only thing I ever finish."

Whiskeytown's debut, *Faithless Street*, was issued at year's end by Moodfood Records. In *No Depression*'s November issue, Peter Black-stock began his review by quoting the opening lyrics to "Midway Park."

I'll ride with you tonight, I'll ride forever
There's no way to predict this kind of weather

"It's the kind of opening line that sets a tone, sticks with you, serves as a harbinger that something significant is looming on the horizon," Peter wrote. "That something is Whiskeytown, whose long-player *Faithless Street* is the best debut album of the year. As word starts getting around about this 'alternative country' thang and folks begin to look beyond the Wilcos and the Son Volts and the Bottle Rockets for further proof that similarly styled young bands are coming out of nowhere, this Raleigh, North Carolina, outfit is at the top of the list."

No Depression had found its niche. "As Peter said, we didn't want to be the next big thing," Grant Alden told me. "We wanted to be the next medium-sized thing. I did not want Whiskeytown to be the next Nirvana. I wanted them to be the next Whiskeytown."

It's not surprising that the people working at *No Depression* had formed a proprietary relationship with musicians that made a certain kind of music. The same condition had been at work in Chapel Hill with so-called indie bands for the past couple years, leading to Ben Folds Five being made to feel like interlopers as well as the push-back against the Sony MiniDisc Festival. Music is great for helping to build an identity construct.

Chew Toy played their farewell show on November 5. "It felt okay to be done," Christina Pelech said. "There wasn't a huge fight. It was just, 'I think we're done.' We didn't go away angry at each other. We went away with this memory of having been able to do this thing together for five years. For me, Chew Toy was a lot of joy, a lot of happiness."

Ultimately, Archers of Loaf declined to pursue a major label buy-out. "Because if it fails, you're done," Eric Bachmann explained. "The hip, underground, indie rock world you came from does not like it when you're on a major label and they give you all this money. If you fail, you can't go back to them and you're sure as shit not going to have another shot with the people you lost money with or anybody else that does that kind of thing." The Archers stayed indie.

1996

THE TELECOMMUNICATIONS ACT OF 1996 WAS ENACTED BY THE 104th Congress on January 3 and signed into law by President Clinton on February 8. It was a big overhaul of American telecommunications code—the first significant one in sixty years. For the first time, the Internet was included for broadcast spectrum allotment. Because the act deregulated telecommunication and broadcast markets and eliminated a cap on nationwide radio station ownership, it became a checkered flag for a small number of corporations to snap up commercial radio stations across the country and homogenize playlists.

Tom DeSavia had been working for the performance rights organization ASCAP since 1989. In January, he was hired to do A&R for Elektra Records. "There was regionalism in music," Tom said. "You knew where your band was from the same way you knew your sports team. We knew The Cars were from Boston. We knew R.E.M. was from Athens. We knew The Ramones were from New York. When you went to Minneapolis, Soul Asylum would be on the radio. When you went to Texas, you'd hear Jimmy Dale Gilmore.

"This was the beautiful part," Tom said. "If a record did well and it wasn't just on locals-only play, then radio stations could see how it was performing in all these different markets. If you looked at the radio charts, you could see the song spider-webbing out across the country.

"Clinton deregulated radio," Tom said. "Then companies like Affinity and Clear Channel got the right to buy all these stations and automate them. Pretty quickly we got Matchbox Twenty World. It used to be I'd go to Chapel Hill, turn on a station, and hear The dBs or Don Dixon. Then suddenly, I'm going to Chapel Hill and hearing Matchbox Twenty. I'm hearing Creed. It's like, 'Wait—this sounds just like the shitty radio in that other town!'"

Southern Culture on the Skids had just finished extensively touring *Dirt Track Date* when they were dragged back out again. "Back then the radio guys had to test markets," Rick Miller said. "Some guy in a modern rock station in Tampa played 'Camel Walk' on a whim because he liked it. Suddenly, people were all over it. Geffen called us up and said, 'You got to get back out on the road. We're doing a big push!'"

"We were tired," Rick said. "On that stretch we did about three hundred out of three hundred and sixty-five days on the road." SCOTS was effectively gone for the entire year.

Spatula's first release of the year was *Medium Planers and Matchers*, recorded in late 1995 and released on Jesus Christ Records. The band was now a three-piece, augmented by Chris Eubank on cello. With its round, low pedal tones and melodic counterpoint, Chris's cello gave Spatula's music a wider aspect ratio. On "Service Entrance Fiasco," Chuck Johnson's introductory guitar part wouldn't be out of place on *The Velvet Underground & Nico*. Then the band launches into a crooked tarantella.

Like Polvo, Ben Folds Five was ready to level up. "We were signed to Caroline, which was owned by Virgin but had a lot of autonomy," Robert Sledge said. "They were the most successful and largest indie distributor in America. They seemed to have a good support network.

"Early on, we realized that there was a ceiling to it," Robert said. "It wasn't the same kind of growth that R.E.M. or The Police had done on I.R.S. Records. Indie records cost $10,000 to make with the expectation to sell perhaps 10,000 records total. It was very college-based. Every good college radio station would get serviced, and you'd do a tour of colleges. If you could get some national touring, then you would go to a major label.

"Early on, someone at Caroline said, 'I hope we sell three thousand Ben Folds Five records!'" Robert remembered. "Ben turned to me and said, 'Three thousand? That's all?' It hadn't dawned on me. We think we're this great band and we wanna go out and play for the whole world, and they only expect us to sell three thousand records? That was a gut punch. The writing was on the wall."

After *Ben Folds Five* was released, several major labels began courting the band. "We were squarely post-grunge," Robert said. "Pearl Jam and Soundgarden were well into their careers. The industry was looking for the next thing. We got a lot of interest from all the major labels when we were touring our first record. It felt like our business was way out in front of us, like we were having to make long-term decisions after just being born." There was an old-school major label bidding war. Sony won.

Ben Folds Five was signed to Sony 550 Music, which operated through Sony's Epic Records division. "The reason we went with 550 rather than another bidder who was higher was because the other bidder wouldn't let us use Caleb," Ben said. "The other label needed someone who was experienced to do it and 550 wanted what we wanted."

The problem was that Caleb Southern quit producing records in 1995. "I was burning out," he said, "and starting to hate music. I didn't want to hate music. It's like when your hobby becomes your job." Caleb decided to go back to what he was originally going to do anyway, which was pursue an academic career in computer science. Caleb sold his Kraptone gear, came up short, and asked his friends to play a benefit concert to settle his debts. Ben Folds Five and Zen Frisbee agreed to help. Caleb resumed his studies at UNC.

"Then I got a royalty check for $7,000," Caleb remembered. "The first Folds album was huge in Japan. I had two points on that record and we were in the black immediately. I'd been somehow living on $7,000 a year, and then suddenly it comes in one lump out of the sky!"

"Caroline got a big payout for the band from Sony," Robert remembered. "When Sony pushes the button on something, it goes global. That comes with a lot of stress. We felt that we had to have a hit. That was us feeling the crunch of this time compression that hadn't happened in the seventies and eighties. Back then, things developed more before you hit that stage. I keenly felt that 'this has to hit now.' There'd been a lot of investment, a lot of negotiation. To 550's credit, they didn't try to mold us into what they thought we were. They just allowed us to be ourselves."

For years, Zen Frisbee's Kevin Dixon and his collaborator Eric Knisley had been drawing a weekly comic strip called *Mickey Death*, published in Dave Jimenez's zine *Trash*. Believing they deserved a wider audience, the two applied for the Xeric Foundation Grant for self-published comic book creators. The grant was instituted by the guys who found massive success with *Teenage Mutant Ninja Turtles*.

"Kevin created the characters and set everything up," Eric told me. "I originally came on board to draw backgrounds, handle shading, and things like that. I eventually became more of a full partner. Mickey Death is an approximately four-foot-tall, undead rodent and an obvious caricature of Mickey Mouse, the Disney character. Mickey Death has a friend The Rabbit, who doesn't have a name. He's just The Rabbit."

"The Rabbit was the character that kept Mickey Death's ego in check," Kevin explained. "I guess Mickey Death was a personification of my frustrations. His ambition was to be a breakfast cereal mascot, like the Trix rabbit or Cap'n Crunch. He had no chance to be a breakfast cereal mascot. They tried and tried and tried to be successful at whatever scheme they had."

Once, Mickey and The Rabbit decided to break into the music business. "They tried to become rap stars," Kevin said, "because you didn't need any equipment or anything. The government's version—the Pat Boone to their Little Richard—was called Vanilla Rice. He was a white rice cereal mascot."

"Kevin Dixon is a fucking genius," Eric said. "That guy is so willing and eager to put in the work. Talent's fine—I don't have a big issue with talent. I don't value it very much, but I don't have a big issue with it. Kevin understands that making this shit is work. It's hard work, and the only way to do it is roll up your sleeves and get down to it. That was important for me as somebody who was involved in this experience as well."

Kevin and Eric were awarded the Xeric grant. "It was six or seven thousand dollars," Eric said. "More money than I ever expected to see." The two collected years of *Mickey Death* strips and self-published a book. One of the biggest lessons they learned from the experience, according to Eric, was that while they might be able to make a good comic strip, they could never figure out how to sell it.

In March, Whiskeytown played the South by Southwest Music Festival in Austin, Texas. "In what's become something of an infamous SXSW tale, a pack of competing major label A&R representatives literally surrounded Whiskeytown's van just moments after the band had finished its showcase at the Split Rail," Andy Langer wrote for the *Austin Chronicle.* "Adams, who remembers being hung over and playing a sloppy gig, says he'd seen the suits in the crowd and retreated to the van precisely to avoid such a scene. Nevertheless, industry weasels swarmed the van, pressing their business cards against the windshield."

"Right after South by Southwest, and probably before that, we knew that labels were interested," Caitlin Cary remembered.

"Immediately, we all felt big for our britches. You could tell that something was happening."

Two members of Whiskeytown, Ryan Adams and Phil Wandsher, were plainly ambitious—Ryan to the point of alienating some people. "I almost got in a fistfight with Ryan," Lud's Bryon Settle remembered, "because my band was playing with his band at Local 506, and Ryan was trying to change the lineup so his A&R guys could get there. It was pissing me off."

"He made a lot of enemies back then," Shark Quest's Sara Bell said. "People who understood what his situation was could see that he was acting out. He had a traumatic childhood. He also had a lot of confidence because he did want to be successful.

"My roommate was in a band with some other really old hardcore guys," Sara recalled. "Ryan was like, 'Yeah, they want their audience to be this big,' and he put his hands close together. Then he said, 'But I want my audience to be *this* big,' and he spread his arms.

"I remember thinking, 'Well, yeah, Ryan. Of course you do,'" Sara chuckled. "There was a lot of trauma among bands that found each other in that era."

"Ryan and Phil were both really volatile and hard to get along with," Caitlin said. "They would fight with each other. There was a weird love triangle between me and Phil and Ryan, because Ryan only has sunshine for one person at a time. Sometimes he would be in the mood to write pretty songs with me, and sometimes he'd be in the mood to write rock songs with Phil. The band would get dragged in those directions. I would hate it when it was the loud, stupid rock songs. I loved it when it was sunny and high and folky. That was the true tension in the band."

By March, Small was still waiting for Alias Records to begin their promised promotional push for *Silver Gleaming Death Machine*, which had now been out for about six months. It was already time to think about a new record and tour. "I hadn't really heard anything," Mike Kenlan remembered. "There was no hype, there was no hoopla. The thought of putting all our heart and soul into another record for nothing was just like, 'You know what? I'd rather not.'

"I talked to Chuck Garrison about it," Mike said. "He was like, 'I've about had it. I don't think it's going to happen. I don't want to put all this effort in again and just have it go nowhere.' So, we decided to pack it in. The other guys were dumbfounded. I don't think they saw it coming. The label didn't see it coming. They were pissed at us."

"It was like, 'What the fuck are we doing?'" Chuck said. "We can either go forward with this and try and cut out an existence or not. Anything more than just, 'Hey, we're here tonight.' I lost interest. I felt like we were spinning our wheels.

"I was starting to think, 'What am I doing with my life?'" Chuck said. "I was twenty-seven. Being poor all those years was stressful for me. I needed some security. I needed a little buffer between me and cold, hard ground." Small called it a day.

Chuck's other band Pipe was still cranking it out. On April 30, the band released their second full length, *international cement*, on Jesus Christ Records. Mitch Easter coproduced and Brent Lambert mastered. Consequently, it sounds great. The songs are all originals except for a faithful if more emphatic cover of Thee Headcoats' "Hatred, Ridicule, & Contempt."

Polvo also released an album on April 30. *Exploded Drawing* was the record the band thought they were recording for Caroline but that ultimately came out on Touch and Go. "Ash Bowie moved to Boston and was dating Mary Timony in Helium," Dave Brylawski said, "and having a great run of music. But suddenly we were a long-distance band. We'd have to meet places to work on music. We weren't playing every week. We weren't practicing at Lloyd Street or at the gas station."

Dave is referring to the abandoned gas station in Chapel Hill's Dogwood Acres neighborhood that John Ensslin and I found in 1991 after we had to leave our old space, the disused furnace room of Durham's Central Leaf Tobacco warehouse. The gas station in Dogwood Acres became the rehearsal room What Peggy Wants shared with Polvo, Metal Flake Mother, Dillon Fence, and related side projects. At $150 a month, the facility was extra deluxe because it had windows and a bathroom. Once, when Metal Flake Mother went on a trip to New York, they left the front door wide open and nothing was disturbed.

One day while I was kicking around the practice space, there was a knock on the door. Outside was a guy wearing a tie and holding a clipboard. "What is this place?" he asked. "It's our practice space," I told him. "It's not here," he said in disbelief, looking at his clipboard. "This place shouldn't exist. It's not supposed to be here."

"Let's let it be our little secret," I said, and went back inside. The man lingered outside for a while before leaving. The building is still there.

"We were all friends before we formed Polvo," Dave said, "so it was important to stay friendly. It never got acrimonious, even when Ash moved away and joined another band. That's Chapel-Hilling It, I guess. It was never a problem, but logistically it became harder."

The Veldt also released a new album in 1996, *Universe Boat*. "I did half of the demos for *Universe Boat* on an eight track," Daniel Chavis said, "because my son had just been born. I would write with him in my lap because he was only two or three. The majority of those songs were written in the fall of 1995."

The Veldt had once again lost a major label deal. They were dropped by PolyGram in June of 1994, just four months after *Afrodisiac*'s release, because of another A&R reshuffle. "We were *CMJ* Top 10 and in the new issue of *Rolling Stone* when that happened," Daniel said ruefully.

After that, the band's management passed on an opening offer for a new Cocteau Twins tour in Europe that would have started in Berlin, instead sending The Veldt out to open for The Smithereens stateside. "It was a real redneck tour," Danny Chavis said. "No diss on The Smithereens, who are great. We played the armpit of the South." For the entire tour, The Veldt draped Confederate battle flags over their guitar amps in order to, as Daniel put it, "troll the rednecks."

The fact is that no major label could figure out how to monetize The Veldt in a segregated industry. "They would compliment and insult you at the same time," Danny remembered. "'You're too unique of a band. We don't know what to do with you.' But they'd put out a white person who could rap."

Universe Boat was recorded back in North Carolina, some in Raleigh, the rest in the Yellow House. Chapel Hill felt different to the Chavis brothers than it did when the band first started. "It was a no-man's-land," Daniel said.

"Everybody was breaking up and doing drugs and shit," Danny added. "Everybody got frustrated, but not us. We had our own personal problems, but we kept the music going."

Universe Boat was released by Yesha Records, a local indie label. "It was run by a guy named Samir Shukla out of Charlotte," Daniel said. "He believed in the band and gave us a little change to make the record. Nothing extravagant." The album's opening track is called "3/5ths a Man."

There are two Southern Culture on the Skids songs on the *Flirting with Disaster* movie soundtrack released April 23: "Camel Walk" and "Red Beans N' Reverb." The soundtrack also features a Squirrel Nut Zippers song—Dr. John and Angela McCluskey's cover of Don Raleigh's "Anything but Love." This was wild to us. I remember Don giving us each a check at Ken Mosher's house for our shares of the synchronization fee.

Don did this because the Zippers had signed a partnership agreement. It laid out that all group decisions would be collectively made. In return, we agreed to divide publishing money equally, even though not all of us were songwriters. Disagreements would be settled in arbitration. The partnership agreement gave Jim and Katharine ownership of the name, which was fine by me. They started the band.

To me, the best part about the partnership agreement was that Jim and Katharine could no longer fire anyone unilaterally. Now the band officially felt like a pirate ship—the only way to go for people who aren't cut out for the navy.

Our second album, *Hot*, was released on June 4. Lane Wurster designed a cover based on the vintage Chinese firecracker labels I'd been collecting. *Hot* was recorded in October and November 1995 at Kingsway Studios, located in famed producer Daniel Lanois's haunted New Orleans French Quarter mansion. Kingsway was wonderful and entirely out of our recording budget, which was something like twelve grand.

"I was like, 'How are we gonna do this?'" Steve Balcom remembered. "To Jay's credit, he was like, 'Yeah.' We could only afford a week to record."

By this time, Squirrel Nut Zippers had toured the country and were doing well. Contrary to Mammoth's wishes but in accordance with Katharine's, we would only go out on the road for two weeks at a time. We saw many of our friends being sent out on burnout tours, and on top of that label hijinks tended to happen when bands were distracted.

"On the first Ben Folds Five record, we learned that if they keep you on the road, they make money," Robert Sledge said. "If you started talking about going off the road, people would get upset. Once we were on tour for three months without coming home and that was fucking painful."

Furthering Mammoth's frustration, the Zippers refused to book shows in new markets where we might lose money. This was seldom an issue. Mammoth was willing to give us tour support, but we generally sold out everywhere we went because of word of mouth. The wind had stayed firmly at our back.

The first time we played San Francisco supporting *The Inevitable*, everyone in the downstairs club Cafe du Nord was singing along. I was amazed. I'd never been to the West Coast before, much less San Francisco, and all these people knew who the fuck we were. That was the summer of 1995. After that show, we wound up in someone's apartment at an after-party. Some guy collared Ken Mosher in the kitchen and talked about how he was editing a new magazine called *Swing Time*.

"He said, 'The swing thing is going to be giant,'" Ken remembered. "His whole thing was how we were properly positioned to make money off this new trend. That's the thing that was absurd. We didn't plan anything." Ken later told me about their interaction, and we had a good laugh.

Beyond the usual intraband power tensions, the Zippers were feeling some real pain. Stacy Guess left the band two weeks prior to our trip to Kingsway. He had started using heroin again and was missing shows. We asked him to leave and get clean, expecting him to return. I didn't understand addiction back then, primarily because I was operating in two modes when touring: high awake and drunk asleep. It never dawned on me that life on the road was as unhealthy for Stacy as it had been for Randy Ward.

We still had a few shows to play in the Midwest before our recording date. "I think the most important thing we ever did was take that vote when Stacy left about completing the tour," Ken said. "It was only four days or something like that. But still, it was like, 'Are we gonna go make money and do these shows without him? Should we go back, figure it out, and get a new horn player, or shall we just go on? These people have never seen us.'"

We decided to continue. Ken, still basically a beginner saxophone player, shaved his head and learned all the lead horn parts in the basement laundry room of a Chicago hotel.

It was a time of savants. For the *Hot* session, a local gunslinger named Duke Heitger came in on the last day and overdubbed trumpet for the whole record. I had never heard anybody play the instrument that well in person. We asked Duke to join the band, but he was making too much money playing the riverboats. *Hot* was also augmented by a violin virtuoso we'd just met named Andrew Bird. We taught Bird several songs at soundcheck before a show in Chicago. Then he got up onstage that night and flawlessly performed a half dozen more, none of which he'd ever heard, much less played.

We came to New Orleans with Brian Paulson but remixed the record in January with Mike Napolitano, who helped engineer the newest Blind Melon record. During the sessions, Mike was down for trying out my idea of recording stuff live with minimal microphones, the way they did before the advent of magnetic tape, which allows for multitracking. Kingsway wasn't soundproofed like a regular studio. It was a big, rambling mansion. You might as well invite those room sounds onto your take because they were getting in there anyway. Mike made it work.

Brian is a fantastic producer, but he was used to the control of making a rock record, a production method that developed after multitracking became available. This kind of engineering and production depends on close miking everything in a more sterile studio environment, ideally by having each musician record their part separately. Then, each track can be manipulated as a discrete entity for mixing, compression, equalization, and the like. Conversely, if every instrument is going into only a few microphones at the same time, you'd better have gotten everything right beforehand: there would be no fixing it in the mix. This idea made most producers itchy.

"Someone has to choose the right mic," Ben Folds said about this recording process. "Then the mics have to be placed the right way. You've got to have the right room and an incredible amount of skill to harness all that stuff to make it live. That's more difficult. Much more difficult. One of the wonderful spandrels of *Hot*'s sound was the trumpet bouncing off the wall."

This old/new approach ended up saving one of my songs, "Put a Lid on It." During recording, we huddled in one room and tracked the song with four mics. I stood behind Katharine on a piano bench and played rhythm guitar into her vocal mic. When the master tape was accidentally erased in January, we used Mike Napolitano's session tape of the recording. He'd pushed up the four faders during the take just for monitoring. That reference tape became the master.

Pitchfork magazine gave *Hot* a score of 9.5 out of 10. "When you first splashdown into the CD ya hit this realization: that people even older than your parents like music like this," James P. Wisdom wrote in his review. "Then, you get over it. *Hot* is exuberant, gin house swing without apologies and it rocks without pretense. If you can manage to resist liking it, you must be dead."

Right before our performance for *Hot's* record release show at the Cradle, I got into a screaming match with Jimbo backstage. The guy we'd just hired as our booking agent and who was staying at Jim and Katharine's was going around the Mammoth Records' release party at Crook's Corner telling everyone he was our manager. Lane Wurster tipped me off. Jimbo said it was his and Katharine's right. I loudly reminded him of our partnership agreement. Our fight was interrupted by a photo session. That night, we played a fantastic set. Such was the fractured nature of the band and the power of compartmentalization.

By the time *Hot* came out, Clear Channel Communications had acquired, or was in the process of acquiring, nearly $600 million worth of broadcast assets, specifically 43 FM stations, 27 AM stations, and 16 television stations. Another 34 acquisitions were pending. In 1990, Clear Channel's stock was worth $2.72 a share. Now it was worth $73.

Dillon Fence's Greg Humphreys formed a new band shortly after getting out of his Mammoth contract. Hobex was a tight, funky three-piece consisting of Greg on guitar, Satellite Boyfriend's Andy Ware on bass, and Johnny Quest's Steve "The Doctor" Hill on drums.

"When Hootie had that big success, all of a sudden there were a million other bands that were getting big record deals and they all had a similar sound," Greg said. "By the time Dillon Fence made our third album we had moved on from that, but that was suddenly a big commercial moment. I had a really hard time pivoting. Like, 'Okay, you've got to go back and write the kind of song that you were writing five or six years ago because that's what's happening now.' Creatively, I didn't want to be thrown into that bag, like, 'These guys are chasing this.'"

Hobex's *Payback* EP, recorded at Reflections in Charlotte, was released on Greg's own Phrex label. "Let Me Live" comes out of the gate in a full seventies funk groove. Somewhere, Jay Faires's ears were burning.

> *You told me you'd meet me half the way*
> *You sold me and now expect me to pay*

"A lot of those songs are kind of pissed off," Greg admitted. "'Let Me Live' is a catharsis. 'I'm not going to let all this bullshit stop me.'"

Hobex hit the road. "Initially, we played with bands that sounded more like Dillon Fence," Greg said. "But then we started playing with other bands and I realized that there was a nascent funk and soul revival going on. Our timing was good for that. The Zippers were retro, and maybe that was an influence on us doing something different stylistically."

On August 2, Spatula released *Under the Veil of Health* on the Squealer Music label out of Blacksburg, Virginia. The band had recently passed on an offer from Alias Records. Label owner Delight Jenkins came out to see Spatula play at Duke Coffeehouse. "She was very LA," Chuck Johnson remembered. "A cool older lady who clearly had some money. She wined and dined us." Alias offered Spatula a five-record deal. The band knew they'd have to tour in support of those releases. Chuck had been watching how things were going with his friends in Small and Archers of Loaf and talked to some of them.

"In the end, we passed on the Alias offer," Chuck said. "There was this attitude that a lot of people had in the nineties that you don't sell out, whatever that means. In hindsight, I'm glad we didn't do it. Our project might have started to feel forced. I didn't want that, because I like to move on from things that no longer feel fresh."

Alias released Archers of Loaf's *All the Nations Airports* on September 24. "Alias was scared we'd leave," Eric Bachmann said, "so they formed a joint venture deal with Elektra Records. It was structured so that if we sold over fifty or a hundred thousand records, Elektra would take over. We were optimistic and said, 'We'll see how it goes.'"

All the Nations Airports was coproduced with Brian Paulson. "We were using expensive studios at the time," Eric said. "So, the money was getting better in terms of paying for recordings. But my financial situation was barely improving."

Archers of Loaf expanded their sonic palette on the new record while keeping their off-kilter pop sensibility intact. There's a piano on it, which evidently went too far for some indie rock fans. "I always liked the idea that we would keep changing the sound of the band," Eric told me. "That was important to me.

"A band is a creative project," Eric said. "It's living and breathing and it's alive. I love AC/DC and bands that do the same thing. They're smart to do that, because that's very marketable. When you don't, you take the risk of falling into a new area that nobody wants to fucking hear. I know what people want to hear from me and I can't do it. I didn't want to write a clever two-minute song about a spider web I ran into at work. I wanted to do something else. I wanted to try different sounds; I didn't want to play guitar all the time. I could play the piano pretty well. I wanted to do things with different instruments."

When *Airports* came out, Archers promoted the hell out of it. "We toured with the Flaming Lips and that was cool," Eric remembered. "They were more like-minded. We toured with the Butthole Surfers in Europe but were hemorrhaging money. It costs a lot of money to go to Europe." The band would grind it out on the road for the next year.

In September, Ben Folds Five began recording their second album. Instead of spending major label money on an expensive studio, Ben's carpenter dad soundproofed the little house on Isley Street and the band tracked in there. "That was just our aesthetic," Robert Sledge said. "We had big ambitions, but the creation stuff—we all wanted to own it. We wanted to feel like we made every single piece of it, every idea of it. We were a very insular band, too: A close little family that didn't have a lot of friends."

Caleb Southern had just graduated from UNC. "They were gonna make the album themselves in Ben's house, which was the dumbest thing a major label could agree to let an artist do," Caleb said. "I was still in touch with those guys. They started it by themselves but decided they couldn't do it and pulled me in. I wasn't sure if I was back in the business or not."

In a way, Caleb had never left. During the sessions, the band did one instrumental take of "Selfless, Cold, and Composed," which begins with a dreamy Vince Guaraldi twirl. After they finished, Ben asked Caleb what he thought.

"It was pretty good," Caleb told him, "but there was a moment in the second chorus where it sounded unfocused and checked out. Then it got back on track again and finished well. I think you can do it better."

"That's funny," Ben said. "I tuned out for a minute during the second chorus and caught myself doing my taxes in my head."

Two members of Whiskeytown, drummer Eric "Skillet" Gilmore and bassist Steve Grothmann, quit the band on the same day as the year ended. Ryan Adams, Phil Wandscher, and Caitlin Cary pressed on. "I almost quit too," Caitlin remembered. "It felt like a faction thing: Ryan and Phil were the rock star dudes, and we were the grown-ups who were gonna be smart and not chase that dream. I wound up thinking, 'Wait a minute. If I don't do this, I'm gonna have regrets.'"

Whiskeytown signed with Geffen subsidiary Outpost Recordings after playing an industry showcase in Los Angeles. "I did not sign the record deal because I waffled," Caitlin said. "So, they signed the deal without me. But then I went along, so I was real dumb. Phil and Ryan got the advance money." A reconstituted band began recording their major label debut in Nashville and Hollywood.

"I really liked Whiskeytown," Steve Balcom said. "Ryan was dating someone who worked for Mammoth. I would see him at holiday

parties. Right after they signed their Geffen deal, Ryan must have
been drunk and called my dad. I had just moved. I was still in
Chapel Hill but now had a Durham phone number. My dad still
lived in town. He has the same name as me because I'm a second.
Ryan must have looked up Steve Balcom in the Chapel Hill phone
book.

"So, Ryan left a voicemail on my dad's machine," Steve remembered. "He said, 'You're gonna regret not signing me! You made
the biggest mistake of your life!' I didn't know about this until six
months later when my dad said, 'I got this weird call from this guy,'
and described it to me. I was like, 'Do you remember his name?' and
he said, 'Bryan Adams?'"

Meanwhile, Squirrel Nut Zippers' *Hot* was doing well. By year's
end it had sold around fifty thousand copies. *Hot*'s performance
mirrored Superchunk's recent album, *Here's Where the Strings
Come In*, which was made for a similar budget and by this point
had moved around sixty thousand units. The difference was that
Merge Records had a $2,000 break-even point. "It was very rare that
we put out a record that didn't make money pretty soon," Laura Ballance said.

Mammoth's break-even point per album was fluid, depending
on circumstances, but significantly higher than Merge's. "Part of it
depended on how much it cost to make the record," Steve Balcom
said. "Part of it depended on what type of marketing we did behind
the record—whether we had to hire independent promotion, or if we
were trying to chase radio, or if we had to do an expensive video."
Mammoth bands would be at least partially responsible for paying
back these expenses before seeing any royalties.

Hot's indie success was a team effort. It's plain to me, more now
than then, how committed Mammoth was to the band. They got us
on NPR's *Morning Edition*. We played the Summer Olympic Games
in Atlanta. There was a lot of day in, day out, independent record leg-
work going on.

"At that point, Mammoth was maybe fourteen people," Steve said. "It was not a huge staff. We had two people doing radio and two or three people in retail and marketing. We had one guy in production and one or two publicists."

From my perspective, Jay Faires was the remote label boss who lived in New York and was mostly interested in furthering his career ambitions at Atlantic. Almost every other Mammoth employee was in Carrboro working their butts off for the roster. Mammoth's office was now located in an old brick coffee roaster's building along the railroad tracks, catty-corner from what used to be Lloyd Street Studios and across the street from the Cradle. I could walk in there any time and meet with Steve Balcom or shoot the shit with Lane Wurster.

The band had grown organically and it was paying dividends. We'd done public radio's *A Prairie Home Companion* and NBC's *Late Night with Conan O'Brien*. We were starting to play these cool-ass renovated movie palaces across the country. People would flood down to the front of the stage in their thrift store finest and dance like they were in *A Charlie Brown Christmas*. It was a beautiful thing.

Considering the critical success of our records and the financial success of our tours, it was not possible in my mind for Squirrel Nut Zippers to do better. For the first time, I thought, "I could have a career at this." I had already quit my restaurant gig. What I wanted most was to be able to put out a record a year, sell seventy-five thousand copies if we were lucky, continue touring, and just keep going. If we could somehow resolve all the internal cloak-and-dagger stuff, there was the potential of having a nice little professional life.

"With Squirrel Nut Zippers, we would put money in and see sales, and we would put money in and see sales," Steve said. "It just kept going and going. With *Hot*, we stepped all of that up. We made videos, we did more types of promotion, and we put the band on the road more, which cost money. At that juncture, we were all thinking, 'We're just gonna keep this trajectory we're on, where we make good records for whatever budget and do the necessary marketing to take the band up to another level.'"

Squirrel Nut Zippers began recording our third full-length album in November. I found a house for rent in Pittsboro, a small town south of Chapel Hill, where I was living with my girlfriend. We climbed in through an open window and looked around. It was big, old, and cheap. The rent was $250 a month. I convinced Ken Mosher to move from Saxapahaw and live in the place. Mike Napolitano, who worked with us on *Hot*, schlepped a bunch of recording gear in there.

We called it Kensway Studios. Jim and Katharine were not particularly keen on the idea. They wanted to record with John Plymale at Overdub Lane. We argued that if we could save money on the front end by reducing recording costs, the resulting album would recoup more quickly and pay dividends on the back end.

Things started going wrong immediately. Don Raleigh was upset because his songs were being overlooked, mostly because Katharine refused to sing them. I guess *Flirting with Disaster* had clued Don in to the fact that publishing money was a source of potentially significant income. Ken and I worked with Don to finesse some of his new material, but it didn't help. He quit abruptly in the middle of the sessions.

We'd already replaced Stacy Guess on trumpet with Sex Police's Je Widenhouse. Probably three different bass players came into Kensway to record on various songs. The vibe was heavy. One day I went home to eat lunch and the band tracked a new Jimbo song without me, one that sounded like what we heard some West Coast swing revival bands doing. I was going to give one of my songs to Katharine before deciding it was too personal and singing it myself.

Worst of all, Ken assumed the role of house mother and stopped contributing any songs of his own. "I still feel bad about that whole era," he told me, "because I literally did not write anything. I felt like I was trying to keep the shit together." Ken had been a reliable co-writer with Jimbo and contributed his own songs to the Zippers since the luminous "Danny Diamond" from *The Inevitable*.

"I think my dysfunctional upbringing prepared me for the dysfunction of the Zippers in the perfect way," Ken said. "In the early days, there was enough care and concern and naivete that I could call Jimbo and stick up for Chris Phillips or somebody. I think every person in that band was from a dysfunctional family."

Speaking personally, I was taught from an early age to accept the unacceptable. I do not recommend this as a life skill.

It seems obvious now that Squirrel Nut Zippers was nearing the end of its natural life. People were starting to move in different directions, personally and artistically. The new album we were making was more eclectic and weirder than the previous two. It would have likely been our last—that is if, like me, you considered the group a confederation of peers.

Because we'd cut so many budgetary corners, the band had three whole weeks to record—triple the time we'd had for *Hot*. Andrew Bird came down from Chicago and stayed upstairs at Kensway, along with Mike Napolitano. My memory of those sessions is negative, but years later Mike played me a compilation of outtakes, and in it all we do is laugh and good-naturedly talk shit.

Tom Osborn was hired to be Mammoth's West Coast rep in 1995. "At no point during that period did I go, 'This is a career,'" Tom said. "If anything, I was just like, 'This is a fascinating endeavor.' It felt like I was on a ticketed ride. This was gonna end and I was gonna do something else." Tom believed his real career would involve teaching art, like he'd studied to do at USC.

"That was my favorite thing about working with the Zippers," Tom said. "It was the first time I felt like, 'This is an artistic experience.' We weren't selling something artificial. There was something very true to what the band was doing. It was experiential, like, 'You're gonna be transformed through this.'"

Tom got us on LA's KROQ-FM's *Kevin and Bean* Saturday morning show before our gig at the Avalon, a 1,250-seater that we'd worked our way up to. It's hard to overemphasize how influential KROQ was at the time. They could make or break anybody. The station's program director was named Kevin Weatherly. "Kevin was the Boy Wonder," Tom said. "He was producing ridiculous numbers out of his marketplace."

Kevin was annoyed with Tom for getting us on *Kevin and Bean*, because KROQ was not playing Squirrel Nut Zippers. But our appearance not only went over big, it helped sell out the Avalon. "Kevin Weatherly went to the concert, but Kevin didn't go to the concert because he wanted to go to the concert!" Tom said, laughing. "He went to the concert because his wife, Margie, went to the concert. Margie loved the idea of getting dressed up, taking a limo to the show with their best friends, and watching these kids dancing. This was a timeless moment. To them, it looked like a scene out of Xanadu."

The Zippers song that *Kevin and Bean* played on the air was not our single. "'Put a Lid on It' was the song Mammoth felt was gonna get the most reaction from college radio and NPR-type radio stations," Steve Balcom said. "We weren't thinking about any format other than that." Instead, *Kevin and Bean* played another one of my songs, a volatile calypso called "Hell." It got an immediate listener reaction—or, in the industry lingo of the time, "great phones."

There was also growing interest in "Hell" from WDCG, a Raleigh Top 40 Clear Channel station better known as G105. "I would call it an alternative-leaning Top 40 station," Steve said. "G105 had a program director, Kip Taylor, who really liked Mammoth. He had played a couple of our bands on specialty shows and put another one in rotation. Kip liked the Zippers and he liked 'Hell' specifically. He came to us and said, 'You know, I think we could get behind this.'"

Mammoth saw a golden opportunity: "Hell" could be put in rotation at a Top 40 station, especially if the Zippers agreed to play G105's morning show as well as their Christmas show in downtown Raleigh. More importantly, KROQ was making noises like *they* were about to add the song to rotation too. The label needed us to play the radio game.

I remember the early days of performing "Hell." We used to close our shows with it. I'd gone to a magic store in Raleigh and gotten something called a Flash Ring. It was a flesh-colored ring that would shoot fire out of your hand. I'd stuff flash paper into a well on the concealed side of the ring and set it off with a flint wheel, like what's on a cigarette lighter. Fire would shoot out of my hand while I sang about people getting fitted for a suit of flame.

I used the Flash Ring when we did our first television show in New York in 1995. Steve was there. "That's a cool trick," he told me. "Can you make the flame bigger?" In the coming weeks, I bought a larger ring and kept stuffing more and more flash paper into it to try to get the biggest flame possible. Finally, it got so overloaded that it stopped producing any fire at all. I'm sure there's a metaphor here.

In the middle of our fraught Kensway recording session, we got a call from Mammoth: Steve wanted to meet with us right away. Maybe Mammoth didn't want to shell out for a new record and video. Maybe we didn't tour enough to their liking. Whatever the reason, they'd never interrupted a recording session before. It couldn't be good news.

"We thought we were going to get dumped," Ken remembered. "I was like, 'Man, Christmas is gonna suck. Are we gonna owe for this equipment? Is Mike Napolitano just gonna leave?'"

When Steve showed up, I was prepared for the worst. We'd set up one room in Kensway for relaxment and called it Club Inferno. Steve and Sean Maxson, Mammoth's radio guy, came in. They were acting strange.

"I remember saying, 'We're really excited about the new record, but we have an opportunity with "Hell" that we feel like we need to pursue,'" Steve said. "I remember being nervous, because any delays in the new record were gonna be met with resistance. I think everybody was like, 'What?'"

I remember Steve saying specifically, "You have a hit song."

"What does that mean?" I asked. We literally could not understand. I'd been talking about bands having singles for years. College radio bands, Chapel Hill bands. I didn't mean actual *hit* singles. I just meant great songs. Steve told us about G105. "This is the Top 40 radio station in town," he said. He might as well have sprouted another head.

"I was like, 'We need to put the new record on the back burner for a little bit and really put our energy behind this single,'" Steve said. "I just remember blank stares!"

Back in Club Inferno, the fourteen-year-old inside of me was elated. But the vibe in the room was heavy. It wasn't what you might expect when a band is told they have a potential hit single. "I think the Seven Musketeers attitude diminished from that point on," Ken said, "because that was not Jimbo and Katharine's plan. It was a song that he didn't write and she didn't sing." The band didn't commit to Steve's radio plan on the spot.

In the car on the way back to Carrboro, Steve turned to Sean Maxson. "I think they'll do it," he said. "They need a chance to talk about it."

Mammoth was in the middle of its own big transition. The multi-Platinum success of one of their signings, Seven Mary Three, had caused tension within Atlantic. Jay Faires found himself in the middle of a new power struggle because of an internal label shake-up.

"It was every man for himself," Jay said. "There was a point where they pulled the plug on Mammoth's Pure record without telling us. I knew they were trying to sabotage us. So, then I had to get the company back."

"At that point, Jay started to try to extricate himself," Steve said. "He had to essentially buy back whatever Atlantic had spent for that joint venture with Mammoth. I remember him saying at one point, 'If this Zippers record takes off, it might fuck the whole deal up,' and me going, 'I have no control over slowing this engine now!' It was intense."

Early one December morning, Squirrel Nut Zippers appeared on *Bob and Madison's Showgram* at G105. Later, we played the station's

Christmas show in downtown Raleigh. True to their word, they started playing "Hell" on the air.

"They had not added it to rotation, but they played it and gave us indications that they liked it," Steve said. "It was testing well. When I talk about 'playing,' I'm talking fifty times a week. They played it a ton." We didn't know it yet, but everything had changed.

1997

I N January, Los Angeles's KROQ put "Hell" into rotation. K-ROCK, as it was known, was more than an industry leader: it was also a Clear Channel station. "When we got KROQ, the chain of Clear Channel stations started to add it immediately," Mammoth West Coast rep Tom Osborn said. "The other stations fell like fucking dominoes." None of us in Squirrel Nut Zippers listened to Top 40, so we had no sense of it.

On January 20, the Zippers performed at "The Youth Ball" for President Clinton's second inauguration. It was held in the Smithsonian's National Postal Museum, an echoey mausoleum. When we came home, we shot a hurried video for "Hell" with former Sex Police bassist Norwood Cheek. We also tinkered some more with our new album, which we called *Perennial Favorites*. There was not a word from Mammoth about a release date for the record.

Meanwhile, Jay Faires was increasing his efforts to end Mammoth's joint venture deal with Atlantic. "In that last year, we had broken Seven Mary Three," Jay said. "The Mammoth cycle was Juliana Hatfield—250,000, cover of *Spin*; Frente! got to 500,000, our first Top 3 music video at MTV, and Platinum worldwide; then Seven Mary

Three came in and did 1.3 million. The tension at Atlantic started on the back end of that. I was an exec there, but I still owned my company. My loyalty was to Mammoth. Squirrel Nut Zippers were bubbling up at 300,000 with *Hot*. That was when I was getting out of there."

Jay had a meeting with Atlantic's new chairman Val Azzoli about ending the relationship. "I had to sign the deal that week, because Squirrel Nut Zippers were about to go into heavy rotation at MTV the following week," Jay said. "The Zippers weren't even on Val's radar. If I'd waited a week, it would have fucked it all up.

"Literally, I had it written down," Jay remembered about the meeting. "It was awkward because I didn't say anything else. I tried to keep it diplomatic: 'I don't think this is working. I'd like out of the deal.' It was prepped on both sides. Val was like, 'We have to have Seven Mary Three,' and I said, 'Okay.' He agreed to let us out.

"My lawyer was screaming at me that there was some deal point that I couldn't let go of in the exit," Jay said. "I remember yelling at him, 'If we don't leave this week, Atlantic will realize what they're giving up and never let us go!' We signed the exit without the deal point and got out."

Once the "Hell" video was featured on MTV's *Buzz Bin*, *Hot* took off in a hurry. The single was already being overplayed on the radio. "There wasn't one market in the US that wasn't playing the song," Tom Osborn said. "I remember the last add we got. The program director was like, 'Look, man, I don't want to play this fucking song. I have no choice anymore.' It was like a gust of wind just took a sail and dragged the boat and all of us with it." Squirrel Nut Zippers became the first Chapel Hill–based band to crack *Billboard*'s Top 200 album sales chart. *Hot* debuted at 197 in February.

Around this time, former WXYC DJ Carrie McClaren came down to Chapel Hill from New York for a visit. "A lot of the WXYC jocks were streaming WFMU out of New York," she said. "WXYC didn't feel crucial in the way it did before streaming media. It saddened me to hear that the jocks weren't even listening to the station they worked for.

"I listened to WFMU when I came up to New York," Carrie said. "I know folks from FMU. It's not a community in the way WXYC was. It was a whole different experience. I talked to one of the XYC people about it. His take was, 'The FMU jocks are more experienced. They're older. Why not listen to somebody who has a broader depth of knowledge than some college kid?' I said, 'Yeah, I get that.' It just destroyed the experience."

After What Peggy Wants broke up, John Ensslin stuck around town for a couple years, despite what his instinct was telling him. "My immediate response was, 'I gotta move away,'" John remembered. "'I can't be in this town without being in a band.' I was unable to be creative in any other form. You have that zero-sum game thing, where you're like, 'Well, if I'm not doing music, then naturally I'll be making short films,' or 'I'll have an exhibition of paintings' or 'I'll write an epic poem' without the drag of being in a band. But, no. In fact it was, 'If I don't have a band, I can't do anything.'

"I was miserable, but I wasn't miserable because I wasn't performing," John said. "It was because I wasn't interacting with musicians. I wasn't doing that nonverbal communication that happens in a band, which connects you to life and other people. It's a special thing to communicate nonverbally at a sophisticated level. It's such a wonderful feeling. With technology the way it is now, people aren't paying attention to the fact that something like four-fifths of all information is nonverbal. You have to be in the same room to really communicate. It's about different stuff than just the words going back and forth."

Sara Bell talked about it too. "It's really hard to give up playing music and what that does," Sara Bell said. "I think maybe it's because I tend to be a solitary person, but music is so communal and social. I don't have any kind of solitary artistic pursuits. They are hard for me to do. I love music because it's collaborative and connected to other people. It's hard to imagine life without it."

John moved away in early 1996 and ended up living in Myrtle Beach, South Carolina. "MTV's Kurt Loder is the man who told me that Tom Maxwell had a cold," he remembered. "'Tom Maxwell, singer for Squirrel Nut Zippers, has a cold, so they're having to reschedule some gigs.' I asked Lane Wurster, 'What the fuck is happening?' and he said, 'Oh my God, they're on fire!'"

Apart from releasing new material from local bands like Capsize 7—a band Glenn Boothe would go on to sign to Caroline—Shawn Nolan's Hep-Cat Records reissued all the Metal Flake Mother recordings from the early part of the decade. "Andrew Peterson and I had a falling-out at the end of Baited Breath," Shawn said, "so I contacted Kelley Cox about reissuing that album. He was fine with it. We added the *Deem-On* seven inch to the end of *Beyond the Java Sea* because it was out of print. 'Scratchin'' and 'Deem-On' were such fucking great songs."

"We didn't have the master tapes," Shawn remembered, "so we basically played it on a turntable and had it recorded. I don't remember if we were in Duck Kee Studios or where it was, but we just had clean copies of the seven inch. You can still hear the crackles in the songs. That's pretty low rent, but I think it actually has enduring quality."

It was around this time that the nineties name curse—which had already claimed Chunk and Small—struck Shawn's Mammoth–funded indie label too. "Unfortunately, there was a ska distribution company called Hep Cat in California that sent us a cease-and-desist letter," Shawn said. "So, then we changed the name of the label to Scrimshaw Records, which I always had very mixed feelings about. We had to make the decision quickly, because we had promo copies of a new release with 'Hep-Cat' on the back and were about to go to print."

One day a few years previously, I was hanging out at Ken Mosher's house in Saxapahaw after successfully getting past his aggressive rooster. (The trick is to wait until they're right against your shin and launch 'em back far enough to let you run inside the screen door.) "Listen to this," Ken said, and hit play on *Ben Folds Five*.

"Holy shit," I said. If all the Chapel Hill bands were high jump athletes, these motherfuckers had just significantly raised the bar. The musicianship was impeccable; the performances fire. The songs were great. The production was exemplary. We cranked it.

The bar was about to be raised again: Ben Folds Five's new album, *Whatever and Ever Amen*, the one recorded by Caleb Southern in Ben's house on Isley Street, was released by 550 Music on March 18.

Mammoth Records, newly freed from their Atlantic deal, was looking for a new sugar daddy. "We started talking to labels at that point about moving to another joint venture," Steve Balcom said. Jay Faires's first idea was to follow Danny Goldberg, who brought Mammoth onboard with Atlantic, to Mercury. MCA also showed some interest; Jay had done a summer internship with them back in the day. "Interscope was in there for a minute," Steve remembered. "Everybody was feeling it out."

Our beloved Crook's Corner colleague Gibson Smith was killed in a car crash in late March. Gibson was one of only a handful of cool lawyers I've ever known. His business card featured the "Get Out of Jail Free" image from Monopoly. I put a small group together to perform at a fundraising event for a scholarship in Gibson's name. One beautiful April day, Ken Mosher, Stu Cole (who'd replaced Don Raleigh on string bass in Squirrel Nut Zippers), and I performed a bunch of jazz standards on Crook's patio. We used my "fake book," which laid out chords, lyrics, and melody.

Just then the Zippers' old trumpet player Stacy Guess walked in. I hadn't seen him for a while. "Hey, man, go get your horn," I said. "We're just running a bunch of songs out of this fake book and could use you." Stacy did and sat in with us. It felt so good hearing him play again. He was a fluid improviser with a relaxed tone. The only thing that bothered me was that he carried his trumpet in a paper bag. That didn't feel right.

Stacy was in a new band now, Venus Flytrap Girls, with Metal Flake Mother's Ben Clarke and Family Dollar Pharoahs' Groves Willer. ("That's how much I liked Metal Flake Mother," Groves said, "that I had to spend the next ten years playing drums for their guitar players!")

"What's beautiful is that Stacy had gotten his shit together after the Zippers," Groves told me. "He went to college and was a philosophy major. He was obsessed with Nietzsche. That was his bag. He would go home and read Nietzsche for hours and hours."

Years before, the Hardback Cafe's Alvis Dunn worked with Stacy at Tijuana Fats on Rosemary Street. "Stacy cooked back there and he was very good at it," Alvis remembered. "He was imperturbable. He would have his trumpet with him. Oftentimes, he would go outside to a nice space out back and play the trumpet if it wasn't busy. Then I'd make the orders.

"Stacy wrote a masterful paper about the philosopher Maurice Merleau-Ponty," Alvis said. "I already had two master's degrees, and he was holding forth about Merleau-Ponty, and there we were rolling enchiladas."

"Stacy started out being Venus Flytrap Girls' trumpet player," Groves said. "I have never seen anybody work so hard to get a horn section together. He made the charts. We had different horn players coming in week after week after week, but we couldn't make enough money to have a horn section. He would get all these fantastic players, but they would leave as soon as they realized how much money we were making." Stacy wound up playing bass.

"We were getting a good batch of songs together," Ben Clarke remembered. "It was taking a while."

Mammoth was about to make a big move. "At the end of the day, it was A&M Records who showed the most interest in Mammoth," Steve Balcom said. "Jay flew me out to meet with Neil Strauss. I thought we were gonna go with A&M. Jay called me that morning and said, 'Disney just came in with this offer that's too insane for us to not really look at. Take the meeting with A&M and pretend like you don't know about this.'

"My problem all along was that Jay would tell us all sorts of things," Steve said. "Some of them would happen in a way that he suggested and some of them wouldn't. It's not his fault. It was a fluid situation. When we first got out there and started talking, we were getting offers that were $3, $4, or $5 million. They weren't big, big offers. They were good offers. Then Disney came along with one that just blew all those out of the water."

On May 16, Squirrel Nut Zippers' second album *Hot* was certified Gold, meaning five hundred thousand units shipped. Around this time, it was selling thirty thousand copies a week. We toured the Squirrel Brand Company factory in Cambridge, Massachusetts. Because of our success, the company had maxed out their production. The place was a time machine: housed in an elderly brick building were big green machines oozing out hot, undifferentiated Nut-Zippers. The employees were lovely. They stuffed our pockets with roasted peanuts and other confections and showed us an ancient delivery van moldering in a garage. Back at the office, the managers produced a large acetate disc from the safe. On it were original Squirrel Brand radio ads from the 1920s. We said we'd get them transferred to a modern format. During one visit, the mayor of Cambridge came out and declared it Squirrel Nut Zipper Day.

Squirrel Nut Zippers performed on *The Late Show with David Letterman* in June. Before soundcheck I approached Paul Shaffer. The *Letterman* house band had been playing "Hell" as a bumper before going to commercial. I thanked Paul for this. "You guys do a great job with it," I said.

"Ah, Tom," Paul replied in his nasally voice. "We sound like a goddamn high school bar mitzvah band."

"The hook with the horns was perfect for my band," Paul told me recently. "Something about the record hit me and I remembered it. I liked everything about it and thought we could pull it off."

I asked Paul if he would sit in with us that night, just like he'd done with Flat Duo Jets seven years before. During soundcheck, he played some great stuff. "Paul, there's no need to hold back," I said with a wink. "You should really go for broke."

Our taped performance was particularly good. Paul was on fire during his solo. He played like he had three arms. When he finished, he looked up at me, beaming. I flashed him a big thumbs-up. Then I looked over to my left and saw David Letterman seated at his darkened desk, holding his head in his hands like he'd just heard terrible news.

That summer, we went out on the H.O.R.D.E. Festival tour with Neil Young and Crazy Horse, Blues Traveler, Primus, Morphine, and some other freaks like Leftover Salmon. Neil's son Ben really liked our single, which is probably why we got the gig. "That damnation record, that's a good record," Neil told me, which made me feel a little faint. Ben Folds Five was on the tour, too, and brought a string quartet. That's when Ken Mosher and I started hanging out with those guys and becoming friends.

I have a distinct memory of standing at the back of the main stage behind the row of Neil Young's amps as the sun was setting one glorious summer day. Ben Folds Five had just finished their closing set nearby on the second stage. As their last note echoed away, Neil struck the same note on his guitar, letting it develop into sustained feedback before launching into Crazy Horse's set. It was sublime.

"Horde '97 comprises a rag-tag assembly of bands with little in common," *Variety* sniffed, "and presents them in such a way as to take all the fun and spirit out of the all-day festival. How else do you explain the timing of the performances here, where one band starts to play on one stage as soon as another finishes on an alternate stage. For example, watching all of Morphine's brilliant but too-short set as second-stage headliners meant missing the first song or two from Neil Young. And who decided that a weak band like lounge chumps the Squirrel Nut Zippers even belong on the same stage as Young?"

Up to this point, the Zippers were considered a "lounge" act and were often compared to bands like Combustible Edison and Pink Martini. It didn't bother me. Combustible Edison had a vibraphone, which was cool. I loved the video for Pink Martini's "Sympathique."

They were like how Ken described the Zippers: a pop band with weird instruments.

Merge Records released Pipe's *Slow Boy* on July 8. "By that point Dave IT had left and we were on a downward trajectory," Ron Liberti said. "It bummed me out. There's a couple of good songs on that record, but we missed Dave. We couldn't really do the tours the way that Merge wanted us to. They got us on the road with the New Bomb Turks, but then Chuck Garrison broke his hand in Louisville. We had to quit the rest of the tour and our booking agent from Seattle dropped us. That was really the death knell."

"Right after Chuck was healing up, I broke my left finger," Clif Mann said. "I got it caught in a garage door. It smashed the tip of my guitar-fingering hand. That put me on hold. I couldn't play for a while. That's about the time that I lost interest in the Pipe thing." Pipe broke up.

The Walt Disney Company formally acquired Mammoth Records for $25 million on Monday, July 21. "Steve Moyer and I very much made the Disney deal happen," Jay Faires said. "He managed two-thirds of the senior execs in the industry. He and I were the critical guys orchestrating it. There was a corporate publicist who crushed it for me. That half page in the *New York Times* bullshit was all her. She did all the corporate PR for it. We had a banker from Bear Stearns on the deal, giving credibility in Disney's eyes.

"I remember going to the Disney commissary and Michael Eisner grabbing me and taking me over to Walt Disney's brother, Roy," Jay told me. "Michael said, 'This is the gentleman who's gonna save our music business.'"

"Jay sold the whole company to them," Steve Balcom said. "At that time, Disney had Hollywood Records, Buena Vista, and their soundtrack things. Hollywood had its own staff. They had some rock acts but no real success. We were brought in to be this freestanding label owned by Disney. We went from being Mammoth Records employees to being Disney employees working at Mammoth. But the real value was that we could go and hire on people. We wouldn't be playing all these games with priorities like we did with Atlantic."

"When the Zippers did break, Val Azzoli was actually a total gentleman about it," Jay said. "I think our buyout price from the Atlantic deal was $2.4 million. Disney ended up paying for that."

One day out on the road, Ken came into our hotel room and threw a newspaper on the bed. "Read this," he said. The headline was DISNEY BUYS MAMMOTH RECORDS FOR $25M, EXPECTS TO RECOUP FROM SQUIRREL NUT ZIPPERS. Not too much later I called Steve and initiated my new career strategy of punctuated hysteria. "Why the fuck did Mammoth sell out to Disney?" I yelled. "They're the cultural devil!"

Back in North Carolina, David Menconi didn't see the Mammoth buyout as a positive development either. "I remember feeling portents of doom," he said. "I thought, 'There's no way this ends well.'"

It might seem counterintuitive, but I couldn't see the Disney deal as good news at all. It stamped a sell-by date on our ass and set up unachievable expectations: If our next record didn't sell twice as many copies as *Hot*, it would be considered a failure. The idea that that kind of growth is sustainable is the logic of the cancer cell. It felt like Jay had grabbed his sack of cash and left us holding the bag.

"Make no mistake about it: Jay made a significant amount of money—a *significant* amount of money—off the Disney deal," Steve told me.

"Early on, Mammoth was very unstable because of money," Steve remembered. "Jay shielded us from a lot of this stuff. He was raising money from Howard Baker. I'm pretty sure we signed a band called Big Wheel from Louisville because this guy in Louisville gave Jay some money! That's one thing about Jay: he has a lot of bravado, but he kept things going in lean times.

"His confidence and bravado are why we did the deal with Atlantic," Steve said. "You meet with Jay and you're like, 'This guy's gonna win.' We got to a certain point with Mammoth where we had the exclusive distribution deal and he said, 'I need something bigger.' So, then it was the deal with Atlantic. Then he was like, 'I'm gonna go move to LA,' then, 'I'm gonna move to New York and be the head of A&R at Atlantic,' and then, 'I'm gonna come back to Mammoth, but if I come back to Mammoth, it has to be bigger.'

"This is part of Jay's ambition," Steve said. "'I deserve this' or 'This is where it's going. I'm gonna win.'

"I was perfectly content to be more like Merge," Steve said, "and have this great label of good artists with a team behind me that really believed. Mammoth had that kind of culture. Had we done a deal with A&M, we certainly wouldn't have gone and hired twenty people and tried to compete at that level. But that's what Jay wanted. I have ambition too, but I'm fine with hitting singles and doubles; maybe a triple and a home run every now and then. I think Jay wants to swing for a home run every time."

Mammoth quickly realized that Disney was not well organized. They were also switching up distributors, from WEA to PolyGram. This caused delays getting the Mammoth catalog out to retail. "There were also weird tensions with the Disney people, who were like, 'Who are these guys?'" Steve remembered. "When we walked in, *Hot* was bigger than any record they'd had. The minute we got to Disney we spent six months trying to figure out how to make it work and hiring all these people. That was not stable, stressful, and hard."

Meanwhile, the Mouse's other musical forays had just become a punch line. On June 24, the Walt Disney Corporation ordered their subsidiary Hollywood Records to recall a hundred thousand copies of Insane Clown Posse's *The Great Milenko* on the day of its release. Disney claimed the band's lyrics were too graphic. If that was a potential issue, they probably would have wanted to investigate it before shipping out a truckload of product.

"Peter Paterno was president of Hollywood Records," Jay said. "He caught so much shit for it at the time. He signed Insane Clown Posse. They had to work themselves out of that one 'cause of the backlash for the Disney brand. Joe Roth's right-hand guy Rob Moore was like,

'Why don't you go work out of Peter's office?' They were trying to get me to take over Paterno's office and I was too dumb to get it. Nor did I want to do it. That roster was just horrific.

"I bought into the synergy idea," Jay remembered about the Disney deal. "If anybody down the Mammoth chain thought Atlantic was political, Disney was more so. Anytime you're inside a corporation, there are more ideas than there is capital to launch things. So, it's always about your division versus somebody else's division."

Josh Wittman put in a ton of time working *Hot* for Mammoth Records. "Disney was like Atlantic times ten," Josh remembered. "With the Atlantic deal we knew we had some time to prove ourselves. With Disney, we were no longer Mammoth Records. We were just trying to find fucking records to put through the machine."

"When we weren't able to call the shots on what the next single would be, or on what artists to sign, that's when it was over," Lane Wurster said. "The fun of it was going to Henry's Bistro, seeing the Zippers' first thing, and calling Jay from the kitchen telephone."

This is the era when Mammoth signed the Teletubbies. "We did things like the MTV *Buzz Bin* compilations and the Teletubbies deal, which is the dumbest deal we ever did," Steve said. "Those signings were made because it made sense on paper, not because it made sense to your ear. They were deals that you talked yourself into instead of, 'I can't go to sleep at night because I'm listening to this record so much.' That's how fractured the label was." *Fun with the Teletubbies* was released in 1997.

Shortly after Disney's acquisition of Mammoth, representatives from the Squirrel Brand Company visited North Carolina and asked us to sign a licensing agreement. It demanded a percentage of our gross receipts, the right of first refusal on what songs we could release, and creative control over our lyrics and album art. Squirrel Brand reps told us that the old man who used to run the company had died.

They wanted to sell but believed that their copyrights were unprotected. Shocked, we refused and made a significantly less onerous counteroffer.

Grant Alden from *No Depression* watched the Zippers rocket take off and gave his verdict. "I thought, 'Another fuckin' Hootie,'" he confided. "That song hit pop radio the same way Hootie did." I'm sure the people at *Pitchfork* were similarly dismayed.

Still, Grant had no trouble trying to center Whiskeytown in a similar spotlight. "If there's to be a Nirvana among the bands that are imprecisely dubbed alternative country," he wrote for *Rolling Stone* on July 24, "look to Whiskeytown." The band's major label debut, *Strangers Almanac*, was released five days later, on Geffen and Outpost records.

"Losering," Ryan Adams and Caitlin Cary harmonize.

Take a second to stop
Think about everything
See what you have been losing

"We toured a good amount," Caitlin said. "We went to Europe. We toured the country several times. We took 6 String Drag out to open for us on a long leg of a tour out West. They blew us off the stage every night."

The RV Tour, so-called because Whiskeytown traveled in an RV, was by all accounts a shitshow. There were onstage fights, abbreviated sets, and general high-dudgeon. Guitarist Phil Wandscher quit in late September after a particularly nasty blowout at a gig in Kansas City.

Shawn Rogers's Scrimshaw Records released Two Dollar Pistols' debut, *On Down the Track*, in August. The band's lead singer and songwriter, John Howie Jr., started out as a drummer: first for Dave Burris's Light in August; then with Raleigh's Finger, who shared that triple bill at the Fallout Shelter with Metal Flake Mother and Superchunk the night Flat Duo Jets played *Letterman*; then with former dB Chris Stamey; and most recently with a group called June, who were signed to a major. Now, John was writing and singing hardcore honky-tonk.

"As a late teen, I'd gotten into Gram Parsons," John told me. "I was a sad young man. I understood isolation, loss, confusion, heartbreak, and all that." Parsons covered people like Merle Haggard and George Jones. John asked his dad about those artists because he was into that music and was duly hooked up with a George Jones two-record compilation.

"It was his 1960s United Artists recordings," John remembered. "The first song on it was the original version of 'She Thinks I Still Care.' As soon as I heard that, that was it." John, a rock-and-roll drummer hugely influenced by New York Dolls, decided he wanted to start a country band.

The Two Dollar Pistols formed in 1995. "Uncle Tupelo got big," John said. "That's when Ryan Adams and people like that came into it." Ryan had moved to Raleigh from Jacksonville, Florida, in 1993 with his punk trio the Patty Duke Syndrome, which folded acrimoniously the following year. He and Phil Wandscher formed Whiskeytown shortly thereafter. ("The rage it takes to make punk doesn't look good on a forty-year-old," Grant Alden noted.)

"Guys like me, Kenny Roby, and The Backsliders had already been into that stuff," John said. "But now there was this little scene happening. For me, it was purely coincidental. I wanted to have this country band for a long fucking time. But what happens is when everybody's listening to it, musicians in our world start learning how to play it. Then you could get a band together."

Shortly after that, John met up with Shawn. "I already knew him and was very fond of him," John said. "He said to me, 'Here's the deal. I have this record label. I'm gonna be getting Mammoth money. It's fantastic because I'm gonna have money to push my acts. I'm gonna be able to give you tour support. But we won't have to answer to Mammoth. It's gonna be great. I don't have to sign bands I don't like.'"

Two Dollar Pistols recorded *On Down the Track* with John Plymale at Overdub Lane. "The thing I liked about Shawn was that he
was no bullshit but nice about it," John said. "He would say to me,
'Here's what's gonna happen. Your record is starting to fall down the
Americana chart. So, you're going to come up to my office, get on
my phone, and personally call everyone who's played it and thank
them. You're going to be super nice—your genuine, charming self.
The hope is that it will go back up the Americana chart.'

"And that's exactly what happened," John said. "Did I want to
do that? Fuck, no! I didn't want to be calling guys who work at radio
stations. But you know what? Shawn was right. He believed in my
band enough to let us make a record at a studio that we couldn't afford
otherwise, take out ads, and give us tour support. We went on the road
for two weeks when that record came out and I came back with money."

Mammoth Records released the Squirrel Nut Zippers' *Sold Out*
EP on September 2. An odds-and-ends assemblage of live stuff and
studio outtakes, it was meant as a consolation to our fans waiting
for new material. Some of the old Squirrel Brand radio ads and jingles are on there, as well as a song I really liked of Jimbo's called "St.
Louis Cemetery Blues," which should have made it onto the new record but somehow didn't. There was still no talk about releasing *Perennial Favorites*, which by this time had been mastered and was in the
can.

Hot was certified Platinum in September, commemorating sales in
excess of one million units.

In function if not form, *Sold Out* feels like Archers of Loaf's only
1997 release, *Vitus Tinnitus*, a mostly live EP recorded the previous
October at the Middle East in Cambridge, Massachusetts. It was also
meant as solace to fans expecting new recordings, a stopgap for an
interrupted release schedule. The Archers stayed out on the road.

6 String Drag's *High Hat* was released September 9. It was produced by Steve Earl. "We were on Fundamental Records for our
first album," Kenny Roby said. "That came out in '95. Then we did a
demo deal with Columbia and they decided to pass on us.

"Shortly after that, we were playing a little festival at the Star Bar in Atlanta," Kenny said. "Steve Earle, his girlfriend Kelly Walker, Jack Emerson, and a couple other people from Steve's label E-Squared Records were there, too. I think they were going to see Whiskeytown. Steve was interested in Whiskeytown, but they were being courted by people with a lot more money. Kelly was a fan of our first record and said, 'Hey, let's check out this band 6 String Drag.' We had horns that night and everything."

Steve asked 6 String Drag to have lunch with him the next day before he left for Nashville. "I didn't expect to sign anybody," he told them, "but after two songs I was like, 'I want to sign this band. They're great. They've got harmonies, they've got a punk rock edge to them. But they also have horns and a New Orleans flavor here and there. Sounds great. It's not like what everybody else is doing.'"

High Hat was recorded in Nashville in January. "When I sign a band," Steve told 6 String Drag, "I wanna make their first record like the thing I saw live." As a result, the band recorded mostly live with a few overdubs. Kenny's vocals were recorded with the rest of the band. "Steve would call it 'lightning in a bottle,'" Kenny said. "It was us at our rawest. I wouldn't say sloppy, but it was more about the energy than singing in tune."

"Soak me in gasoline," Kenny and bassist Rob Keller harmonize on a particularly spirited stomper, "if you need more fire, Maybelline."

Superchunk also released an album on September 9. *Indoor Living* was engineered and coproduced by John Plymale. Like Archers of Loaf, Superchunk were expanding their sound. *Indoor Living* has an organ, a Mellotron, and, on the reflective "Martinis on the Roof," a marimba. "Trick night and Halloween," Mac McCaughan sings.

> *An April Fool's bad dream*
> *Cigar smoke over the moon*
> *And you were leaving way too soon*

Cheetos and a hundred proof
Martinis on the roof

You can sense an accumulated emotional weight listening to
Indoor Living, probably because the band had been cranking out
an album a year for eight years and touring almost the entire time.
When they weren't doing that, Mac and Laura Ballance were running Merge Records.

"Our shows got bigger and bigger and then peaked out at some point
and started going back down," Laura said. "*That* made me feel bad, more
than 'Oh, we never got to be Nirvana' or whatever. Once we weren't
attracting as big a crowd as we once did, that's when some sort of ambition set in, like, 'Oh, this is supposed to just keep going up, isn't it?'"

Polvo's new record *Shapes* came out on September 23. "The critical reaction to *Exploded Drawing* was fine," Dave Brylawski said, "but
Shapes was *derided*. It wasn't well received." The album was created
during a time of upheaval. Eddie Watkins quit before the sessions.

"We had to figure out our next drummer and decided at that
time—me, Steve Popson, and Ash Bowie—'Let's do one more record
and one more big tour and then call it,'" Dave remembered. "That
record was *Shapes*. Ash drummed on a couple tracks. Brian Walsby
drummed on a couple tracks.

"Sonic Youth's Thurston Moore said to me, 'I think it's cool that
you announced you were going to do one more record and one more
tour,'" Dave said. "Because that's not how it goes. We knew that it
was harder to keep it together, but we still had some music in us. We
didn't want to stop. It freed us, in a way.

"The tour we did for *Shapes* was our biggest," Dave said. "We
toured the whole country. Everyone knew they weren't gonna see us
again. Bands didn't get back together at that time. Everyone came out
to say goodbye. At the end, I think Steve, Ash, and I were content and
ready to move on." Polvo disbanded.

Southern Culture on the Skids also came out with a new record
on September 23. *Plastic Seat Sweat* was another Geffen release, but

its sales of around 60,000 units didn't come close to *Dirt Track Date*'s quarter of a million. This kind of thing usually resulted in a band getting dropped, but this time it was SCOTS who walked away.

"I remember when we ended up leaving Geffen," Rick Miller said. "We had a two-record deal and were up for another. I thought, 'We've recouped. They'll want to re-sign us.' They did, but stipulated that they needed more sales. It wasn't enough to make money. They wanted big money. They wanted to go after this market, they wanted us to work with this producer, they wanted to make sure that we had a radio-ready song.

"We thought about it in the band," Rick said. "We had our disagreements. But my feeling was that if we'd gone with them, we wouldn't have lasted. They would have started to put more pressure on us. I mean, they were going to give us the same amount of money we used to make a whole record to just make one demo with some producer who was going to take probably 90 percent of it. We were like, 'Forget about it. We'd rather do it on our own again,' which we did.

"The most important thing for us was to maintain control of our destiny," Rick told me. "When we signed with Geffen, they said, 'You have to have a manager. We won't talk to the band.' We had a good booking agent, a good lawyer, and a good accountant. That's all you really need. I kept all my publishing, too. I wouldn't sign that away." SCOTS continued recording their own albums economically and touring vigorously.

Jimbo Mathus made use of the Zippers' career doldrums by releasing a benefit album called *Jas. Mathus & His Knockdown Society Play Songs for Rosetta*, issued by Mammoth Records on October 7. The beneficiary was blues legend Charlie Patton's daughter Rosetta, who not only had never seen a nickel from her father's work, but helped raise Jimbo as a child back in Clarksdale. *Songs for Rosetta* contains Patton songs as well as several Jimbo originals. A mess of people played on it, including Andrew Bird, the Zippers' Stu Cole, and original members of the North Mississippi Allstars.

On October 14, Merge Records released Shark Quest's first recordings, a seven inch of "Blontzo's Revenge" b/w "Pig River Minor." Kevin Dixon illustrated the cover. The label tried to help the band be a little more professional and found them a booking agent. "We were all so busy with other bands," Sara Bell said. "That made it hard because we had other commitments. The booking agent gave up on us."

By the fall, Shawn Rogers's brief career as head of an indie label ended. "We put out three records as Scrimshaw," he said. "After a while, I remember feeling overwhelmed. I went to Jay Faires and said, 'Hey, I don't think I can do this anymore.' He was disappointed. He was always very supportive and nice about the whole situation. I know we didn't make money for him.

"Jay was like, 'No, that's totally cool. Well, would you want to work at Mammoth?'" Shawn remembered. Jay was fine with Shawn keeping his management side hustle as long as he got the work done. Shawn started at his third local music label.

On November 21, 550 Music released the Ben Folds Five song "Brick" as the fourth single from *Whatever and Ever Amen*. Caleb Southern remembered recording that track especially. "Darren Jessee wrote most of it, including all the music, melodies, and the chorus lyrics," Caleb said.

> *She's a brick and I'm drowning slowly*
> *Off the coast and I'm headed nowhere*

"Ben wrote the verse lyrics at the last minute," Caleb said. "We had a deadline to finish the tracks. Ben finally finished writing with a couple of days left. Darren and Robert were standing with me in Ben's kitchen, the control room. Our jaws collectively dropped to the floor. It was a heavy and personal story about an abortion. We all got it, without saying a word.

"Robert Sledge might be one of the most underrated musicians ever to come out of Chapel Hill," Caleb said. "He never fucked up. He could play anything on demand. Robert played the bowed stand-up bass on 'Brick' and he fucking nailed it. It wasn't even his natural instrument, and he did it, cold, on the first take."

For his part, Robert never embraced the singles mentality. "I thought of us as more of an album band," he said. "I still have an album mentality. I was like, 'Single, shmingle! Check out this group!' But singles were super important. I still have a hard time investing too much in one song.

"When 'Brick' was released, Ben left the country," Robert remembered. "He went to Australia. I didn't quite understand it at the time, but interpret it now as him not wanting to see the first reviews coming in. He wanted to come back to America and see if it had succeeded or failed. We all knew it was a make or break."

1998

O N JANUARY 10, BEN FOLDS FIVE PERFORMED "BRICK" ON *SATUR-day Night Live*, becoming only the second Chapel Hill act besides James Taylor to do so. "We were terrible," Ben later told David Menconi. "I was so pissed. We'd slayed ten thousand performances before that, but it sure didn't look like it on TV. Afterward, I was beat. I was in such a bad psychological state that I left the country the next morning and stayed away for a month. The weird thing was, I sucked on that show and we left feeling like we'd been a failure. Then I came back to the US and we had a charting album and sold forty thousand records the week after *Saturday Night Live*. 'Well,' I thought, 'I guess that's what it's all about.'"

Three days after their *Saturday Night Live* appearance, Caroline Records issued a "new" Ben Folds Five album called *Naked Baby Photos*, a kitchen-sink compilation consisting of live performances, the band's first single, and outtakes from *Ben Folds Five* and *Whatever and Ever Amen*.

Norton Records released their third Flat Duo Jets record, *Wild Blue Yonder*, on January 27. It's a live album recorded at venues all over the country. About half of it is cover songs.

Flat Duo Jets ended their relationship with Dick Hodgin's M-80 Management and went with a new outfit, Slick Winston. The brainchild of Paul Laughter and Ben Wingrove, Slick Winston was located in Carrboro near the Merge Records office. Paul had been a Mammoth intern during the Atlantic years.

It was a promising time for Flat Duo Jets. In 1996, Outpost Records' principal and long-time R.E.M. producer Scott Litt was at a Duo Jets show in Seattle with his friend Peter Buck, guitarist for R.E.M. "You should work with these guys," Peter told Scott.

Litt began producing a new Flat Duo Jets album with former dB Chris Stamey. Their vision was much more highly realized than what Norton had been capable of doing. On some songs, Dex and Crow would be accompanied by a string section. Ken Mosher and I played saxophones on another.

"There are people out there who say, 'Why are you doing this?'" Litt told *Billboard*. "It is what the Flat Duo Jets are. It's never been fully realized, and it's not fair for those people to hold these guys back and say, 'You have to make these three-day records for your whole career.'"

"Put it this way: it's a dream come true," Dexter added. "I was hoping it would happen and it finally did."

Hobex was also being managed by Slick Winston and making a new record. "There were a lot of people our age that were in the game," Greg Humphreys said. "Then there was another generation coming up after us. These management guys were part of that. They had seen the scene developing and wanted to get into the music business. We decided, 'Well, we're going to expand from this trio sound. We're going to add some keys.' There's percussion. The Kletter sisters sang on it." The Zippers horn section is on there too, credited as "The Carrboro Horns." The new Hobex album was called *Back in the 90s*. It was recorded at Overdub Lane and produced by John Plymale.

Meanwhile, Dillon Fence's drummer Scott Carle was in a new band called Collapsis, named after one of Greg's Dillon Fence songs.

Scott met singer Mike Garrigan when he was at Carolina. "He did a monumental record with John Plymale at Overdub called *The Lessons of Autumn*," Scott said, "and that record blew my mind." The band got permission from Greg to use the name. Ultimately, Collapsis would include Mike, Scott, and two ex-members of Queen Sarah Saturday: Ryan Pickett and Chris Holloway. The band would go on to release *The Chartreuse* EP.

Ben Folds Five had offered Squirrel Nut Zippers the opening slot for their European tour in late '97. Mammoth said no. It didn't make sense to us. Why go break European markets the hard way when you could open for two thousand people a night? "We wanted all our energy here," Steve Balcom explained. "We felt like if we had success here, it would be easier to break the band and have a pathway over there."

Instead, we toured Europe in March by ourselves, often performing to small crowds of people who had no idea who we were. One day, I cornered the Mammoth rep about not being able to find our CDs in any of the local shops. "Tom, your records have been released over here," he told me. "They're just not in the stores." I think about that line all the time.

Jimbo Mathus was sick during the whole European tour. I was told that he was trying to quit smoking and was taking a drug to help him do that that had nasty side effects.

There were so few people in the audience during one gig in Stockholm that we had them all gather around and tell us their names. Then we dedicated a song to each one. In Malmö, I got a call from back home. Our former trumpet player Stacy Guess had overdosed on heroin and was comatose in the hospital.

"After *The Robust Beauty of Improper Linear Models in Decision Making, Vol. II* came out, we formed the Robust Beauty Band to go play the Knitting Factory and Maxwell's in New York," Kirk Ross said. "Stacy was part of that. He and Chris Stamey did all the melody lines that Chris had come up with. They did 'em in unison. It was really a nice sound. During the day between the two shows, Stacy really wanted to go find 81 Mulberry to get some 'cough syrup.' That was supposedly where the band 81 Mulberry got their name: it was a place where you were able to get heroin in cough syrup.

"I wandered around town with Stacy while he tried to score," Kirk remembered. "I was trying to not be supportive, but also not lose him. Just stay with him. He was unsuccessful, so we sat outside into the wee hours talking. This was like three, four in the morning in New York. He told me his theory that heroin is your inner fascist. It will not stop. It is relentless. Then we went back, crashed, and got up and played the show.

"We had another gig scheduled in Chapel Hill a week later," Kirk said. "Stacy showed up for a rehearsal but didn't make the show. Chris put a spotlight on the microphone stand where he would have stood. He didn't call any of us." Stacy died a week later, on March 11. He was thirty-three.

After getting the news about Stacy's death, I felt utterly disconnected and alone. It was cold. Chris Phillips and Jimbo were getting into voluble fights backstage. I was a million miles away from the people I loved and too close to this substitute family who had, by degrees, sacrificed the things that made our experience together precious. Zippers shows were still fun to play, but our offstage camaraderie was gone. I could hardly get on the bus at the beginning of a tour because of crippling panic attacks.

I was mad at Stacy for dying and furious with myself for being an insufficient friend who couldn't even talk to him about his addiction, much less be of any help. When I told the rest of the band the news about Stacy one bleak afternoon in Germany, no one said a word. We couldn't even grieve together. The reality of his death was an unapproachable void.

Back home, Mammoth's deal with Disney had already gone to shit. "It was dope as fuck to meet Roy Disney," Jay Faires said, "but six months later I was so in the doghouse with them it was ridiculous. I was trying to sign bigger acts. I did the Dust Brothers deal and their label was called Nickel Bag. Disney corporate PR were already trying to get me, so they put in the *Wall Street Journal*, 'How is the Walt Disney family-friendly fare gonna deal with an executive who's signing deals with marijuana references?'

"I called my manager Steve Moyer," Jay remembered. "He said, 'Dude, you took the money. Just ride it out for a year and a half.' I had to sit on my hands. It sucked."

On Saturday, June 20, the Zippers played Birmingham, Alabama's massive outdoor City Stages festival. Katharine was sick and didn't perform. We decided to go on without her, which felt weird. It was so hot that generators were blowing up down the street. From the side of the stage, I looked out at a sea of fifty thousand undifferentiated faces. It was then I felt certain that I had no right to be there.

I thought of Metal Flake Mother and all the other bands I admired and came up with—all populated with incredibly talented people—who had fallen by the wayside without proper recognition. I thought of John Ensslin, who taught me how to write a smart lyric and be a compelling front man, now exiled to South Carolina.

Then it hit me, on a molecular level, that none of this had anything to do with me or the Squirrel Nut Zippers. We just happened to be representing. It was our little moment to carry the baton before passing it off to someone else. The most comforting thought was the understanding that where I came from *was* who I was, not some brittle little rock star doing it all by himself. That's what got me onstage that afternoon.

"In 1998, I started a tech column for *HITS*," Joe Fleischer said. "There were now MP3 players. The music industry tried to sue them into nonexistence but lost. Now they were rapidly trying to come up with proprietary codecs that they could wrap security around so that you couldn't freely play MP3s. They were working on very early, crude versions of conditional use. I covered a lot of that."

"I was involved with founding a software company called M-PAK," mastering engineer Brent Lambert said. "We were figuring out a way to securely share media from computer to computer without copyright infringement. College campuses had just started these networks where students could have accounts and share files. They were downloading records and burning them onto CDs. Computers had CD disk drives in them back then. So, you could take data off the CD and share it for free. Record companies were freaking out and nobody had a solution."

In May, Jack Campbell completed his degree at Carolina. He started actively looking for someone to buy Poindexter Records. "That last year, I was starting to sell an awful lot of blank recordable CDRs," Jack remembered. "It didn't make any sense to me, because CD burners cost six hundred bucks. Well, it turns out that at least one enterprising guy in every Duke University dorm had one, because suddenly we weren't selling CDs in the kind of numbers we used to. For a $1.25 recordable CDR, you could have the newest Dave Matthews or whatever. Just write the band's name on it with a Sharpie."

Tim Harper, former Cradle soundman and producer of What Peggy Wants' *Death of a Sailor*, came up with a fix for the file sharing problem. "It was just a way to package MP3 files securely," Tim told me. "We could include album art, lyrics, and other media. It would also track plays since the media player was included."

"Adobe Flash was a multimedia presentation platform," Brent explained. "Tim figured out a way to put it in a wrapper around a wrapper, software-wise. You could deliver an album to somebody and it would look up the machine code of the computer it was playing on. It would only play if it saw that machine code. If you sent that album to somebody else, it would look for the same machine code. If it wasn't there, it wouldn't play.

"Tim came to me and said, 'I have this great idea,'" Brent remembered. "'Can we start a business and do this?' I got this high-powered law firm on board. They said, 'This is an amazing idea. In lieu of legal fees, we want to exchange preferred stock in this company so that if it goes public, we're going to make bazillions of dollars.' We refined the software. I rented a building in Carrboro on Weaver

Street and moved these guys into it. They were working there all the time." M-PAK was born.

"It became clear that we would need either a large media company to buy M-PAK from us immediately, or we would have to keep developing it and grow in the venture capitalist methodology," Brent said. "Every single major record company was interested. We were also getting calls from IBM, Microsoft, and all these other people. We started getting offers but none to buy the software."

Zen Frisbee resurfaced momentarily to release the retrospective compilation album *Eat at the Burrito Bunker*. Burrito Bunker was a Mexican restaurant on East Franklin Street in Chapel Hill. "The record was called that so we could have free burritos for life," Kevin Dixon told me. "It was a deal Laird worked out."

Eat at the Burrito Bunker contained songs from the shelved Ardent sessions, the 1990 Merge single, and much in between. Its CD insert came in three different colors—green, yellow, and red. A dried red pepper was placed inside the spine of each jewel case. "I haven't listened to *I'm as Mad as Faust* as much as I've listened to *Burrito Bunker*," John Ensslin said. "I really like that record."

"When the Ardent thing fell through, it was like, 'We're never going to have any luck,'" Kevin recalled. "'We're never going to get anywhere.' So, we stopped doing it for a couple of years. It was a lot of fun while it was all happening, but also very frustrating to feel left behind."

The other reason Zen Frisbee took a break was bassist Andrew Maltbie's heroin addiction. "The majority of the Zen Frisbee boys smoked pot," Laird Dixon said. "I don't, but have always considered it a very docile and harmless drug. Brian Walker and I brought Andrew in when he was a child, literally. He was going to high school and we needed a bass player. He used to come over and visit me and Brian every day at Basnight Lane.

"Andrew loved rock-and-roll music and seemed to know a hell of a lot more about it than us," Laird said. "He was one of those people who, like Chuck Garrison, Kevin, or Groves Willer, are encyclopedic over it. Andrew was that and a blossoming bass player. We thought, 'It would be cool if we got a high school kid to do it,' sort of like the Bad Checks did with Hunter Landen.

"We brought Andrew in and very quickly his whole persona changed," Laird remembered. "He started going toward this rock-and-roll slant with his look and attitude. The scarves came out. He started drinking alcohol and that's absolutely our fault. Unfortunately, he developed an interest in harder drugs. He loved the idea of junkies. Rock and roll goes hand in hand with junkies. I was dreading the day. The more he talked about it, eventually, someone got him high."

"I moved away from Chapel Hill for two years, from '95 to '97," Evil Wiener's Bill McCormick said. "Things seemed to be winding down. It was time to start another chapter of my life. So, I went off to Asheville and got certified to teach elementary school. When I came back, things were different. Some bands were hanging on, but most had broken up by then. There was a new set of bands, and they were good, but it wasn't the same. A lot of the people who were still there, trying to get a band together or even playing in successful bands, were having heroin problems. People I played music with in the eighties, who I knew from a long time ago, were also getting into it. They were older than me. It got dark. I stuck my toe in that pool and it immediately sucked me in up to my knee. I moved away again."

After fifteen years, Zen Frisbee called it quits. "The 'star-crossed' explanation rings a little truer to me about what happened with Zen Frisbee's career than 'if they'd only been able to get their shit together,'" Jolene's Dave Burris said. "We're fucking musicians. We all can't be player managers. There's always gonna be some element of chaos with any group. Yeah, Laird is a bit ethereal. Brian has one of the highest IQs of anybody I've ever met and that creates its own problems. Maybe this is lazy, but if they could have gotten connected

with a label, an A&R person, a manager, or something that could
have focused that chaos, they would have been okay. They just
weren't fortunate enough to have that happen. That was maybe true
of The Veldt too. They didn't get the right manager or A&R person
who could have helped them choose the right paths."

The principals in The Veldt don't disagree. "My opinion is that
had we not been so shortsighted, we would have stayed with Jay
Faires, worked that out, and then waited to go to an indie," Daniel
Chavis admitted. "Whereas, we had all these people coming at us
and making deal offers. We wanted to go with a company that would
take us to England."

The Veldt were also closing a chapter. The band released *Love at
First Hate* on May 19, subtitled *a guide to romance and misery in the
21st century.* "Those were a bunch of demos that Danny didn't play
on," Daniel said.

"At that point in time, I thought the band's sound should be
advancing," Danny Chavis explained. "In New York, I'd been
exposed to a lot of DJ culture stuff like Tricky, Portishead, and
Massive Attack. I was working with a programmer up there named
Charles Reeves. We began to do a new set of demos. Marvin Levy
and Daniel didn't really agree with the concept, so I just said, 'Fuck
it. I'll do it my damn self.'" The Veldt disbanded.

Dana Kletter and her identical twin sister Karen released *dear
enemy* on Joe Boyd's Hannibal Records. It was a fulfillment of what
Joe had asked Dana to do back when he produced the first blackgirls album. "My sister came to do backing vocals on our first record, *Procedure*," Dana said. "Joe told us that me and my sister were
at all the same places on the dials and gauges. He said, 'What I
really want to do is make a record with you and your sister.' But
we already had an agreement that he was gonna produce the second blackgirls record. Joe kept coming back and saying, 'You need
to make your own record.' But at that time, I wasn't ready to do
that."

Even though Hobex was still indie to the point of self-releasing *Back in the 90s*, G105's program director Kip Taylor—the same guy who helped break "Hell"—loved the record and played its undeniable single "Groove Baby." This was a ballsy move for a Clear Channel station in the late nineties, even though that's exactly how regional radio used to work.

Once again, Kip Taylor's instincts were right. "'Groove Baby' became a Top 10 hit on the station," Greg said. "That was an aberration. He was breaking the rules and doing it anyway. So, it took Hobex from being like, 'Oh yeah, that's the band that guy from Dillon Fence is in,' to 'Wow, Hobex has a lot of momentum!'"

There was interest from Capricorn Records, but Hobex was made an offer by London Recordings. "We signed the London deal and I made more money on that day than I had in the previous six years of working for Mammoth," Greg said. "It wasn't obscene, but it was a major label deal. We paid off our lawyer, paid our management, and split the rest." The band went back into the studio with John Plymale to rerecord some songs from *Back in the 90s*. London wanted a single and Hobex had one in "Groove Baby." A little polishing was in order.

"M-PAK did our dog and pony show around the country at various big media companies," Brent Lambert said. "It became clear to me that most of the people running these large record companies were just MBAs who had no music industry experience. They knew nothing about music. The senior vice president of BMG said, 'I see on your CV that you were in the music business. What do you think of our current roster?'

"I thought, 'You know what? I'm gonna be honest with this guy,'" Brent remembered. "I said, 'Well, I think your A&R staff is too young and don't really understand what's going on. They're just chasing what's already popular. They don't have any vision, and there's nobody of relevance on your label right now.'" Offended, the BMG guy stood up.

"He said, 'Let me tell you something, son,' and walked up to this whiteboard," Brent said. "He wrote down the names of a dozen

magazines and said, 'Look. When I want to make a band successful, I just pick up the phone and call the editors of these magazines,
because we own them. We have over two hundred attorneys on staff
here. It doesn't matter how good the bands are. I just make them
popular.'

"He was proud of this," Brent said. "I thought, 'Wow, you're so disconnected from the whole concept of creating art. No wonder your
label is suffering.' It summarized what I suspected, which is that the
corporate music industry was not really interested in reflecting or promoting individual scenes or subtle gradations of creativity. They were
just interested in selling toasters."

Ultimately, no one was buying what M-PAK was selling. "The
record companies were all so greedy that they didn't just want to solve
the problem," Brent said. "They wanted to solve the problem in a
way that all their competitors would have to pay them. They could
never come to an agreement and work with each other. There were
three other companies doing parallel things, but they didn't really
have software engineers on their staff. They didn't have the foresight
to think that brick-and-mortar distribution could go away."

Instead, M-PAK decided to pursue the venture capitalist route.
Goldman Sachs flew two guys down to discuss terms. "These suits
from New York City were sitting in my mastering studio," Brent
remembered. "I was asking for $1.2 million for development. I had
a completely commonsense route for how we were gonna make M-
PAK more marketable and sell it. They said, 'Look, we read your business plan. This is an amazing idea, but we need you to rewrite it for
twenty times that much.'" Brent spent the next two years doing just
that.

The Squirrel Nut Zippers' third full-length album, *Perennial
Favorites*, was released by Mammoth Records on August 4, nineteen
months after it had been completed. "Up to the point where the Zippers suddenly blew up, I don't recall reading a discouraging word
anywhere," the *News & Observer*'s David Menconi remembered.
"The coverage was always very friendly, very favorable: 'Here are

these cool underdogs doing this oddball punk rock take on a retro style,' and, 'Isn't this fun?' Suddenly, 'Hell' hits and I remember *Spin* just dumping all over the band when *Perennial* came out. They gave it a four out of ten or something."

To me, *Spin*'s disdain was a sign that we were on the right track. But it was also part of a justifiable backlash against us being shoved in everybody's face for a year and a half. Worse, the Zippers had been dubbed the vanguard of a new trend. In 1995, people called us lounge music. Now they called us a swing revival band and compared us to a cadre of Los Angeles groups who basically played Kansas City Jump Blues with a Gene Krupa floor tom pattern. Like Archers of Loaf and the Maverick Records roster, I did not want to be associated with those bands. Not that it mattered.

"That was the clown version," Ben Folds said. "The Zippers had a punk rock aesthetic—a do-it-yourself, 'We're going to express because we have to' thing. It's by necessity. When you hear something that's expressed by necessity, that's one thing. When you hear someone who has a fuckin' hobby, that's another."

Seattle produced some great popular music in the late eighties and early nineties in addition to Nirvana. Pearl Jam made gargantuan records and took it to Ticketmaster for gouging fans. "I wanted to *be* Mudhoney," Laura Ballance told me. "I thought they were so cool. They had this dark edge but were goofy and fun. That appealed to me more than the Nirvana thing, honestly."

But when the media invented grunge as a lifestyle choice, things became stupid. Soon, there were silk flannel shirts in the Perry Ellis spring 1993 collection. If anything, the burgeoning swing movement was less diverse, more cynical, and devoid of enough good music to even make it interesting. All of this, to me, felt like a reversal of the Zippers' great good fortune, if not an outright negation.

One day, watching TV at home in Pittsboro, I saw a Gap clothing commercial. It featured a bunch of kids throwing themselves around doing the Lindy Hop like we'd been seeing at our shows. The *Charlie*

Brown Christmas dance crowd had been aggressively sidelined by a new crop of people. The dudes wore fedoras and zoot suits. The girls all had Bettie Page hairdos. They'd been taking swing dance lessons and felt entitled to be dicks about it. After the show, some of them would criticize us for playing our songs too fast, which always put a little murder in my heart.

The Gap commercial was called "Khaki Swing," because these kids were wearing khaki pants and white T-shirts instead of the swing Nazi uniform. I remembered seeing Nirvana perform on *Saturday Night Live* with Jimbo years ago. "That's it for swing," I said to myself.

Perennial Favorites shipped in excess of six hundred thousand units, which was mind-boggling. I went up to Steve Balcom's office shortly after the album's release. He congratulated me on our instant Gold record status. I asked him how things were looking at radio. "Not too good," he winced. "Radio says there aren't any swing songs on the record." Just like that, *Perennial* was considered a failure.

Archers of Loaf's constant touring was destroying Eric Bachmann's voice. "I was going to ENT doctors because my throat was so messed up," he said. "I could only do seven days in a row of belting it out on a song like 'Wrong.' It was a bad scene.

"There were cracks in the hull of the ship," Eric said. "We were starting to get burned out. After the whole *Airports* push, record sales declined. It was like, 'You've sold forty-five thousand copies of *Vee Vee* but only twenty-five thousand of *Airports*.' It was a cleaner record, a poppier record. I got made fun of for bringing a piano out on tour. It's comedic now, but there were piano Nazis."

"I was sick of touring," guitarist Eric Johnson said. "I wanted a break. I think we were all done with it. Not in a bad way at all. We remained good friends, but none of us were really into it that much anymore. We didn't have time to practice and come up with new songs. It was constant, man: six weeks here, two weeks off, six weeks back out on the road. It was a grind. I was like, 'I don't ever want to play another show in my life!'"

"We had one record left on Alias," Eric Bachmann said. "The band wasn't living in the same town anymore. I had moved to DC to be with my girlfriend, who was in medical school. Eric Johnson had moved back to Asheville. Matt Gentling and Mark Price still lived in Chapel Hill. I'd scavenged up enough songs—like ten to fifteen ideas—and had finished a few of them, enough to get back together. We all agreed, 'Okay, let's make one more record just to get off the contract with Alias and see how it goes.'"

The new album was recorded with Brian Paulson at Ardent Studios in Memphis. "The record was piecemealed together," Eric remembered. "It was totally not like the process we'd ever done. I worked with Brian by myself most of the time and EJ would go in by himself. People were not motivated. We did a few rehearsals and played together to some degree. There's a lot of stuff we played live that we recorded, but for the most part after the initial three or four days of tracking, everybody scattered. Nobody was into it."

Archers of Loaf's swan song, *White Trash Heroes*, was released on September 22. It caught flak for not sounding like an Archers of Loaf record. The band went back out on the road. By this time, drummer Mark Price had developed carpal tunnel syndrome. "At the end of the whole thing, Mark's like, 'Man, I think I'm done,'" Eric remembered. "He was really beaten down. He's a smart guy, so he was like, 'I'm not going to be anybody's bitch. This is ridiculous.'"

"After that tour, that was it," Eric said. "We were done. I was working at Gumby's on Franklin Street delivering pizza right before I moved to DC." Archers of Loaf broke up.

Despite this, Eric Bachmann wasn't finished making music. "I had other things I wanted to do," he said. "Creatively, my tank was full. I had no doubt that I wanted to keep going. I knew that the band was changing. Mark didn't like what I wanted to do with the sound of a few of the songs I'd written. I don't blame him: you like what you like. Matt Gentling and Mark were more into Jesus Lizard kind of stuff.

They wanted to get more rockin' that way. Eric Johnson wanted to do his own textural thing. I wanted to write. It was the song for me. It was always about the song. So, I wanted to do something like loops and strings and electric guitar." Soon after, Eric initiated a new project called Crooked Fingers.

Squirrel Nut Zippers' *Christmas Caravan* came out on October 6. It was our second record released in 1998, scarcely two months after *Perennial Favorites*. It sounds odd to turn out two full-length albums back-to-back after a year and a half of radio silence, but this one was the product of a quid pro quo. The Squirrel Brand Company sued us after we wouldn't sign their licensing agreement, meaning the nineties name curse had darkened our door as well. Our immediate response was to consider changing the band name to Squirrel *Not* Zippers, but Mammoth wouldn't hear of it. Instead, they agreed to help pay for litigation in return for a Christmas album.

Christmas Caravan was recorded in sullen little clutches in July in Kingsway Studios down in New Orleans. Ken Mosher and I joked that it would be our last Zippers record, but then again we always joked about things that were painfully true. Contrary to Mammoth's expectations, the album contains mostly original material. It had been so long since we'd written anything new—the songs on *Perennial Favorites* had mostly been composed by the summer of 1996— that Jimbo, Ken, and I cranked out a stack of new ones without discussing it.

"I remember seeing Jay's face when he saw that there were no standards on it," Steve Balcom said. The poor devils had no idea how destructive it had been promoting *Hot* for so long with nothing new to work on or look forward to. It wasn't immediately profitable for them to know something like that, essential though it is to the life of an artistic project. After all, the contingent clause of Mammoth's original motto was "We'll take care of the business."

When Jimbo sent me a cassette tape of his *Christmas Caravan* song demos, Katharine's solo record was on the other side. We had never officially been told about *Katharine Whalen's Jazz Squad*. I'd heard about it from Andrew Bird, who's on it, but Jimbo denied its existence.

"I remember it being presented as, 'If you want another Zippers record, we need to do this *Jazz Squad* project,'" Steve said about the album's origin.

The Zippers had been artistically dormant for a long time. It makes sense why Katharine would want to do her own thing with other people like Jimbo had done with the Knockdown Society. It wasn't like it was some huge production. I'm not claiming to have been good at Chapel-Hilling It. At that point I was devoid of chill. But it bothered me that Katharine's solo record wasn't going to be done on her own time.

Sometime in late summer, Jim and Katharine announced in a band meeting that the Squirrel Nut Zippers would be taking the first six months of 1999 off. When I pointed out that doing this would cause Mammoth to have a meltdown because of the *Perennial Favorites* touring cycle, I was told that Steve Balcom had been informed and that the label was cool with it.

"I don't remember that at all," Steve told me years later. "There's no way that would have been cleared by us." Steve and I figured out that he first heard about the six-month hiatus when I mentioned it during a meeting with him sometime after the *Perennial Favorites* release. I remember it too: it was the only time Steve ever screamed at me: "*Why the fuck are you guys killing this record?*" Katharine would go on to turn down an opportunity for the Zippers to play the Macy's Thanksgiving Day Parade because she said it would be too cold.

The Scott Litt and Chris Stamey–produced Flat Duo Jets album *Lucky Eye* came out in October on Outpost Records, a subsidiary of Geffen. The record got mixed reviews, mostly around the band exploring new instrumentation and arrangements. "I think it's a fine record," Dexter Romweber told *Perfect Sound Forever* in 2001. "I can't understand why someone would not like the production. I like records with horns and strings and stuff. I don't like being tied to one thing. I like opening up new instruments and vistas."

Lucky Eye didn't sell particularly well. After a career encompassing fifteen years and ten records, the Flat Duo Jets broke up abruptly on the road shortly after the album's release. During the *Perfect Sound Forever* interview two years later, Dexter admitted to not having spoken to Crow once since the breakup.

In October, Joe Fleischer began addressing the digital revolution in his music industry trade magazine. "I wrote this thing on Napster for *HITS* because I got the beta version," Joe remembered. "I brought in a bunch of people and said, 'This thing is called Napster. You can get anything you want, burn it to a CD, and play it in your car. It's the coolest thing I've ever seen.' Half the people were like, 'This is cool!' and half the people were like, 'This is straight evil. It has to be stopped.' I said, 'I don't think you can stop it. That's the Internet.'

"The idea of going track by track and cherry-picking songs via Napster unbundled the album," Joe said. "That was the part I thought was so groundbreaking. I'm like, 'You realize you can just acquire the one song you want. You're no longer having to buy the entire Natalie Imbruglia record for "Torn" because you don't want the other eleven songs. You're reducing the addressable margin of the recorded music industry by 90 percent. That seems super important!'

"So, I wrote this column about it to no reaction," Joe said. "No one said anything. It was like, 'Whatever.'"

Spatula put out a new album at year's end. *Despina By Land* was recorded at Overdub Lane and produced by Bob Weston. "He'd worked with Polvo and that's how we got his contact," Chuck Johnson said. "But he was based in Chicago and was working with a lot of artists that I felt a strong affinity for. He worked with Gastr del Sol and Rachel's and a lot of other bands that later might have been called 'post rock.' So, I knew his work. I really loved his drum sounds in particular.

"At the time, in my mind, it was the drum sounds that made the record," Chuck said. "I still think that, really. That was the tell that something wasn't recorded well, or with good gear, or in a good room: the drum sound wasn't happening. So, that was something I wanted to have. With Matt Gocke and me—even with Chris Eubank in the band—there was a lot of space in the music. I wanted each element to be treated in a more orchestral way. I knew that Bob could get that huge sound from the drum kit."

Writing for the English psychedelic music magazine *Ptolemaic Terrascope*'s November 28 issue, reviewer Phil McMullen had this to say about *Despina By Land*: "Spatula are a band on the seashore staring in toward the traumatized, brooding, rain-sodden post war landscape, a group struck mute by the awfulness of it all who can only interpret what they see through colourful, cavernous rhythmic structures, every chord a fractal raindrop, every melody a fluttering retreat."

Despina By Land would be Spatula's last record. "It was certainly not an interpersonal thing with Chris or Matt at all," Chuck told me. "We were all getting along great. It's just something that happens with me and bands when it's like, 'Okay, we have this one night a week where we practice.' If I'm not feeling it that night, I don't want to be there. Then I get frustrated about what comes out of that practice session. I also wanted to be able to tour more and we didn't have a booking agent. I guess I had expectations from that record—that it would help us access some things that we didn't have access to—and it didn't happen. We all recognized that Spatula had hit, not exactly a dead end, but a place where it wasn't clear that it had anywhere else to go."

Chuck paused. "I guess that's the definition of a dead end!" he added, laughing.

"It doesn't have to be a negative thing that a project reaches the end of its life cycle," Chuck continued. "I think it's a mature thing to recognize that. After Spatula, I didn't have an audience of that size for a long time, as meager as it was. It's a very adult thing to recognize, 'On some level this is going well, but now's a good time to call it.'"

MTV News wrote about the impending multi-billion-dollar merger of PolyGram and Universal Music Group on December 4.

"The deal, which will create the world's largest music company—from two of the world's 'Big Six' music corporations—is expected to jettison dozens of bands from the rosters of Mercury, Def Jam, Geffen, Island, Interscope, and other labels owned by the two companies," they wrote. "After the merger, there will be five major music corporations: Universal, Sony, Time Warner, EMI and Bertelsmann."

Hobex was no longer indie. "The other bands on London's roster at that time were like Rammstein," Greg Humphreys remembered. "They were an end-stage capitalism, corporate rock label. It was like, 'What are we doing here?' We had a meeting with our A&R guy. He had a TV tuned to the financial channel and was distracted by the ticker tape running stock prices. We realized, 'This is the guy who's gonna determine our future.' I don't think he had anything invested in us at all."

Producer John Plymale remembered that meeting. "We were in the studio working on the new versions of 'Groove Baby' and 'Windows,'" he recalled. "It was a Monday or Tuesday. The A&R guy calls and says, 'We really need to talk about this record. I'm gonna buy your tickets. Y'all come up here to New York.' It was the next fucking day! We were like, 'Oh, shit. Okay.' We even canceled a studio day. Greg and I flew up there together. We felt like we were being called in because we were in trouble."

Once they landed in the city, Greg and John caught a cab over to London's office. "We went to dinner with a few of those label guys," John said. "They were talking about all their investments. Then we went back and spent a couple hours in their offices listening to music. We came back the next day and hung out in their offices for another couple hours. Nobody ever—one single time—*ever* sat down and said a single thing to us about anything. There was never, 'Okay let's close the door. Here's why we called you here.' They spent a few thousand dollars getting us up there to say 'Hi.'

"I asked Greg," John remembered, "'Did anybody say anything to you when I wasn't in the room?' and he said, 'No! Did anyone say anything to you?' No one ever said anything about anything."

Mystified, John and Greg returned to Chapel Hill and continued working on the music.

London Recordings interfered with Hobex telephonically. "The label said, 'We can't really work with these regional managers,'" Greg remembered. "'Either you instead let them go, or we're gonna have to drop you.' So, we went to Ben and Paul at Slick Winston and said, 'Look, we can't work with you guys anymore. We're being given this choice and we feel like we're too far down the line to walk away from the deal.' They were very bitter." London released the Hobex single.

One of the last things the Zippers did before the year ended was play some radio thing in Charlotte. By this time, I was so over everything that I was incapable of even pretending to be nice. Beyond that, some commercial radio people could be real assholes.

I remember playing a summer outdoor radio festival for a big commercial station in San Francisco. The DJs brought musicians up onstage just to push them into a kiddie pool. A station manager in Boston vowed to ruin us because we refused to play their show with other swing bands. We had to pee in plastic buckets backstage before a performance for another station because they didn't bother providing proper facilities. Commercial radio had a literal sense of ownership over artists.

Ken Mosher remembers the Charlotte event better than I do. It was a prime example of what Chris Phillips once called "biting the ass that feeds us."

"I was so fed up with the band at that point that I was riding with the equipment truck driver," Ken said. "We drove overnight. This muckety-muck from the station was there in the morning when we loaded in. I didn't have to load in. I was sitting there when she came in. She went up to our tour manager and said, 'I'm certainly glad that this band is going to follow through with their agreement this time, because they were supposed to be here for that holiday show. It really sucked that they canceled on us.' Then she stormed out.

"I'm like, 'Okay, this is great,'" Ken said, "and I go get a beer. So, I'm sitting in the audience in the only chair that's not on a table. She came back in, and I pretended to be drunk. I said, 'Yeah, I'll be right there to help you guys as soon as I finish this beer!'"

Then I showed up. Ken was telling me the story when the woman walked up to us and reiterated what she said earlier. "I'm glad you're playing this show," she said in an acid tone. "You don't seem very radio friendly. Bob So-and-So, the program director, was *very disappointed* that you didn't play the holiday festival." She made Bob So-and-So sound like a mob boss instead of a commercial radio program director.

I couldn't understand why this person was banging on about a show we didn't play when we were there for this one and why she was so remonstrative. I didn't like her patrician attitude and had no idea who this Bob So-and-So was.

"Well," I said emphatically. "Bob So-and-So is a fucking asshole!"

"That's my husband!"

1999

IN JANUARY, WHISKEYTOWN BEGAN RECORDING A NEW ALBUM, *PNEU-monia*, at Dreamland Studios in Woodstock, New York. Dreamland was located in an abandoned church. The recent merger of Poly-Gram and Universal Music Group put the album's release on indef-inite hold.

London Recordings was also part of the PolyGram/Universal merger. Consequently, Hobex was dropped. "London signed the Roll-ing Stones," Greg Humphreys said. "They put out ZZ Top records. So, to 1998 Greg Humphreys, London was fucking cool. But what I realized is that it's just a catalog of music. There's nobody left at the company that had anything to do with those signings. It's just a brand."

Meanwhile, the Zippers had begun our six-month hiatus. In Jan-uary, Ben Folds Five invited Ken Mosher and me to come put horns on the new record they were making in New York. It was great to see the guys and Caleb again. They were installed in a big, cushy studio. Having done everything we could in the Zippers to keep recording costs low, Ken and I were shocked to find out that the album was being written on the clock.

"It's decadent as fuck," Ben said. "It was pressure. It was the only way I would finish it. I was like, 'I don't even have a single song. I've got to set up a situation where I come in from ten to two, then have something to play that doesn't have a title or any words or the chords are changing every five minutes.' That was extremely stressful and a big waste of money." When we talked about it during the sessions, Ben said, "I work best with a gun to my head."

Ben was pushing for a concept album of continuous music with one side break rather than a collection of songs. This ran counter to label expectations, to put it mildly. They were looking for a follow-up single to "Brick."

"Honestly, the three of us were pretty united on that front," Ben said. "We weren't gonna do that. Caleb was trying to coax it out of us. Darren Jessee brought in the only song—never mind that it's a great song, but it just happened to be the only song, which made it the best song—which is 'Magic.' I hadn't finished anything. We'd been in there for three weeks. Darren brings in something that's got a beginning, a middle, and an end and makes people cry. It was really good. Caleb was like, 'Let's do that. Let's just go with that. Please, God!'"

"Magic" is a mournful waltz. "Saw you last night," Ben sings, "dance by the light of the moon."

> Stars in your eyes
> Free from the life that you knew

"'Magic' was the second song of ours about Stacy Guess," Ben said. "We were in the studio contributing a song to the *Godzilla* soundtrack when he died. We'd recorded an instrumental. I brought a string section and everything. And, I don't know, Disney or Bill Clinton or whoever was putting the record out called us and was like, 'We need words.' We had one more day. So, I wrote a song from scratch. Stacy died that day and I thought, 'Okay, I didn't know him very well, but here is what I think about life before death.'" That song is called "Air."

There's an ugly buzz that hovers just above the quiet
Found a way to make it silent
I'm comin' up for air

In February, I started making a solo album called *Samsara* after reading that it's the Buddhist term for the endless cycle of desire and dissatisfaction. Principal tracking was done at Kingsway Studios. Ken Mosher came along, as did fellow Zippers Stu Cole and Chris Phillips. Producer Mike Napolitano found an amazing piano player named Tom Loncaric. He knew Tom would be the right fit for my record when he started explaining the difference between Fats Waller's piano and pipe organ techniques. Duke Heitger, who played on the Zippers' *Hot* album, came out too.

Samsara is a record made by a person who wants nothing to do with Top 40 radio. It's got a gospel quartet and hot jazz pipe organ on it. There's also Chinese opera. The Pittsboro antique store owner who turned me on to vintage firecracker labels once gave me a cassette tape of Chinese music. I decided to cover one of its songs for *Samsara*. Because I don't speak Cantonese, I wrote down what it sounded like the vocalist was singing phonetically in English.

Death can be noiseless
Taken one stung by one needle
Oh your face is sad

"Oh shit," I said, looking at the lyric sheet. "It's about Stacy." I called the song "Some Born Singing" and asked Holly Harding to sing it if she was okay with the lyrics. Holly dated Stacy for years and almost married him. They were in a band called Soma together. At different times, both Jimbo and I both drummed for Soma.

Later, I took a copy of the original album to someone in the Chinese department at UNC. I wanted to know what that song was about. The professor called a few days later. "This opera is called *According to One's Heart's Desire*," he told me. "That particular track is about betting on a horse and losing everything." This was around the time I understood synchronous events as clear, if unnerving, signs that you're on the right track.

Stacy's memorial album *Legacy* was released by Mammoth Records on April 6. It's a collection of recordings Stacy made with Pressure Boys, Sex Police, Squirrel Nut Zippers, Venus Flytrap Girls, Chris Stamey & Kirk Ross, and Soma, as well as some solo stuff. Proceeds from sales went to the Stacy Guess Memorial Fund, a music scholarship at his Chapel Hill high school.

The Squirrel Nut Zippers songs featured on *Legacy* are both Stacy originals: the instrumental "Bedlam Ballroom" as well as "The Puffer," cowritten with Jimbo. Both *Legacy* versions are rough-and-ready live recordings Ken made during a performance at Spaceland in Los Angeles in the summer of 1995. It's likely that these two songs would have appeared on *Hot* had we not parted ways with Stacy two weeks prior to recording the album.

Contrary to what was suggested by *Hot*'s twentieth-anniversary reissue in 2016, we did *not* track a version of "The Puffer" at any time during those sessions, even though a "remastered" version of the song appears on the recent reissue. We also didn't record the song in 1991, despite what Jimbo told *Billboard*, because that was two years before the band existed.

Ben Folds Five's *The Unauthorized Biography of Reinhold Messner* was released on April 27. It's a fantastic record that didn't translate into sales or stir up much more than a lukewarm critical reception. It's a point of honor that my barking laugh appears on the single "Army." Caleb played a rough mix of the song through our headphones while we were tracking horns. I lost it when I heard Ben sing, "My redneck past is nipping at my heels." Caleb caught it on tape and left it in the mix.

"Reinhold Messner" was the name put on fake IDs in Houston when Darren Jessee was coming up. The band had no idea that it was a real person—in fact the first guy to climb Mount Everest without oxygen.

In the spring, Ken and I flew overseas to do promotion for the new Ben Folds Five record. We started in London. One night, when we were all being taken out to dinner by the band's record label, I found myself sitting next to Ben. "You like to smoke pot, don't you?" he asked. This was a rhetorical question.

"I could never get into it," Ben went on. "I went to Darren's hotel room one time and smoked some weed. It didn't make me feel good. I went back to my room and felt bad for a while. Then I looked in the mirror and realized that I was an ape. All this stuff about trying to be a person and having a job—it was all bullshit, because what I really was was an ape. So, I did ape stuff: I jumped around on the bed; I kinda trashed the place. At some point, I went to sleep. But you know what the funny thing was?"

"No," I said.

"The funny thing was, when I woke up, I realized that there was no mirror."

Polvo's Dave Brylawski and Spatula's Chuck Johnson, along with Black Taj's Grant Tennille, formed a group called Idyll Swords. "Toward the end of Polvo and Spatula, Dave and I realized we had this mutual interest in music from India, the Middle East, and Eastern Europe," Chuck said. "We were buying CDs and going to see classical Indian music concerts. Grant was as well. I was also really interested in that post–John Fahey style of acoustic guitar that had been brewing for a long time. As soon as I became aware of who Elizabeth Cotten was, I thought it could be interesting to meld those interests. A lot of our songs were based on modal music and drone."

"Chuck was a good friend," Dave said. "Polvo toured with Spatula and loved them. Chuck is like Ash Bowie. They both came into themselves and metamorphosed in a way that you couldn't believe. I was right next to it and couldn't believe it."

Idyll Swords came out on the Communion label on May 25. "I recorded it on an eight-track tape machine," Chuck said. "Some of it was recorded in my apartment and some of it in Dave's parents' house in Durham. We mixed it at the Yellow House. I brought in my tape machine and we mixed it through their console. We were able to add some effects and get a more polished sound on what was pretty much a lo-fi recording.

"Some of *Idyll Swords* leaned more toward the blues, some of it leaned more toward Arabic music, but all of it was our own," Chuck said. "It was a naive way of trying to approach these musics in a way that was respectful but also playful and creative. We felt like, 'There aren't rules that we have to adhere to. We can blend these things.'"

After months of agonizing, I quit the Squirrel Nut Zippers on June 30, the final day of our professional timeout. My lawyer wrote a formal letter to the label and I wrote a personal one to the band. I told them that it had been a good run, thanked them, and said that I was leaving because we couldn't make group decisions. I was terrified of stopping but incapable of continuing, so in that sense it was an easy choice. I wanted to be in *our* band, not Jimbo and Katharine's band.

Afterward, I drove a few blocks across town to Ken's house. "I'm quitting," I told him. "Well," he said, sighing. "That sucks."

"That was a shock," Steve Balcom said. "It was the beginning of, 'Okay, where is this going?'

"If you shine a light back on *The Inevitable* and on the first part of *Hot*, we were all working together," Steve remembered. "There was at least a feeling that we were in this together, and then obviously that completely deteriorated. So, by the time you left the band, I was like, 'I don't know who's who and who's doing what.' I like Jim and Katharine, but it was a lot harder."

Mammoth had an option to pick up *Samsara* and declined. In my opinion, the album was far too disjointed and strange to ever work for the Disney version of Mammoth Records. There was too much downward pressure on them to produce another hit.

6 String Drag had broken up in 1998. "The label used to call us '6 String Dad,'" Kenny Roby said. "I got married and had a kid. Ray Duffey was the only one who didn't have a kid. There were a lot of changes in what people wanted to do and how they looked at it. I was all in. I wanted to be a touring musician. 'This is what I'm gonna do as well as be a father.' Some of the people in the band were cool with it going either way. I got frustrated."

Kenny started work on a solo record called *Mercury's Blues*. In addition, he and another guitarist named Neal Casal released an album called *Black River Sides* on Glitterhouse Records on August 2. Kenny had recently opened for Neal during a European tour.

"We did a live record in New Jersey at a little venue called Bernie's Black River," Kenny said. "So, that's why it's called the *Black River Sides*. We did two nights and took the best stuff from those performances. It was basically like we did on tour: we played together on each other's songs and did a couple of covers."

On August 10, Superchunk released *Come Pick Me Up*, their seventh full length. The CD cover was painted by Laura Ballance. The album is augmented with strings and horns—one of those horn players being Polvo and Spatula producer Bob Weston. "Grab us by the neck, I volunteer as prey," Mac McCaughan sings in a descending falsetto on "Hello Hawk."

We could leaf the world in gold
If this muddy road would only wash away
Hello hawk, come pick me up

I was asked to give the keynote address for *College Music Journal's* 1999 Change Music Conference. "There are only five major labels," I told the conference attendees, "and they have something like a million-unit break-even point. That's fine for the top two or three bands that get $20 million advances, but everybody else becomes a loss leader. This system isn't working anymore. I'm going to self-release *Samsara* and have much more control. I'll use the Internet to sell copies.

"There must be a way for musicians to do it ourselves," I told them. "It's already getting easier for us to make decent records without a studio. The Internet can be a great distribution tool, even though it's unclear how to use it for promotion. At any rate, it's time to drop out of the traditional record label structure. It's too top-heavy and about to collapse.

"At last," I concluded, "I have the keys to my own car. I don't know yet if it's a Cadillac or a Pinto, but it's mine." Later, a guy on a panel about the future of music insisted that, one day, all songs would be composed and performed by robots. I digitally released *Samsara*.

Katharine Whalen's Jazz Squad came out on Mammoth Records. It's a collection of jazz standards first performed by the likes of Billie Holiday, Nina Simone, Nat "King" Cole, and Alberta Hunter. Jimbo contributed the instrumental original "Badisma."

The late-century music industry was facing a mass extinction event. "A year or so after I sold Poindexter, I was living in New York and working at ASCAP," Jack Campbell remembered. "I was in the Public Affairs Department. Public Affairs looked after legislation that was going to be favorable or unfavorable to songwriters and publishing companies—not the labels so much, but the intellectual property behind the songs. One day, my boss stuck his head in the door and said, 'Figure out what Napster is.'

"I started researching it online," Jack said. "My report to him at the time was, 'I don't think it's gonna affect publishing, but labels are done.' I went home to my girlfriend's house. We were having a party. I invited a bunch of people into my little computer studio and downloaded an early version of Napster. I said, 'Name a song you'd like me to download,' and somebody said, '"Smells Like Teen Spirit" by Nirvana.' I typed it in. When the little progress bar was all the way across, I hit my spacebar and the song played. I said, 'That's the end of the music industry right there.'

"I saw how easy it was for me to steal any record," Jack said. "It was like, 'The record store is no longer locked. I can walk in and take whatever I want, any time I want.'"

"The record industry's response was, 'We're gonna shut it down,'" *HITS* magazine's Joe Fleischer said. "'The MP3 is gonna get shut down, Napster's gonna get shut down, we're gonna stamp this stuff out, and it's gonna be over.' What was apparent to people outside the record industry was that the Internet was *designed* to facilitate communication among peers. But you couldn't go into a record company and say that without being escorted out as a pirate. The first thing major labels tried to do was compete on their terms: no MP3s, no singles, no free use, only conditional use, no shareability—none of those things. Of course, those are the things that made it great, so they lost on the merits and began to sue people.

"The thing that everyone missed is what indie music was and why it was so cool is community," Joe said. "There was a culture that hung together around the music in the early to mid-nineties that I don't think had happened since seventies punk rock. What drives music, what connects music, and why people consume music is community. I think that was totally lost on everyone in the nineties. The technologists didn't really understand the power and importance of credibility and community. They just wanted to make killer apps.

"I'm sorry the technology didn't come earlier," Joe said. "If you'd had Napster in '95 when you had this bursting-at-the-seams beautiful indie sound, the majors might have been irrelevant and artists might have had more control of their destiny. The early version of Merge Records is a great example: if those guys had the means of distribution at their fingertips via the Web in the early nineties, they wouldn't have had to worry about getting physical records into hard-to-reach places that were expensive to deal with. If they'd had that sort of democratized distribution system in the nineties, the world could have been very different."

But it wasn't, and the dinosaurs of the major label record industry continued towering over the cultural landscape, ignoring the asteroid hurtling toward them.

"There was an artist named Mark Lizotte that Mammoth was trying to sign," Lane Wurster remembered about that time. "He had big hits in Australia in the early nineties under the name Johnny Diesel. The closest he was playing was New York. By this time, Jay Faires had access to a private jet. He would use that plane to sign deals. He would take artists up and they would fly out over the Atlantic for an hour or two and discuss deal points. I remember him doing that with the Dust Brothers when he was trying to sign that development deal.

"Three or four of us flew on this private jet at 7:00 p.m. from Raleigh to Teaneck, New Jersey," Lane said. "We took a limo to the club, saw Mark's set, and were back home by midnight. It was the same amount of time it would have taken to drive to Raleigh to see a band at The Brewery and come back. It was crazy, drinking champagne and beer on this private jet. I was flashing back to the tear in the checks from the early days!"

Regardless, Mammoth Records was also about to go the way of, well, the mammoth. "I started hearing rumblings in the trades about how Mammoth was struggling," Shawn Rogers said. "Then there were rumors that Jay may be looking for another partner. It felt like something was going on underneath. Over time I was like, 'I am not happy. I gotta get out of here.'

"One day a friend and I were talking," Shawn remembered. "She said, 'Hey, we've got a film and TV position potentially opening out here at SubPop. Would you be up for interviewing for it?' So, I went out there and got along famously with everybody—the owner in particular. In September they offered me the job, which started on January 1, 2000. Y2K."

Ken Mosher quit the Squirrel Nut Zippers in October. "We had a meeting with Mammoth," he said, "and agreed to do all this stuff for the next record. In my mind, I wanted to try and have a bit of our past on there. I would have been just a sideman at that point, so it wouldn't have mattered anyhow. But we had that meeting and I found out that Katharine was pregnant. All the stuff that they said they were going to do—the schedule for the release, the publicity tour, that whole thing—was right when she was supposed to deliver. The end of my email when I quit was like, 'This is fraud and fraud is bad. Therefore, I can't be a part of it.'"

Disney fired Jay Faires in November. "They pushed me out in two years," he said. "We had six to nine months to make it work. If I'd sat down with Steve Balcom and Chris Sawin and said, 'Hey, let's go take another run at this and do five more years,' we could have made it work. We got schooled along the way. Finally, we didn't outsmart 'em and they caught up to us."

"Disney fired Jay, but Jay didn't tell me," Steve said. "I'm pretty sure he was trying to figure out, 'Okay, what's my next move? How can I do what I did three years ago—buy the label back and then negotiate another mega deal?' He didn't tell me until two months later. I remember having a meeting with the Black Crowes, who I'm very tight with, about possibly signing them and having no inkling. It was hardcore."

"Whiskeytown had a big show for New Year's Eve," Caitlin Cary remembered. "That was the last show we ever played. We thought the record was about to come out." In fact, *Pneumonia* wouldn't be released until 2001.

Whiskeytown disbanded. "Every solo thing Ryan Adams has done that I've listened to has been halfway to being good," *No Depression*'s Grant Alden said. "He didn't have the creative friction without Whiskeytown. Ryan without Phil Wandscher and Caitlin Cary is less disciplined. He's less challenged. When you're working with hired musicians, you're not gonna get the same 'That fucking sucks, dude. Go write it again' that you're gonna get in a rehearsal with people who are your equals."

"I have absolutely no regrets about having done it," Caitlin told me about her time in Whiskeytown. "I blew up whatever academic career I was heading toward and it changed my whole life. It allowed me to be a musician as a career for a number of years and also very much know what I *didn't* like about that. I got in bands with nice people henceforth, for sure! But it was magical to have that sense that you were making music and people cared. At the end, it felt like being a part of a big, happening moment. Even when we were in it, it felt that way."

The New Year came, bringing the curtain down on the decade, century, and millennium. This is where our story ends. Well, not quite: most of us are still kicking around. Here's what the people who I talked to for this book are up to as of the time of writing. Some of the following is in their own words.

Seconds Before the Accident, a live Archers of Loaf album recorded in November 1998, was released in June 2000. The band reunited in 2011 to play an unannounced set at the Cat's Cradle. Before that, Eric Bachmann's Crooked Fingers released several albums on Merge Records. Eric Johnson released one EP and is now a decidedly cool lawyer. The Archers issued *Reason in Decline*, an album of new material, in October 2022.

"Being in the Archers of Loaf gave me the confidence that I didn't have when I was younger," Eric Johnson said. "I think a lot of musicians get into it for that reason. When I look back on it, I'm proud of it, which gives me confidence and makes me feel good about it."

Sara Bell, who performed with the Angels of Epistemology, Dish, and Shark Quest, is now a folklorist. "I always saw myself as being stateless," Sara said, "constantly traveling between Raleigh, Durham, and Chapel Hill. Then I left at this really significant time in our little music world and went to school in another country. I came back and went to school to study folklore, which is all about community and how communities express their experience. I was like, 'Oh, my God! I'm a part of an amazing community and have been for a long time.' It was a homecoming to realize that."

Bicycle Face's Mitch McGirt tells me he hasn't written a song since the band broke up but still thinks the world of those guys. "My wife is the most interesting thing about me now," he wrote, "and my daughters are the most remarkable thing I did in my life."

In addition to a bunch of other things, you might recognize actor, comedian, and former Bicycle Face bassist Brian Huskey from such television shows as *Bob's Burgers* and *Veep*. After his brief but uneventful career in music, Brian went on to work with fellow North Carolinians Zach Galifinakis and Jody Hill. He later learned that musicians like Nina Simone and Thelonius Monk were also Tar Heels.

"It makes sense," Brian told me. "There's a relaxed observance that comes from North Carolina's creativity. It's something about being at ease with what's around you and then letting that ease and observation turn into something else. When it turns into something else, it's unusual. It's not based on what's popular. It's not based on what's going to necessarily work. They're doing it from a place of curiosity. It doesn't come from a fraught place. It comes from a communal, easy place."

Former WXYC program director and Caroline Records rep Glenn Boothe currently works for Merge Records and runs the Triangle-area independent concert promotion business Andmoreagain Presents. Over the past two decades, Glenn has been involved in live music— first as the owner of Local 506 from 2004 to 2014, then by working for the Cradle and Durham's Motorco Music Hall.

Jolene's and The Veldt's Dave Burris is a film director, producer, and writer. He's also a television showrunner, having worked on *The Mole*, *Survivor*, and many other series. In 2015, Dave directed and produced the independent feature film *The World Made Straight*.

After gigs for labels and tech companies, Pressure Boys and Johnny Quest bassist and Poindexter Records owner Jack Campbell works from home. "Now I am national brand manager for two lines of cutting-edge air-conditioning units," he wrote. "So, I'm still cool." Jack left The Triangle in 1998 and lived all over the country. Now he's happily ensconced in a big home in Chicago with his daughter, son, son-in-law, and grandson. Jack still plays music, having been involved in everything from indie rock, ska, polka, alt-country, and bluegrass. Now he's holding down the low end in "Chicago's premiere Halloween band."

"There's a thing that happens between a song and lots of people," Jack said. "I think it's the same thing that happens in a room full of people when everybody's really connected with a band. That's the thing you can't put your finger on, that you can't bottle up and sell. I will never believe that anybody is skillful enough to promote something into making it a hit. Millions have been spent trying. If people don't want it, they don't want it. It cuts across the whole major versus indie debate; it cuts across all formats. It's a human societal group phenomenon that is essentially mysterious."

More than almost anyone I can think of, Dillon Fence's drummer Scott Carle is the ambassador of the North Carolina scene. "I'm incredibly fortunate," he told me, "because I've played for so many groups of all types of music for so long." Collapsis went on to have a Top 40 hit in 2000 with "Automatic" from *Dirty Wake*. "I got a little redemption," Scott mused. "I thought it was over. I thought, 'That's cool. I've done this. I'll go do something else.'" That was never gonna happen: Scott's been in twenty local bands since high school. His continuing enthusiasm for all things music and musicians is infectious and undiminished.

"I'm a fan of all these bands," Scott said, "and not because I'm acquainted with them. I've gotten to know people through their music. I really care and get what a lot of these people are doing around here. I love supporting 'em."

Caitlin Cary married Whiskeytown's first drummer Eric "Skillet" Gilmore. She formed Tres Chicas in 2000 with former Let's Active member Lynn Blakey and Hazeldine's Tonya Lamm. Caitlin has also been in Small Ponds, made a record with Thad Cockrell, guested on about three dozen albums, and is a member of the NC Music Love Army, a group of musicians fighting against regressive politics. She makes two-dimensional artwork using repurposed upholstery fabric and a "pretty nice sewing machine." Caitlin shows her work, along with other artists, in the Pocket Gallery, which she owns and curates. *While You Weren't Looking*, her first full-length solo album, was released on YepRoc Records in late 2002.

The Cat's Cradle is still located at 300 East Main Street in Carrboro. Frank Heath still runs the place, is still soft-spoken, and still has shoulder-length hair. Pretty much everyone I spoke to for this book—and everyone I know—considers Frank to be the patron saint of the Chapel Hill music scene. Thank you, Frank, from all of us.

Sex Police's Norwood Cheek is still making music as well as working in film and TV. In the nineties, he was involved in creating music videos for Archers of Loaf, Ben Folds Five, Dillon Fence, Flat Duo Jets, Pipe, Johnny Quest, Sex Police, Small, Squirrel Nut Zippers, Superchunk, What Peggy Wants, The Veldt, and Zen Frisbee. There are more, but those are just the bands that appear in this book.

"What's beautiful about that time to me is that none of us were doing it for fame and fortune," Norwood said. "That became a by-product later. It was an accidental thing, like, 'What? I thought we were getting dropped from the label. We have a hit song?' We were clueless! It's the beauty of that unbridled energy of being in your twenties."

After Satellite Boyfriend disbanded, Phil Collins sold his guitar and married his sweetheart, Grace. They had, and continued to have, two delightful daughters. Phil and Grace went into the legal profession. They then spent decades dreaming of a life outside the legal profession but enjoyed every sandwich. Every seven years or so, Phil is struck with a creative burst of energy and writes some songs. Other times he just lies down until the feeling passes. Phil and Grace live in Raleigh on the same street as the old Duck Kee recording studio where a portion of Satellite Boyfriend's album was recorded. Requests for a historical marker have been rudely ignored.

Moist Records' Kelley Cox lives in Louisville, Kentucky. "I'm still married to the wonderful woman I left Chapel Hill with so many years ago," he wrote. "We have two children who have grown into amazing young adults. I still buy lots of records and listen to music every day, all day.

"In Chapel Hill, you didn't have to be in love with a band if they were your neighbors," Kelley said. "You supported them anyway. Some of my absolute best friends in that town played in bands that I liked *okay*, but I went to the shows and hung out with them because that's what we did. When my band played, I would look down at the crowd. It would be Superchunk and my roommates and the people from the restaurant where I worked. They would all be in the front row dancing. That's what that place was. In any other scene, that support and non-competitiveness doesn't happen."

During the Wifflefist days, Skip Elsheimer started showing old 16 mm educational films at clubs and galleries that the collective got from school auctions. They named the project A/V Geeks and now Skip does this full time. A/V Geeks has over thirty-six thousand 16 mm films, does daily streaming on YouTube, and sells stock footage to documentaries and TV shows.

John Ensslin moved back to North Carolina in 1998. He's still a visual artist and a poet as well as a writer and filmmaker. Before What Peggy Wants, John and I were in two side projects called Enormous Boy and the Pecking Order; at the same time, he was also in a 1976–1982 cover band called Fast Times with Greg Humphreys, Jack Campbell, and Jon Wurster. Since What Peggy Wants, John's fronted for The Breaks (with ex–Emperors of Ice Cream's Steve Carr), Marat (with Scott Carle and ex–Snatches of Pink's Michael Rank), London Dungeon (with legendary local guitarist Terry McInturff), Arrow Beach, and his current band Cage Bird Fancier, who counts Scott Carle and Pipe's Dave IT among its number.

"The primary function of going out to see music was social," John said. "One of the things I really loved about it—and I think most people hated—was the attitude. Chapel Hill was famous for nobody dancing. Everybody stood in the back with their arms crossed and just *judged* that band. You'd only know later if it went over or not. They were not giving an inch. I loved it because it cut through a lot of the friendly bullshit. I did not see performances as auditions. In a lot of scenes, that's the thing: 'Hey, I can play guitar! Check out these chops.' That is not what led to the Chapel Hill scene at all, in my opinion. It wasn't people trying to display any kind of individual musical prowess necessarily. It was creating music that was exciting, engaging, and cool."

Ben Folds Five broke up in October 2000. Ben then proceeded to crank out a mess of solo albums. The band reunited in 2008, when they performed *The Unauthorized Biography of Reinhold Messner* in its entirety. In 2012, they released an album of new material, *The Sound of the Life of the Mind*, followed by a live album the following year.

Jettison Records' Todd Goss runs his family's construction business and is also a cat rescuer. He's working on several creative endeavors.

Dick Hodgin has spent a lifetime in the music business fulfilling various roles: manager, booking agent, publicist, tour manager, soundman, radio promoter. Since 2001, Dick has been the co-owner and chief engineer at Osceola Studios in Raleigh.

"If record companies knew, beyond a shadow of doubt, what a hit song was, that's all they would put out," Dick told me. "They don't know. They are speculating, just like everybody else. One might think that the record companies may have a little bit of a leg up on the general population when it comes to speculating on what a song could do. But in the end, people still have to like it and buy it. There were so many missed opportunities for record companies to just give it a try. Just *try* it. I saw so many great bands fall by the wayside when they could have done a lot better."

John Howie Jr. released two more records with the Two Dollar Pistols. After that, he fronted John Howie Jr. & the Rosewood Bluff. His first solo album, *Not Tonight*, was released in 2018. When performing at the memorial of A Number of Things, Schoolkids Records, and Sex Police stalwart Steve Akin, John sang a countrified version of The Clash's "Bankrobber" that blew my goddamned mind. He lives in Hillsborough with his partner and son.

Greg Humphreys has never stopped making music. Hobex released three more albums in the aughts. Now he appears in

Greg Humphreys Electric Trio as well as the occasional Dillon Fence reunion.

Blackgirls' and Dish's Dana Kletter is still a musician. She's also a writer, teacher, Stegner Fellow, and, at least according to her, "the girl with the least cake."

I asked the Hardback Cafe's Grant Kornberg what he wanted to say for this bit. "Don't forget to tip the band," he wrote. Jamie McPhail told me she is happy, healthy, and painting away at her country estate. Alvis Dunn continued bartending for over twenty years and earned his doctorate in Latin American history.

Former Cradle soundman Tim Harper and his partner Beth Boylan founded Starpoint Brewery in their Carrboro garage in 2012. It's a much bigger operation now, with beers named after (among other things) Tim's "misspent youth as a touring musician and sound engineer." As of this writing, Tim is currently working on a new record by The Connells.

Spatula's Chuck Johnson joined Shark Quest in 2000. Idyll Swords released another album in 2000 and an EP in 2002. Music is Chuck's life. He scores for movies and television, releases solo and group albums, and is an engineer and mixer. Chuck's website says he "approaches his work with an ear toward finding faults and instabilities that might reveal latent beauty." He's based in Oakland, California.

"There was a part of me that knew well before the early nineties that I wanted to make music," Chuck said, "but it's hard to imagine that I could have ended up where I am now—where it is the focus of my life—had I not had that experience of being in a small, extremely supportive community at that time and place. One where I could pick up an instrument and within a year have ideas that are worth sharing with people on the stage and were well received and encouraged. The next thing I know, people want to invest money in releasing the music. Had that not happened, I don't know what I'd be doing. I wouldn't be doing what I do now."

In addition to helping WXYC become the first ever radio station to simulcast, Paul Jones founded ibiblio.org. A faculty member of the UNC School of Journalism and Media for several decades, Paul is also a poet. His poetry collection *Something Wonderful* was published in 2021.

Jerry Kee still runs Duck Kee Studios, though it's now more of a part-time operation. He also plays music in Stray Owls as well as Regina Hexaphone with his friend Sara Bell.

Mickey Death cocreator Eric Knisley moved away from Chapel Hill in the mid-nineties to escape people he termed "The Ubiquitoids." After becoming a 3D animator in the United States and England, Eric now works for the Science Museum in Raleigh. He still draws comics.

After the Pressure Boys disbanded, Robb Ladd moved to Los Angeles and played drums on Alanis Morrisette's debut, *Jagged Little Pill*. Since then, he's toured with Don Henley and played with Roger Daltrey, David Crosby, Stevie Nicks, Don Dixon, The Connells, the Bad Checks, and a boatload of other people. Although Rob's worked on Grammy–, Emmy–, and Tony Award–winning projects, he doesn't lord it over anybody. He just gets paid.

The stock market crashed the day after Brent Lambert submitted his multi-million-dollar M-PAK business plan to Goldman Sachs, negating his yearslong investment in the project. Brent continues to own and operate The Kitchen Mastering, though it moved out of his house to a proper building in Carrboro long ago. He's mastered many Grammy Award–nominated and –winning projects. Brent is the cofounder and principal partner in Arthur-Lambert, LLC, an acoustic consulting and design firm specializing in studio, theater, audiophile listening rooms, and immersive theaters.

Former WZZU program director Kirsten Lambert lives in Saxapahaw and paddles a lot on the Haw River. Her debut album, *From a Window to a Screen*, was released in October 2022. Chris Stamey wrote and produced it. Brent and Kirsten's son Julian plays piano on one song.

As of this writing, Kirk Ross and Bryon Settle's band Lud is working on their ninth studio album and making a documentary. After decades as a reporter, including a long stint in the state capital press corps, Kirk mostly blogs about music and politics. He still lives in Chapel Hill. Bryon describes himself as "a large man who likes to rock out with his friends from time to time."

Pipe's Clifton Lee Mann still performs with his first band the Bad Checks. In the nineties, he cofounded Demonbeach Records, which released quite a few albums by local groups like Dexter Romweber Duo, Butchwax, and The Spinns. Demonbeach's first release was a long-overdue reissue of the Bad Checks' 1985 album *Graveyard Tramp*.

Chew Toy guitarist and Sony MiniDisc Festival survivor Karen Mann blogged about local music for several years at mannsworld.com. She still writes about beer and mead for other publications, plays guitar around the house, and lives in Raleigh with her husband and cats.

Mammoth Records was the first independent label anywhere to produce two Platinum records. Disney came in and fired everyone in April 2000. Steve Balcom's contract ended on September 30, 2000. The next day he founded a marketing agency called the Splinter Group with Lane Wurster. Jay Faires went on to become President of Music at Lionsgate. Now he's head of the Wellness Agency, a company that "works with founders and CEOs of wellness companies to help scale their businesses globally."

Evil Wiener's Bill McCormick, also known as Billy Sugarfix, has spent most of his adult life teaching elementary school and selling books but never stopped playing or writing music. In the aughts, he helped pioneer the niche industry of custom songs and still provides the service on a boutique basis through customserenade.com. He also continues to perform, geography permitting, with Evil Wiener. His current projects include releasing music with the Early Girls and working on a theremin Christmas album. At the time of this writing,

Bill is honing his skills as a fiction writer. He's based in Krong Siem Reap, Cambodia.

"When I lived in Asheville, people would always talk about how crowds in Chapel Hill don't dance at shows," Bill wrote. "They even had this mock Chapel Hill dance where they'd cross their arms and stand still. It always made perfect sense to me. I saw our scene as a collection of bookworms and wallflowers. We were the shy kids who didn't have the social skills to navigate school dances. I always tried my best to hear the lyrics when bands were playing. That's easier to do if your booty is not shaking. I know it sounds pretentious, but I wanted a deeper experience out of live music. I figure that if you want to dance, you should just go see a cover band. You already know what they're going to say."

Carrie McLaren published *Stay Free!* for over fifteen years. After six years at Matador Records, she left the music industry and has worked various jobs, mostly in media. Carrie is currently Senior Associate at Dot Connector Studio, a fancy way of saying she does design and editing in her pajamas. She lives in Brooklyn with her husband, a wily teenager, and one mean-ass cat.

David Menconi spent thirty-four years writing for daily newspapers, twenty-eight of them at the Raleigh *News & Observer*. The 2019 North Carolina Piedmont Laureate, David has published several books, including *Step It Up and Go: The Story of North Carolina Popular Music, from Blind Boy Fuller and Doc Watson to Nina Simone and Superchunk*. These days David edits a new series of music books that launched in the fall of 2023 on University of North Carolina Press with his *Oh Didn't They Ramble: Rounder Records and the Transformation of American Roots Music*, a history of the independent folk label Rounder Records.

Through unerring discernment and committed perseverance, Merge Records became a Chapel Hill institution. In addition to documenting the local scene, they released landmark records by the Magnetic Fields, Neutral Milk Hotel, Spoon, and many more consequential acts. Though still an independent label, Merge scored big with Arcade Fire's *Funeral* in 2004, breaking the Billboard 200. Their partnership with Touch and Go lasted until 2009. "We like to pride ourselves on long-term relationships," Mac McCaughan said.

Metal Flake Mother's Ben Clarke works with big data in the cloud for the Department of Defense. Quince Marcum lives in upstate New York with a cell of forgotten soldiers who still believe the war never began.

"You can come at Chapel Hill from the angle of a bunch of people trying to start bands and make music, or you can come at it from the angle of a bunch of people trying to individuate at the same time," Quince told me. "That was my experience—the music was a function of people trying to be a certain kind of person."

"To save my own life, I gave up my passion," Ben said. "Passing it on to my nephew is meaningful to me. I've had a lot of creative pursuits outside of music, but I haven't found that again. I was obsessed with music since I picked up a guitar. I like my job now. I'm good at it. I've done well, considering everything I've been through. But *Beyond the Java Sea* is the best thing I've ever done in my life. As far as a creative statement, that's the one I made."

Former WXYC station manager Todd Morman lives in Raleigh, works at Duke University, and reads everywhere he can.

Ken Mosher and I scored for television and films for six years after leaving the Zippers. We also made two albums: *Brother Seeker* with Robert Sledge and *Maxwell/Mosher*. As of this writing, Ken is director of operations at the Hampden Family Center, a nonprofit organization in Baltimore, Maryland. The center helps people with economic insecurity through SNAP benefits, utility support, and handing out daily snack bags. He's also got a side hustle making stained glass windows.

"Chapel Hill at that time was as close as you could get to a socialist, artistic, creative environment," Ken said. "The great thing about it was the feeling that everyone who raised the bar raised the bar for everyone. Everyone was supportive of everyone else, but also in competition in a loving and nurturing way."

I once told Ken that I thought he was the heart of the band. "I thought we were all the heart of the band," he said.

Shawn Rogers Nolan still manages Archers of Loaf. He has been a licensed attorney for over fifteen years, assisting Grammy-nominated and award-winning artists, producers, songwriters, record labels, publishing companies, and other entertainment-related entities in their respective career pursuits. He and his family reside in Chapel Hill, where you can catch him at a Cradle show now and then.

No Depression's Grant Alden is the supporting partner in Coffee Tree Books/Fuzzy Duck Coffee Shop in Morehead, Kentucky, and dabbles in writing speculative fiction. Peter Blackstock left *No Depression* in 2009, working as associate editor at *Indy Week* (formerly the *Independent Weekly*) from 2010 to 2013, then as on-staff music writer for the *Austin American-Statesman* from 2014 until 2022. Peter currently lives in San Diego.

Flat Duo Jets' Dexter Romweber has been prolific in the new century. Since *Lucky Eye*, he's released fourteen albums, some solo, some with the New Romans, and some with the Dexter Romweber Duo, which ultimately included Dex's wonderful sister Sara, formerly of Let's Active and Snatches of Pink. In May 2023, Dexter released *Good Thing Goin'*, his first new album in seven years. On the title track, Dex sings like his life depends on it. It always has.

Chew Toy's singer and lyricist Christina Pelech currently lives in Durham with her husband, her mother, and one to three cats. After twenty years working in various bookstores and publishing houses, Christina changed careers and now owns a hair salon. Many of the people mentioned in this book are her clients.

Baited Breath Productions' Andrew Peterson ended up in Vermont, "married a Yankee girl," and had two boys. Andrew still sponsors the occasional band that comes through town, but now mostly farms and malts grain for local breweries and distilleries.

"I went to Chapel Hill, found this community, and found my people," Andrew said. "We all have friends from high school who will be some of our best friends for life. But you go off to college and you find the people who think like you do and love what you love. There were just tons of them in Chapel Hill. I loved every minute of that. I loved being a part of it. There was brilliance everywhere."

Pipe released a self-titled album on Third Man Records in 2023 featuring both Mike Kenlan and Dave IT. Ron Liberti is still making beautiful art, including the cover for this book. Mike Kenlan lives in coastal North Carolina and works as a design engineer for a giant telecommunications company.

Former Pressure Boys and Sex Police front man John Plymale produced and engineered records out of Overdub Lane for twenty-five years. Now he's the director of implementation for DroneUp, a drone flight services innovation company that, among other things, is responsible for Walmart's residential drone deliveries.

"If the Polvo story had just ended in the nineties, it would be completely different," Dave Brylawski said. "A little sadder, maybe." Instead, the band re-signed with Merge Records in 2009 and released *In Prism*, a new album of original material. Dave is now a psychotherapist living in Washington, DC.

"DIY taught me to make some noise and make it yours," Dave told me. "That's what you do. That's what being a musician is. The nineties allowed me to admit how important music is to my identity and my life. If there's anything in common with everyone you're talking to, it's that they're all music obsessives. Music is one of the biggest worlds they inhabit in their thoughts and mental real estate. If it wasn't for what I went through in the nineties with Polvo, I don't know that I would be here now: comfortable in the world of music."

Kenny Roby continues writing and performing, releasing four albums since 1999. 6 String Drag reunited to make *Roots Rock 'N' Roll* in 2015.

Early Cat's Cradle partner and chef Bill Smith is basically a living legend. "When your email came in, I was at the Cradle seeing a splendid show by Yo La Tengo," he wrote. "I still go there all the time. I retired from Crook's Corner in 2019 but still sometimes do cooking things—usually fundraisers for things I support. My second career fell in my lap. I'm a guide for food tours of Oaxaca and am in Mexico about a third of the year now. This is better than running a restaurant. I also write occasionally for magazines, usually about food. The only official music thing I do now is serve on the board of WXYC."

Southern Culture on the Skids still tours and makes records with the same lineup they've had since the mid-eighties. The band has released eleven more albums since 1999 and will celebrate their fortieth anniversary in 2024.

When we conversed in late 2022, Caleb Southern was a lecturer in the College of Computing at Georgia Tech in Atlanta. Although he no longer produced records, Caleb had lost none of his former energy, insight, or attachment to cigarettes. He died from an infection on July 6, 2023. A memorial Cradle show held in Caleb's honor that August featured Ben Folds Five, Bicycle Face, and Mind Sirens reunions, most of Archers of Loaf, half of Superchunk, Shark Quest, Todd Goss's band Blue Green Gods, me, and many others. Those who could not be there in person attended in spirit.

"At the beginning, I couldn't see it because I was in it," Caleb told me about the scene. "I thought, 'Well, of course it's like this because I care, and these people care, and we're all here. Of course we're gonna do something big.' I was young and naive and ambitious, and took it for granted that the sheer force of will from me and all the people I respected that were doing this was normal. But no, it really wasn't. In hindsight, it does seem magical—and unusual, in that it worked. It would not have happened but for the Cradle. If the Cradle wasn't there, it couldn't have happened."

An ever-changing cast of characters called Squirrel Nut Zippers still perform and sporadically record. Jimbo Mathus is the only remaining original member. As of this writing, there are eight other people in the band now. On the group's Wikipedia page, Ken Mosher and I are included in a list of past members along with twenty-six other people. "I had nothing to do with any real version of Squirrel Nut Zippers after that *Bedlam Ballroom* record in 2000," producer Mike Napolitano said. "After that, I just recorded Jimbo. Whatever he called it I don't know."

Superchunk continues to make records and tour, interspersed with some needed breaks. Since *Come Pick Me Up*, the band has released nine albums, including 2022's *Wild Loneliness*. Mac McCaughan founded Portastatic in the early nineties. After drumming with Superchunk for more than three decades, Jon Wurster left the band in February 2023. He's a member of the Mountain Goats and has toured with Bob Mould, Katy Perry, the New Pornographers, The Connells, R.E.M., among others. Jon is also a comedy writer, known for frequently appearing on WFMU's *The Best Show with Tom Sharpling*.

"I've spent more time with my bandmates than I did with my family growing up," Laura Ballance, who has stopped touring with the band, said. "I've been with them more intensely for more time than anyone else in my entire life. I love them so much, but there have also been times when I hated them. They're my brothers."

After a long hiatus in which they released two albums as Apollo Heights, Danny and Daniel Chavis reformed The Veldt. *Entropy Is the Mainline to God* was released in 2022, the same year The Veldt was awarded the Raleigh Medal of Arts. In September 2023, the band released the shelved Capitol Records version of *Marigolds*, a remedy both long overdue and well worth the wait. Drummer Marvin Levy owns his own house painting company.

"We went on tour in 2022 and all these little white kids came up talking about the Cocteau Twins," Danny said. "And these young Black kids, too, coming out talking about how we influenced them and whatnot. It trumps any kind of bad history we might have had because they're out there."

Chapel Hill's Other Drummer Groves Willer performs with Shark Quest, tends bar at basement institution The Cave on West Franklin Street, and lives in Hillsborough.

Zen Frisbee's Kevin Dixon still makes art and comics, most recently a full-length graphic novel adaptation of the *Epic of Gilgamesh* in collaboration with his father. Despite the band's legendary career-spanning streak of misfortune, Zen Frisbee somehow manages to play a gig every year or so. Kevin considers himself extremely lucky to still play music with his best friends from the eighties. He continues teaming up with his brother Laird in the band Shark Quest, which he joined after Chuck Johnson's departure.

Laird Dixon wants you to know that he's happy and a snappy dresser.

Chuck Garrison married "Tom Maxwell's former hot roommate" Sue Hunter and had two kids. "Although the stresses of coaching youth soccer are taxing," he wrote, "I do find time to work, mow the yard, and even hit the drums occasionally." Chuck is still Chapel Hill's Drummer. As of this writing, he's in Spider Bags, Mad Crush, Pipe ("every third year"), and "the zombified corpse of Zen Frisbee when someone dares to raise it from its slumber." Chuck claims to have an upcoming snare drum solo album called *Whoomp! (Snare It Is)*.

The Eternal Present

Harold H. Anderson, research professor of psychology at Michigan State University, published "The Nature of Creativity" in the Spring 1960 edition of *Studies in Art Education*. "It is axiomatic that Creativity must represent the emergence of an original, something unique," Anderson wrote. He continued:

> One approach to a definition can be made by thinking of Creativity as *product* and of Creativity as *process*. If we make this distinction we find that on the one hand we are emphasizing a concern with *Things* and on the other hand expressing an interest in *Persons*....
>
> There are...important distinctions between Creativity as product and Creativity as process. The product exists only in the past; the process is the instantaneous moment of *now*. The process is the flow between the past and the unknown, unpredicted and unpredictable future. The product not only belongs to the past; it takes on the characteristics of the crystalized closed system of static unchanging immobility. There is no Creativity or growth in the past, nor in copying, imitating or conforming to the past. Similarly, it is un-Creative to resist the flow of life into the open future or to fear the unknown.

Philosopher, author, and scholar Alan Watts combined this concept of creativity existing in the now with the Buddhist doctrine of *anattā*, or nonself. "To understand music, you must listen to it," Watts wrote in 1951's *The Wisdom of Insecurity: A Message for an Age of Anxiety.*

> But so long as you are thinking, "I am listening to this music," you are not listening. To understand joy or fear, you must be wholly and undividedly aware of it. So long as you are calling it names and saying, "I am happy," or "I am afraid," you are not being aware of it.
>
> For the perfect accomplishment of any art, you must get this feeling of the eternal present into your bones—for it is the secret of proper timing. No rush. No dawdle. Just the sense of flowing with the course of events in the same way that you dance to music, neither trying to outpace it nor lagging behind. Hurrying and delaying are alike ways of trying to resist the present.

As a chronological retrospective, this book has thus far been concerned with creativity as product and therefore things: who put out what record when, who sold which company for how much money. Some of us raised in this materialist society will think this is all there is to it. But there's a strong argument to be made that the past is a mental construct, linear time doesn't exist, and all we have is Alan Watts's eternal present, Harold H. Anderson's instantaneous moment of now.

An early proof of this concept in the Western world was presented by English idealist metaphysician John Ellis McTaggart in "The Unreality of Time," published in *Mind*, a quarterly review of psychology and philosophy, in October 1908. "I believe that time is unreal," McTaggart wrote.

> Positions in time, as time appears to us prima facie, are distinguished in two ways. Each position is Earlier than some, and Later than some, of the other positions. And each position is either Past, Present, or Future. The distinctions of the former class are permanent, while those of the latter are not. If M is ever earlier than N, it is always earlier. But an event, which is now present, was future and will be past.

Since distinctions of the first class are permanent, they might be held to be more objective, and to be more essential to the nature of time. I believe, however, that this would be a mistake, and the distinction of past, present, and future is as essential to time as the distinction of earlier and later, while in a certain sense, as we shall see, it may be regarded as more fundamental than the distinction of earlier and later. And it is because the distinctions of past, present, and future seem to me to be essential for time, that I regard time as unreal.

I'm not competent to summarize McTaggart's following argument on my own, so I ran to the *Stanford Encyclopedia of Philosophy* for an explanation. "McTaggart distinguished two ways of ordering events or positions in time," it reads.

First, they might be ordered by the relation of earlier than. This ordering gives us a series, which McTaggart calls the B-series. A second ordering is imposed by designating some moment within the B-series as the present moment. This second ordering gives us a series that McTaggart calls the A-series. According to McTaggart, in order for time to be real both series must exist, although McTaggart holds that, in some sense, the A-series is more fundamental than the B-series.

Although there are various ways to reconstruct McTaggart's argument, for our purposes it will suffice to consider the following one:

1. Time is real only if real change occurs.
2. Real change occurs only if the A-series exists.
3. The A-series does not exist.

Therefore, time is not real.

Setting aside the potential unreality of time, I align myself with Harold H. Anderson's definition of creativity as process, both in the sense of that definition being interested primarily in people over things and on that process operating solely in the existing moment.

Having given a sense of the nineties Chapel Hill music scene in terms of creativity as product, let's now turn to it as process. The last thing that I want is for this book to be considered merely a sentimental reverie of vanished youth or an argument that our music was the best and therefore all kids should absent themselves from our lawn. Fuck that noise.

Everything we did was created in the eternal present, even if the results assumed the characteristics of, and are relegated to, the last decade of the previous century. Now that we're talking about creativity as process, let's dispense with the idea that each artist is some kind of hyper-individuated superhero. On a foundational level, art is the product of a collective process.

"People look at art as the product of the artist and study things in that way," John Ensslin said. "Then the artist's personality becomes all mixed up with the art and no piece is individual: Each work fits in relation to the artist's other works. Because of that, you get an idea I despise: that art is just the cool detritus of amazing people. It's detrimental to the appreciation one can get from an individual work of art."

John coined a marvelous term for the role of the artist: Midwife to the Unmanifested. "To my mind and process, I'm not creating the art," he said, "because that's going to get in the way of producing good stuff. The best stuff is the most itself. That is the highest criterion when you're judging something. There's no yearning for anything beyond the contours of the work. It is itself.

"The artist-as-midwife idea is very simple and useful if you want to make art versus being an artist," John said. "Every work is a compromise between intention and medium. The less important component is the intention. It is completely disposable at the point the material comes to life. Then, all the practice in the medium and the experience with intuition is there to help as you plop this thing into the world as smoothly as possible, whatever it is, itself. No artist should ask, 'What am I trying to say here?' That's useless and profane. It's not a code to be figured out. It's a thing already. Get out of the way. It's not about you."

What John calls the unmanifested is just that: all things without form, all potential yet to be realized. The unmanifested is beyond genre because all genre exists within it. It is not bound by linear time's by-products of expectation and precedent. It is, I would argue, the entirety of culture and society, ever renewing, waiting to be accessed and articulated.

Building on John's argument, I would suggest that no artist truly works alone. The riff to "Hell" popped into my head at a stoplight. While it's true that I didn't collaborate on that series of notes with anybody else, I can hardly claim to have written it by myself. It emerged fully formed almost without effort. Such a thing would have never entered my mind unless by chance I heard the 1937 recording of "Seven Skeletons Found in the Yard" by Lord Executor on WXYC in 1990 and found *Calypso Breakaway*, the CD it had been recently reissued on, at Schoolkids Records.

Further, "Hell" was the result of listening to hundreds of hours of prewar calypsos and internalizing the form. It came into being because the Squirrel Nut Zippers encouraged me to write material like that and needed a show closer. The process of creating that song also required a car and a red streetlight and an almost infinite number of other variables. It assumed form only in the sense that it was revealed to me, the artist prepared to receive it.

I feel privileged to write this book and appear among the people featured in it. I regard each of them on a spectrum ranging from deep respect to awe. But it would be dishonest to claim that, even in their astonishing creativity and wonderful diversity, this crowd was somehow better than any other group who came before or will come after. That's silly. The real genius of the nineties Chapel Hill music scene is the community that created, nurtured, and sustained it.

I talked to Love Tractor's Mark Cline about his experience in Athens, Georgia, in the 1970s and '80s with fellow bands like The B-52s, R.E.M., and Pylon. "If you think of the scene as a cold, we were the sneezes," Mark said. "It was a collaborative effort of a group of about two hundred people. It was very Carl Jung in the sense of a collective consciousness."

In Chapel Hill, we thrived in an infrastructure that empowered and supported us. It forgave failures and encouraged experimentation. It provided platforms of expression, from the Cat's Cradle to WXYC to *Stay Free!* magazine to a half dozen indie labels. It facilitated creativity through sufficient employment and affordable housing. It gave us what urban sociologist Ray Oldenburg termed "third places"—public spaces that aren't work or church—like the Hardback Cafe, where we could gather, relax, be inspired, or, as Alvis Dunn put it, simply "think of string." Most importantly, it was made up of people deeply committed to its existence.

It's been occasionally jarring to write this book. It's shocking to remember a time without cell phones—when you could not only get lost as hell or have to look for pay phones to call your loved ones from the road but also end up seeing the exact person you wanted to see purely by chance, when they'd suddenly pull up beside you in their car and say, "Get in."

It's unnerving to write about a time when you could work a restaurant or copy store gig and make enough money to feed yourself and pay rent, even if you lived in comparative squalor. It's difficult to write about modern luxuries like affordability and walkability when, at the time, we considered them the bare necessities, if we considered them at all.

It's depressing to document an age when one could consciously opt out of creating inside a corporate system—albeit even then with some difficulty. The indie label infrastructure, so pervasive and influential in the decade that preceded the setting of this book (and absorbed during it), seems as quaint as a wax cylinder. What made the indie mentality so vital, however—community, regionalism, and instinctively valuing artistic expression over profit—are also the foundations on which to build the next scenius.

The healthiest artistic ecosystem produces the most beautiful and diverse forms by collectively encouraging individual expression. This kind of self-reinforcing creative environment is available to you if you want it and are willing to work for it. If nurtured through intention, these garden-variety elements of community will recombine and engender another artistic hothouse. When that happens, every action each person takes in furtherance of that collective's vitality and renewal—even if done by themselves with a guitar in their bedroom—will be a sacred act.

This is because artistic creation, no matter how humble, is the genesis of all other cultural expressions. Everything that follows—criticism, physical or digital reproduction and distribution, publicity, profitability, emotional resonance, and any fool's definition of cool—not only exists in relation to the act of creation but is dependent upon it. As any creator will tell you, these postliminaries are also the things that can make you feel separate from or insufficient for the act of creation because they are so often used to measure value or worth. This is no accident: It's a tactic employed by the ownership class designed to make those who create the wealth feel powerless. Don't buy it. This is your time. Connect with like-minded people, occupy the physical spaces available to you, and inherit your rightful creative kingdom. As Christ told his disciples in the Gospel of Thomas, "It will not come by waiting for it. It is not a matter of saying, 'Here it is' or 'There it is.' Rather, the kingdom is spread out upon the earth."

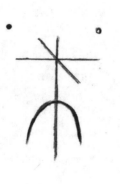

In Memoriam

Steve Akin
Stacy Guess
Steve "The Doctor" Hill
Andrew Maltbie
Michael McKinney (Jack Whitebread)
Dave Robert
Joe Romweber
Sara Romweber
Marc Sloop
Caleb Southern
Cy Vance
Randy Ward
Eddie Watkins

Acknowledgments

Bill Smith's quotes were first published in an interview I conducted for *The Bitter Southerner.* Used by kind permission.

Jon Wurster's quotes were provided by kind permission of his interviewer, Emil Amos.

Kirk Ross hepped me to "The Unreality of Time" because he's cool like that.

I am indebted to Michael Benson, Monica DeClay, Andy McMillan, Maura Patrick, Melissa Swingle, and others whose generous contributions were not possible to include.

In addition to sharing his indispensable perspective, David Menconi's several informed corrections to the manuscript kept me from looking like a complete idiot.

Thank you, Emrys—whom I love more than love—for your wise counsel, unflagging support, and willingness to listen to me read everything I write out loud.

Thank you to my agent David Patterson, my editor Ben Schafer, senior production editor Sean Moreau, and the good people at Hachette Books and the Stuart Krichevsky Literary Agency, without whose belief and labor this book would not exist.

Finally, thank you to all those beautiful souls who made up that extraordinary community, the totality of which this limited effort can scarcely describe. There are few things more precious in this world than a mutual benefit society. My love to all.

Index